THE
TEMIARS
OF THE
PUYAN RIVER

HISTORY, CULTURE AND SITUATION
OF THE ORANG ASLI OF POS GOB

VOL. **1**

BY

DAVID P. QUINTON

SUPPORTED BY

  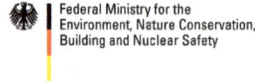

PUBLISHER

Layout by Tong Kar Yew, Mediarc Communications

Cover art, Illustrator: Mun Kao, Colourist: Tan Vei Xhane

CONTENTS

Chapter 4

Appendix 1

Bibliography

List of Tables

List of Maps and Figures

PREFACE

Many good books and detailed research papers have been written about the Orang Asli peoples of Malaysia, including some on the Temiars, who have lived in the Ulu (upriver) valleys of Kelantan and Perak for many centuries. These publications (see my bibliography for a few titles) contain a wealth of insights into the traditions and beliefs that are held by these original peoples. But I wonder, how many of them discuss the peculiar history and origins of a specific community of forest-dwellers, and especially of a remote Temiar one?

In this two-volume book I piece together the origins and ancestry of the Temiar community of Pos Gɔɔb (normally written, Pos Gob[1]) and its dozen or so surrounding villages, together with a description of their traditions and life-style, before and after its interruption by war, relocation, logging and religious campaigns.

My intentions for visiting Pos Gɔɔb, the first time back in 2010, were to learn about Temiar customs and to study their language, but I soon found myself unearthing details of their distant ancestors and many stories about the past, what they had been through in the last hundred years and how they had survived even longer than that in this region of dense rain forest. I found them eager to share with me the tales of their great predecessors, who, only a hundred years ago, were walking the hills and mountains bare-foot, clothed with tree-bark loin cloths, and carrying the blowpipe and quiver full of poison-tipped blow-darts.

There was no one at Gɔɔb to take the initiative and sketch out for me on paper who their forefathers were and where they came from. I had to dig up the information little by little, while their stories side-tracked into the old way of life or the times of the communist insurgents, or the threats and the bribing of the loggers, who were pushing them aside at the time. It seemed that every time someone gave me a description, I had to cancel out my previous notes because they never gave me the whole picture in one narrative, and I had to be careful to compare stories from different sources. The Temiar mind assumes most of the time that you already know something about the topic at hand, and if you don't yet know anything you are inevitably going to misunderstand what they are talking about. After a couple of years I found out that one forefather actually had more sons than they had first told me, and what I had understood for a long time to be father and son, among their ancestors, was actually the same man, but with two names.

0.1 I spell Temiar place names as they are pronounced by the Temiars. They would never pronounce Gɔɔb as 'Gob', but with the sound as in 'orb'.

Finding a knowledgeable person was a task in itself because most of the old men who knew so much had already passed away, taking all their knowledge with them, if they hadn't told the stories to their children. All history, ancestry and traditions are passed down orally among the Temiars, there are no written accounts. This means that if the next generation fails to listen to the stories their grandfathers and grandmothers tell, or the older generation lose interest in telling, then the history is simply lost. There is also no one person who knows the whole story, but the history is shared out in pieces among different ancestors and these fragments must be found and constructed together to make a more complete picture, as I have attempted to do here.

Pəŋhulu^k P′di^k K′lusar,[2] the late headman of Tɛmagaa^k village, was by far the most helpful of his generation, while others in the villages told me they had forgotten to ask their fathers or grandfathers to tell the stories they knew, and sometimes even their real names! But with P′di^k getting old, his knees seizing up, and his eyes growing dimmer, his stories often rambled up and over many hills, and to understand everything he said (in Temiar) was a challenge indeed. Fortunately his sons would come and sit with us and they proved very helpful with clarifications of what he said and they could answer many of my questions about their forefathers. Pəŋhulu^k P′di^k died in 2019, soon after after a bomb explosion shook the valley (an unexploded ordinance from the 1950s, detonated by the police) and almost caused his heart to stop, or else caused him to remember the days of his fathers, which were shaken by bombs as well. He will be remembered as a dear, friendly man who loved his land and his people. Pəŋhulu^k Bɔŋsu of Gɔɔb was another of those few remaining men of old, but he passed away in 2014, while I had barely begun my research. Had he lived on for another four years I would have discovered much more of the intriguing story they knew, and this record would be even richer for detail. I met him a number of times and listened to what he had to say, which was mainly his complaints about how *gob*, or outsiders, were encroaching on his land.

P′di^k K′lusar, late Penghulu of Tɛmagaa^k village, who was born at Lawaar, 1940, on the Jɛŋhuŋ River, in the Bərtax River valley, close to where his great-great grandfather, Taa^k Galoŋ, had first settled perhaps a hundred years earlier.

Fortunately again, Bɔŋsu's nephew, Jambu ʔAlaŋ, had spent time with his father and uncles to gather the stories they knew and he gave me much help with the Upper Puyan side of the history. Down at Pinaŋ village, Taa^k ʔAdi^k R′masa was a tremendous help detailing the history of the Píɲcɔʊŋ River Temiars. At Gawíín village, Taa^k ʔAbaaŋ ʔAnjaŋ, descended from the same Temiar line as Pəŋhulu^k P′di^k, gave me such clearly remembered details of his ancestors that he seemed as if he were a book.

The research turned into more than mere stories however, when the villagers of Tɛmagaa^k started leading me out on long treks up the Bərtax River and into the more remote valleys, where it seemed as if no outsider had ever laid foot (but for soldiers during the Emergency years). They took me up Sɔ̆id mountain, with its four 2000m-high peaks, and Bərlɛɛy mountain, to show me the land where their forefathers had lived, dreamed, planted and hunted a hundred or more years ago. With the aid of a hand-held GPS receiver we could plot the locations of the old swiddens, caves, rivers and hills with pin-point accuracy and soon other groups were camping out, far from home, reaching the boundary of mountains surrounding Pos Gɔɔb, to collect all the points they could. The map started to fill up, area by area, as much as our energy permitted, and all the interruptions going on, of the rainy season, the rice harvest, and not to mention frequent child-births and illnesses. Logging companies were active at that time too, bulldozing roads and felling the ancient trees for timber, and those areas where they operated were danger zones to be avoided.

0.2 See my notes on language in the next section for an explanation of the symbols I use to spell Temiar words.

I persisted with the work at Tɛmagaa^k, seeking out from them any historical homesteads they might have missed, and soon the people of B′rɤg and Kacaŋ villages started involving themselves, hiking up-river to the sites of their last century dwellings at the Puyan River source.

It was a lengthy and slow process, discovering where the old settlements had been, as the land area was so large, hundreds of square miles of it, with hundreds of ridges to walk up and rivers to cross, with fallen trees and bamboo lying across the paths, that needed climbing over or hacking through, and dangling thorns that would snag one's clothes, or one's face if not careful. Each area to be surveyed was reached on foot and then a team would spend usually three or four days visiting sites in the nearby forest, until they needed to return and rest. The hike from Tɛmagaaᵏ or Bʼrɤg up to the Perak border would take a whole day, setting out at five in the morning with a heavy back-pack, and making camp on a mountain ridge-top or a valley of a cool river source by four in the afternoon. We camped under a tarpaulin stretched over a pole and spread leaves out on the ground to sleep on, sometimes using one campsite, or sometimes breaking camp and moving on each day. I once joined a team mapping the Puyan River sources and we walked up and down five paths to the mountain border, taking us nine days and five campsites, and just as we had located an amazing waterfall on the Ragas River, they were beginning to complain of leg aches and so we had to leave it.

The rainy season practically canceled all activity away from the villages as the wet weather made walking treacherous. And then there was the swidden cutting (the term for shifting cultivation), planting and rice harvest that involved the entire population and no one was available to make expeditions. In the Bərtax and Upper Puyan River regions we managed to plot almost 80 pre-war dwellings and 50 post-war swiddens in the closer vicinity of Pos Gɔɔb. After a two year effort, putting a ton of enthusiasm into it with a good crowd of volunteers, the Píɲcɤʼɤŋ River region, six miles down the main river from Gɔɔb, was explored. By the next year, in 2016, we

Temiars from Tɛmagaaᵏ village, trekking through the dense forest along the boundary between Kelantan and Perak, that marks the edge of their traditional territory.

Some Temiars from B'rơg village sit by the camp fire as they prepare their meal of langur meat, after arriving in torrential rain to survey Rɛnipuy cave, high up on the Ragas River.

Hunters in the mapping teams took every opportunity to track animals while walking and camping, and this wild boar was chanced upon as it wallowed in a mud hole, right on the path.

were able to plot the swiddens of the Lower Puyan, which rounded up the whole territory and gave us a total of 143 pre-war and 95 post-war swidden sites.

But the work didn't stop there. The Temiars took me up to the boundary, which follows the back wall of mountains that encircles the Puyan valley like reclining giants, and we walked its entire length (almost 60km long), first from the northern point round the western side, and from the same point round the eastern side. This involved several week-long hikes, camping in cool temperatures in the dense forest, which felt freezing at night, even with our fires burning. Most of the boundary to the north is high-altitude, over 1400m ASL, and the vegetation is markedly different, with wrangled and twisted, moss-covered trees on the highest paths, and flowering bushes on the mountain peaks. Blow-pipe bamboo was plentiful on the altitudes between 1300-1800m and our path seemed to wade into it, so that it had to be hacked with parang, our steel

Palm leaves from the forest are laid out to make a bed at this temporary camp.

A group of mappers walk along the border of their ancestral land. The vegetation here is typical of high altitude forest.

Crossing the Bǝrtax River at its sandy and slow-moving river-source, on the path to P'gǒy Mountain, an old route that leads to Perak.

bush knives. Up on the mountain summits we were rewarded with breath-taking views of the valleys far below (if one could keep the biting ants off one's feet!), of the Puyan and Pɛriyas Rivers and often the head-rivers of Perak. My companions would scramble about picking the leaves and flowers, only found on these high-altitude peaks, to weave into headbands and stuff in their belts.

All the long-house locations that we pinpointed, together with the mountains we climbed, are shown on the maps I have drawn here, each point having been plotted by its recorded GPS coordinates, accurate to three to five meters. Only at waterfalls and caves did the GPS signal go a little haywire. Which means that any of these places can be located simply by geo-caching the points and walking in their direction, except that one would be advised to have a local guide and not wander off alone into the forest here, because it's easy to get sincerely lost. The ridges and gullies appear and meander in ways that one wouldn't expect and you can end up among thick clumps of bamboo or in a stream that seems to be flowing in the wrong direction, with steep sides impossible to climb.

All the rivers on the maps, that are like roots spreading out from a trunk toward the north, I drew by hand, using a topographical map (of National Mapping, Malaysia, or PNM, 1990) as an underlay. The PNM map rivers were drawn many years ago, from aerial photographs I believe, and sometimes rivers join other rivers in the wrong places (as found out by GPS data or local knowledge) and sometimes a river appears when there is none in reality. Therefore some of these errors may have been carried onto my maps, but I have adjusted the course of rivers in a few places, such as of the Píɲcờờŋ, at its mouth, which on the PNM map cuts right through the hill top where today's Pinaŋ village is located! To plot all the rivers using GPS tracks would have taken us twenty years or more, with ample supplies of food, pairs of shoes and batteries! The river names given on the PNM map are good only to be discarded as even the twenty percent of them that are nearly correct are badly miss-spelled. I labeled most of the rivers, those from the northern regions, from my own experience, having walked there so often and been told the river names whenever we crossed them. Toward the south I created sketches

Fig. 1. Map showing the location of Pos Gɔɔb and its river territory, in western Kelantan state, Malaysia.

The coloured areas show the extent to which the Temiars and surrounding indigenous people groups can be found settled or are known to roam (green shades: Senoic groups; purple shades: Jehaic groups). The 'Pos' villages were established as Army forts in the 1960s and today represent the centres of the different communities. RPS denotes a relocation scheme area. I have tried to piece together the names of rivers in Perak from people's knowledge here, at the Puyan, and taking clues from previous maps.

of the rivers for the Temiars to identify and occasionally, I had to double check the names they gave with GPS points collected in the field, or vice versa. With the more knowledgeable old men unable to walk far because of their aching joints, it was left for the younger men to go and point out places, and sometimes they might have confused the river source of one river with another. Such errors would not have been made if they had followed the river from its mouth to its source, but that kind of work would have demanded days and days of extra walking, and not considering the villagers still needed to work, collecting forest products, to provide for their families.

Without the geographical survey work to aid us, we who were not born in this land would only be able to imagine what the stories of their ancestors tell us. We wouldn't be able to grasp at the size of the land that they had roamed, for generation after generation, to preserve their lives. It would also be hard to prove that Temiar customary land follows an oral law of inheritance, each forefather entrusting his land to his own sons and grandchildren. The points on the maps show us that the Temiar groups of the Puyan valley have each continued to exist in their own forefather's land, even until today, and have not spread out beyond those inherited bounds.

It was also a great experience camping out with the Temiars and seeing a little of their handywork skills in the jungle, and their sense of direction, their knowledge of trees, plants, medicines, fruits and birds, and how to source foods to eat when in trouble. Just to see them so at home out in the wild, even though humanly they are vulnerable to the elements, to hunger and to biting creatures, is a real eye opener to the way things might have been for the whole human race, thousands of years ago (if the world had been so forested as it is here!).

ʔAríf Panda^k points to a tree that is scarred with a hack mark made by a Temiar perhaps eighty years ago, on the path to Rɛmŋoʼo̱m Mountain.

0.3 Of note, in May 2023, I made corrections to my description of traditions (i.e. the *s'lombaŋ* underground dragon dance, on pp46-49), after more discussions produced needed clarification.

0.4 I follow Geoffrey Benjamin's use of the word 'medium' and 'mediumship' to describe the communication and invocation of spirits as it describes the activity of communication with the spirit world on behalf of others in the community, as opposed to manipulating the powers of that world for personal use, which would be described as shamanism. In Temiar belief, most spirits are wandering souls (and hence I refer to them as souls throughout). They are the soul or inner person of natural entities that have wandered away from their physical home, whether it be it a tree, mountain, animal, or human, and can be seen and interacted with by persons in their dreams, and especially by the spiritually adept, or mediums. A soul-medium can interact with the souls of nature while in a trance state during a ritual dance.

I can only say that I regret not finding my way to Gɔɔb fifteen years earlier, when I first heard of the name, and when the forest was still intact and the old men of the people were still alive who held so much knowledge. Even more so, I wish I could go back to the 1930s and see what their life was really about and capture their customs on video camera.

In 2018, I received a copy of Geoffrey Benjamin's book, Temiar Religion, sent to me by the author himself, for my study. It was a thoroughly interesting book, especially for me as I was in a place to directly weigh its ideas with the Temiars around me. And thus my research work on Temiar beliefs began in earnest (from which Chapter 1 of this book is written). Through the next two years I discovered much, and I found it fascinating uncovering the true traditions that are upheld by the Temiars, that lie underneath all the normal activities that are carried out. After several months of intensive investigation, I found that many areas of research in the book didn't accord well with the Temiars here in the Puyan Valley, and the story they gave me seemed much more robust, coming from Temiars who haven't had their traditions watered down by interference of outside society. Hence, if you have read the book, you will find that the record of Temiar traditions I give here is different in many regards. It is my hope that I have been able to correct what was distorted and paint a more vivid picture of Temiar beliefs and customs (if somewhat summarised here in this book), so that the traditions of the Temiar may be better known and preserved.

While I have no doctorate in anthropology to back up my own research, the facts that I have given can be proven by anyone who has the opportunity to speak to Temiars who are knowledgeable of their traditions. They will be the ones to prove or to disprove what is written here—and hopefully they will do so, in good time. I have certainly not tried to fabricate anything myself but there are bound to be discrepancies that will need ironing out in due time, as I or anyone else among the Temiars continue to dig for clues to their history. I am not a Temiar and do not have half of the inborn knowledge they have, and it is easy for me to misunderstand the concepts that they talk about. But at least I can refer back to them at any time and learn where I have made my errors, as I am not removed from the Temiar environment.[3]

It is interesting that the author of the book aforementioned, in response to my feedback on his published research, said that we will never find two Temiars saying the same thing, and thus our research will always differ from each other's. And I agree that this is partly true, as two Temiars may apparently have two ideas about the same concept which they are both describing, but it is not the whole story. If one lives with the Temiars for an extended period one should realise that they only ever describe a concept partially at best (in their mind they are providing what they feel is important at the time, not a categorical breakdown of the entire subject), and the gaps need to be filled in by further careful investigation. As well as that, some Temiars claim to know every detail when in fact they can be proven by others to be ignorant of the traditions they claim to know. It takes much time, even years, to find persons who are consistent with their knowledge and who can be trusted with what they tell. But even a trusted person may need to be asked about something on multiple occasions in order to gain a full picture of the lore that lies hidden inside his heart.

One good example is with the Temiar concept of '*kɛnlo'ox,*' a word that by itself means a glass ball or eyeball. I had difficulty in discovering the true significance of this word to the area of soul-mediumship[4] and at first I heard that it was the eyeball of the soul-guide that the medium took in a dream and thereafter kept in his pouch. Later on the picture became clearer and I found that it is a stone that a medium keeps from his/her soul-guide, to make it a 'pet'. The soul-guide, which has a real animal form in waking life, then becomes the 'eye' of the medium and can see for him or her as it roams in the forest and thus it is the guide itself that is called the 'kɛnlo͂ʼo͂x'. The idea in the book was much more cloudy, simply saying that the 'kɛnlo͂ʼo͂x' was one of the medium's souls, leading to an assumption that humans have multiple souls.

Also inferred in the book, Temiar Religion, is the idea that the ritual taboos that are held on many actions and foods and that are stringently adhered to in every-day life, help to provide moral guidelines for Temiar society. But in fact, I found that they do nothing to constrain inter-human behaviour, they only serve to prevent actions of human behaviour that might interfere with the souls of nature around them. Furthermore, the deity that resides over these souls and metes out punishments on breaches of the code of non-interference is not interested in the slightest regarding the ups and downs of human morality. But this idea about taboos and morals is not a Temiar-born one, but is an imposed hypothesis. The taboos do not really constitute part of the Temiar religion either, as they do not direct attention toward the Creator, who is very apparent in Temiar thought, or to any of the other souls that are ritually celebrated, but to an evil being in the heavens who booms with anger, causing thunder from above.

The picture of the Temiars is well in need of repainting or re-colouring anyhow, as they are a people who are hardly heard of and the advancing, modernist society all around them still knows very little about them. Their faces are seen at town when they make day-trips to collect their small benefits[5] and to visit the market or the hospital, but where they come from, how they live and what traditions they hold all remains a mystery. They are deemed a bush-people, who lag behind main society, refusing to pick themselves up and learn about the modern 'scientific' life that makes the world a 'better' place. Visitors to the Temiars will see their 'poor' living conditions (evidence of a dependence on natural materials, not of squalor), and may assume they are idle most of the time, noting also the absence of money-making activities going on, such as commercial farming or rubber plantations, especially in the upriver valleys. When they clear off, daily activities can resume and a perpetual list of jobs that are necessary for maintaining a forest existence, such as foraging fern shoots and fruits, cutting and burning new swiddens, planting and tending crops, collecting materials for house-building, gathering medicinal plants to treat ill persons, sometimes venturing far off in the mountains to find what they need. Some go hunting, fishing and setting traps, to bring back food for their families.

Social activities also go on, like the night-time dances, the celebrations of the first fruits and rice planting, or the sending away of a deceased person's soul. Discussions of important issues are held by the elders, such as regarding land-encroachment by loggers and development companies, or regarding the settlement of a dispute between villagers. That the Temiars posses a *hukom*, or code of conduct, that the elders uphold and teach in their community, is probably completely unheard of to outsiders. If those visitors would hang around a while they might see that the Temiars do not sit idly watching the sun rise and then set each day, but they busy themselves, as much as their energy allows, providing for their families and maintaining the spiritual life of their society. They might also see that life in the last twenty years has become increasingly difficult to maintain, with widespread deforestation and the loss of many natural resources. In the old days the Temiars could make a living by collecting forest products for

0.5 A government benefit scheme, started recently in 2019, called Bantuan Sara Hidup, which is available for married women and allows them around RM1000 (US$250) a year, plus some extra (US$30) for each child. Before this scheme came out there was Datuk Najib's BR1M (Bantuan Rakyat 1Malaysia) that offered households around RM450 (US$125), three times a year. Another scheme, dubbed "*dowít mískín*" or poverty money by the Temiars, doled out RM200 (US$50) a year to people over 50 years of age, but in 2020 this was closed down with a final deposit of RM5000 (US$1250). Also, if children attend the government school, families can receive a child allowance, called 'Saham', but it only amounts to another RM200 a year for each child.

Dense angular ferns grow rampant on an old logging track near Tɛmɛnkaaᵏ Mountain.

trade, such as manau rattan, but in recent years even these resources have been reduced to very little, due to serious damages inflicted upon the landscape.

I begin this book, then in Volume 1, with a discourse on Temiar traditional beliefs and their observance of rites that stem from these, as these are what make the Temiars a true indigenous people group of the Malaysian Peninsula. The Temiars are recorded as the second largest group (after the Semai, a sister people group living further south) of original peoples in Malaysia, who are termed 'Orang Asli,' having a population reaching 25,000 in 2008, compared to 42,000 for Semai (Gombak Museum figures). There are some 19 people groups of the Orang Asli, that have been classified by the government (but there would be more if language division is appreciated), and, undoubtedly, some of them will be found to hold similar beliefs and observances as the Temiars. For example, while the Temiars practise ritual celebration of the souls of the forest, including that of the tiger and those of the trees and mountains, the Menriq people to the east of them celebrate the tiger soul, and the Jehai, to their west, celebrate the souls of trees and nature. Therefore, parts of this discourse may provide an introduction to the beliefs of not only the Temiars but also of the neighbouring indigenous people groups.

0.6 Especially in the paper 'Who gets to be called 'indigenous', and why?', Geoffrey Benjamin, 2015.

I should state that my usage of the title 'indigenous' follows the traditional understanding of the word (as discussed by Geoffrey Benjamin in his papers on the Orang Asli[6]), where it is applied to those whose ancestors have lived in a land since time immemorial. That people still live there and speak the same languages and hold the same traditions as their ancestors,

even while a different ethnic majority lives around them. This view is often not held by all, with indigeneity (the indigenous identity of a people) instead being ascribed to the majority people, or the definitive people—those who founded the modern nation. In Temiar terminology, they call themselves *sɛnʔoóy sɛŋroʻx*, or forest people[7], and they hold that they resided in the land long before the arrival of other ethnic groups, and have maintained their own social and religious frameworks that originated only with themselves. They see themselves and all other tribal groups, who carry the blowpipe and invoke spiritual power through agency of *sɛwaŋ*, ritual dance and spirit-invocation, never having migrated to the Peninsula (which they call Tanyux, or Tanjuŋ, 'peninsula'). Their ancestors, traditions and cultural identities have their beginnings right here in the land of Tanyux, originating from the survivors of a catastrophic flood, which they call the *límbaŋ* (see section 1.4).

This notion originates purely from the Temiars themselves, and has been confirmed also by various Semais and Bateqs I have met. The Temiars often remark that if the majority ethnic groups were indigenous to the land, they should know all the names of the rivers, hills and mountains, and not need to ask the Temiars, Semais, Jehais and so on what they are. When outsiders use a place name learned from the Orang Asli, they can't help alter its pronunciation, and when they think up their own names they use ideas like Batu Putih, 'white rock', or Gunung Ayam, 'chicken mountain', which carry little cultural or historical relevance. In Temiar and other Aslian customs a river confluence is always named after the river that terminates there, which means that Kuala Lumpur, 'muddy confluence', would be named by them, Boʻox Gombaᵏ, after the Gombak River. According to the Temiars and Semais, the name Selangor comes from the name of a tropical plant species, *s'laaᵏ ŋoʻor* (pictured on p118). The locality of Gua Musang, now a small town in southern Kelantan, was originally known to the Temiars and Mendriqs inhabiting the area of limestone stacks, as Gəəp Tɛnyuᵏ, or bear cat cave.

0.7 The Semai call themselves, and all the other blowpipe-bearing tribal groups, simply *sɛnʔoóy*, or native people. In Temiar, *sɛnʔoóy* means 'person', regardless of race or origin, and *sɛnʔoóy sɛŋroʻx* refers to the original peoples of the Peninsula.

In Chapter 3, I then begin to describe how the lifestyle of the Temiars once was, with their inherent knowledge of natural species and their techniques for utilising the materials in the environment around them. I discover how the knowledge they possess did not spring from schools or books, but it was gained by observation, as each followed their elders. I have attempted to condense here everything I have learned from the Temiars regarding the methods

A natural rock outcrop, called Batu^k ʔAsaad, that takes the shape of a pumpkin. (Credit: ʔIdris ʔAsod)

A Temiar from B'riix village stands on ʔAyaap peak. This stretch of the boundary runs between Gawíín and B'riix villages over the rocky Sakoʼb Mountain. (Credit: Wahab ʔAlʉj)

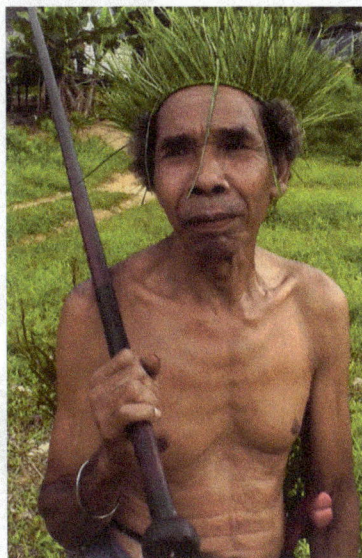

Alʉj Soʼid, of Tɛmagaa^k village, holding a blowpipe in 2011.

A hunter takes aim at a monkey, high up in the trees. (Credit: Rapi)

of forest survival which they practise, though there is still much more to discover and document from them.

In Chapter 4, I describe a particular area of Temiar survival skills in greater detail, one which they have preserved well until today, their ingenious trap tying.

Appendix 1 gives a list of 1000 names of natural species known to the Temiars. Of trees and plants, the names were listed by brainstorming them with a group of Temiars, whereas the lists of animals were made by identification, using picture books. My list of birds was first amalgamated into a list published by Lim Teckwyn (Malayan Nature Journal, 2017) but here it can be found hopefully more accurate and complete.

In Volume 2 of the book (containing Chapters 5-11), I describe in the first chapter another area of Temiar knowledge, a truly exceptional part of their culture that is vital for maintaining health, their practice of herbal medicine. In Chapter 6, I discuss the concept of land and how it is perceived in the eyes of the Temiars, as being granted to their forefathers by Nyʉ^k ʔAlʉj, the Creator, and passed on to them to be perpetual guardians. I discuss how places received their names long ago, whether from the presence of trees and plants or from events in real life or in dreams, which remain until today (and in Appendix 2 I list over 1000 names of mountain, hills, rivers, gullies and swiddens in the Puyan valley and their origins).

In Chapter 7, I reach the historical part of the book and detail the ancestry of the Puyan Temiars, and the geography of where they cut their first swiddens, looking back over a hundred years ago from today. I continue the story, in Chapter 7, into the 1950s, when the Temiars' peace was shattered, by the Chinese communists taking advantage of them, by the bombing of the RAF, and by the British Army following after thee insurgents, to hunt them down. Life was soon upheaved even further when the British lured them with food and deported them down-river, out of their own homeland, to prevent them from supporting the communists. Then, in Chapter 9, I describe the return of the Temiars to their own river, after some five or six years away, and how they resettled it, under the observation of the Army. Their forest was still intact and the rivers were still clean, but their traditional lifestyle had been rudely interrupted and hundreds had died during the shifting about downriver.

In Chapter 10, I then describe how the logging companies moved in, back in the 1990s, under the guise of building roads, to extract timber from vast areas of Temiar hereditary land, leaving behind bare earth on the hillsides and causing devastation to the natural environment. Finally, in Chapter 11, I mention what has happened in the present day, with outside influences and pressures from religious groups putting wedges into Temiar society, seeking to pull them away from their mysterious and misunderstood traditional lifestyle.

NOTES ON THE
TEMIAR LANGUAGE

As of today there is no formalised way of writing Temiar. The Senoic language has some complex word forms and difficult vowel sounds and attempting to write it with plain Roman letters, as has been attempted before, proves totally inadequate. It also does little to help the non-Temiar with correct pronunciation of Temiar words. The Temiars use plain letters, such as in their short-hand messaging on their phones, because they recognise words without the need to write them so precisely. But to do the language some justice, and to help us non-Temiars, I use some special symbols that allow us to differentiate between vowel sounds (which can all be short, long or nasalised) and to add some special consonants. My grasp of Temiar is not yet perfect, however, and my spelling of Temiar words may still be experimental sometimes!

Vowel symbols are as follows:

a	aa	front vowel, as in pat, but 'aa' can tend to a lower sound as in art.
ə	əə	mid-central vowel, as in her.
ɛ	ɛɛ	unrounded 'e', as in pet.
i	ii	high-front vowel, as in feet.
í	íí	unrounded 'i', as in pit.
o	oo	a rounded 'o', as in poke, but 'oo' can be higher, almost at 'uu'.
ɔ	ɔɔ	a half-rounded 'o', as in cord.
ɤ	ɤɤ	back, unrounded 'o', as in pot.
u	uu	rounded vowel, as in do.
ʉ	ʉʉ	mid-central 'u', as in 'ew'.
ù		a half-rounded 'u', as in book.

Most vowels can be pronounce short or long.

Consonants sounds that are different to English are:

c	is pronounced similar but shorter than an English 'ch', and word-finally it is shortened even more.
j	is like English 'j' except word-finally where it is usually unvoiced (it positions the tongue against the palate).
ŋ	'ng' as in ping pong, Ŋ when capitalised.
ɲ	a nasalised 'y' (different to 'ny'), Ɲ capitalised.
x	is a pronounced (velar) 'k' at word-final, often as 'kh', having slight aspiration by many Temiars.
ᵏ	(a raised 'k') is the glottal stop at syllable-end, which marks a truncation of the vowel sound before it. I refrain from introducing glottal stop marks (ʔ or ˀ) here because they would not be recognisable to Temiars, who grow up with the use of k, as it is used with the Malay language. It is raised so that it isn't confused for a pronounced consonant (the velar k) by a non-Malay-speaker.
ˀ	is a glottal stop pronounced before a vowel at word-beginning or mid-word where a consonant does not begin the vowel sound. It is marked here to show that words in Temiar do not run into each other.

Diphthongs, especially of vowels at word-end, which are usually closed by w or y:

ay   as in fly (long: aay)
εi, εy   as in say (long: εεy)
aw   as in how (long: aaw)
ow   as in snow (long: oow)
ớy   as in toy (long: ớớy)
uw   as in flew (long: uuw)

Also, there are ớw, ớớw, əy, əəy, uy, and uuy which are not found in English.

Vowels can also be pronounced nasalised and these are denoted with a bar over the letter, e.g. ō.

When words begin with two consonants together, the first consonant makes a short sound (basically a half schwa), in order to prevent it joining with the proceeding consonant. This does not happen in English because consonants can join together. For example, the word 'try', in Temiar the equivalent word would be 't'ray,' where the 't' and the 'r' are separated by a very short sound. These are found in Malay also, for example, the 'e' in Kelantan, which is not a full vowel; the name could actually be written K'lantan.

Some Temiar words that you may find in this book are:

jɛlmớl	mountain	j'huuᵏ	tree	dɛix	house
taŋkớl	hilltop	k'bəəᵏ	fruit	Taaᵏ, tataaᵏ	grand-father
luwag	gully	s'laaᵏ	plant	Jaaᵏ, jajaaᵏ	grand-mother
l'gəb	valley	pɛnlaay	medicine	halaaᵏ	soul-medium
tɛŋkớh	waterfall	nớŋ	path	bɛlyan	spiritual power
²ớớx	river	l'mog	former swidden	sɛn²ớớy	person
guwɔɔᵏ	cave	s'laay	swidden	r'waay	soul

It should be noted also that the language I use here among the Temiars in the Puyan valley is considered different in certain regards from that spoken by Temiars further south or those in Perak state. From Pos Gɔɔb, the farthest Temiar community northward in Kelantan, to Pos Balaar, several river valleys south, the kind of Temiar spoken is considered plain and direct, and because of that fact these Temiars would call themselves, *Tɛmɛɛr*, meaning 'plain and clear'. Temiars further south in Kelantan, from Bớớx B'tʉs (Kuala Betis) to Pos Haw, speak with intonations that gain them the label of *Gɛnləəl*, 'wavering'. Further south still, and akin to the Temiars of Perak, the Temiar is mixed with Semai, the language of a sister indigenous group, due to the proximity with Semai communities in the Cameron Highlands. Over in Perak, the Temiars speak slowly and slur their speech, thus giving themselves the title of Temiar *p'lɛɛh*, which comes from the word *p'lɛnhɛɛn*, 'slowly'.

While ethnographers try to explain that the real divide between kinds of Temiar speech is North-South, regardless of the Central mountain range, the Temiars here in the Puyan Valley do place a certain lingual divide along that mountain border. There are countless different words used by Temiars in Perak and their formations of words from verbs follow the Semai rules. One obvious aspect of morphological difference, is the nomilisation of verbs, to create nouns. For example, the Perak Temiars' *cɛbniib* 'a journey', from the verb *ciib* 'go', as compared to *nɛbciib*, the same word as spoken in Kelantan. Perak speech largely follows the Semai rule of infixing verbs whereas Kelantan speech nearly always affixes to the front of words.

Temiars from Tɛmagaaᵏ village stand on P'naŋoᵂ Mountain. At 2180m, it is the highest point in their territory and the most revered of their mountains. (Credit: ʔIdris ʔAsod)

A fire is lit after a team makes camp on the ridge-top, along the boundary with the Bayur River valley, near ʔAboŋ Mountain.

ACKNOWLEDGMENTS

The following members of the Pos Gɔɔb community have made this work possible, giving valuable contributions from their oral record, without whom I would have nothing to put on paper. Given in order of their contribution, chronologically:

Pəŋhulu^k P'di^k K'lusar, ʔElan P'di^k, ʔAnyɛh P'di^k, ʔAŋah Pando^k, ʔAlaŋ Panda^k, ʔAnjaŋ Sud, Norman ʔAlʉj, ʔArif Panda^k, ʔUda ʔAloŋ, ʔAdi^k ʔItam, ʔAlʉj Cɛrloy, ʔUda Siyam, Jambu ʔAlaŋ, ʔAso̒d Panda^k, Yusman ʔAndo^k, ʔAndo^k ʔAwih, ʔAdi^k R'masa, ʔAbus Sisam, ʔAlʉj Sisam, Samsudin B'kəd, Roslan ʔAŋah, Busu Lo̒ŋ, ʔAbaaŋ ʔAnjaŋ, Latíf ʔAbaaŋ, Jani ʔAyob, ʔANít ʔAlí^k.

I make a special mention of the late Rtd Sgt ʔUda Siyam, who passed away on the 6th September, 2018. His knowledge of the old swiddens on the Upper Puyan where he lived with his father while a young boy, and of the mountain paths that he followed with the commando unit he was attached to while in his twenties, was crucial to the survey teams exploring the jungle locating these sites. The many interviews he gave helped fill in important details of the history, and, with ever-full jugs of sweet tea, his hospitality to all those in the team was never lacking.

I also make mention again of the late Pəŋhulu^k P'di^k, whose love of the land and his forefathers added life and feeling to the history and helped me grasp at the things they hold deep in their hearts.

Over 130 other persons, from all 13 Temiar villages of the Puyan valley, helped to make this work complete by sacrificing their time and energy while hiking up rivers and climbing mountains to collect geographical data. Without their contribution and enthusiasm, very little of the kind of data gathered here would have been possible to obtain.

I make mention of Geoffrey Benjamin, who encouraged me to seek publication of this work, back in 2018, at a time when I didn't think it was likely to happen. Many thanks to Colin Nicolas, for giving us advice and direction with preparation of the work for publishing.

A million thanks to Caroline Quinton, my mum, for proofing this work (several times over) and for correcting my grammar in so many places. Many thanks also to our designer, Tong Kar Yew, who has done an outstanding job putting the book together.

Thanks must be given to the GEF Small Grants Programme for funding the publication of this book, without which I doubt that it would have been possible to finish writing it or bring it to the printing press. Thanks also to the GEF National Coordinator for Malaysia, Shin Shin, for her tremendous help and enthusiasm in in the project.

This project was completed using open source software: notably, two geographic data plotting programs, Viking and Quantum GIS, running on GNU Linux. Map contour lines come from an open source satellite imaging project, openDEM (http://opendem.info), and are used in my maps under the Database Contents License (DbCL). More information on that can be found on my GPS page at my **website: http://dquinton.github.io/debian-install/**

All images in the book are taken by the author except where credited otherwise. A fair number of images are credited to ʔAnɛl Samsudin, my fifteen-year-old Temiar brother-in-law, who with an artistic eye has captured some great pictures, even with the basic compact cameras he's had so far. He also has the time, and the young companions with whom to roam around, to see things that I don't look for. There are also many pictures acredited to his older brother, Rapi Samsudin.

ʔAnɛl Samsudín, who has contributed many pictures to this book.

Lɘruw waterfall, on the Píɲcɔ̌ʼɔŋ River. (Credit: ʔAnɛl)

"RANTOꞋW PUYAN – THE RIVER GIVEN US BY NYUᵏ ꞋALꞀJ THE CREATOR."

Taaᵏ ꞋAmpís Galoŋ, around 1900

1 | SPIRITUAL HARMONY AMONG THE SOULS OF THE WILD

1.1 THE DIVIDE

A hundred years ago, the land of the Temiars stretched from the Galas River in the east, where today's Gua Musang town is situated, and encompassed what is today called the Nenggiri River with its entire watershed, westward, toward the Central Range. This watershed comprises of seven main rivers, considered iconic to the Temiars and their homeland. The first river, at its source in the south-west, is the B'roʊ́x, a highland river that, in recent times, runs clear at the source but red with soil sedimentation after flowing through land development at Lojing. The B'roʊ́x is joined by the Bəər as it flows north-east, and further down by the B'tʉs, at which point its name changes on maps to the Nenggiri (but to the Temiars it remains the B'roʊ́x its entire length). Further downstream, the remaining four rivers, the Pɛriyas, Jɛnrol, ʔUyas and Lɛɛw, take turns to merge with the river. Over in Perak, their land extended to meet with the territories of Lanoh and Jehai peoples, and as far as the B'roʊ́x river-source in the south, where it met with Semai populated areas.

Gɛncol B'roʊ́x, the source of the B'roʊ́x River: a Temiar floats building materials downriver on the crystal clear water.

In those days the land was covered with thick forest, crowded with towering trunks and a myriad of tropical palms, ferns, zingibers and bamboo. Wild animals abounded, from branch-swinging langurs, gibbons and siamangs and night-creeping civets and bear cats, to herds of sambar deer, the ox-like gaur, the cave-dwelling serow, elephant-nosed tapirs and packs of hunting dholes. The armoured pangolin and land tortoise wandered from their holes in the rocks. It was no park with neat pathways and tidy flower beds, not in the least, as gullies and swamps abounded, infested with giant pythons, rearing king cobras and striking pit vipers, haunted by the powerful tiger and ghost-like leopard, and shuddered by the heavy feet of Asian elephants and the Sumatran rhinoceros. This is the environment in which the indigenous peoples of the land have inhabited the last three or four thousand years, and have proven well their ability to survive in it while keeping their traditions preserved.

The B'roȯx River towards Kuala Betis, flowing red with silt, which is the result of unchecked land development (photo taken the day after the photo at the source, in June, 2016). The Temiars at B'tʉs remember when it was also clear and deep, and teeming with fish.

They have, of grave necessity, acquired and stored an extensive knowledge of the natural world around them, be it of edible plants and fruit species, of herbal remedies, of animal and bird habitats, and of the lie of the land itself. The human is an alien in the tropical rain forest, a soft-skinned creature lacking fur and claws, and and the ability to digest many fruits and plants that other animals eat. Without intrinsic knowledge of what to look for, how to identify it and how to make use of it, he could never prolong life very long. He must find shelter and make fire to provide warmth, he must avoid poisonous plants and creatures on his way, and keep safe at night from hungry beasts. The divide that separates human life from the wild is indeed vast, and yet the Temiars, and other forest peoples inhabiting this land, have mastered how to

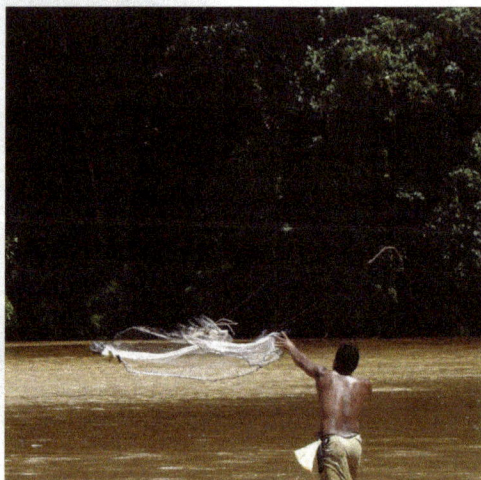

A Temiar throws a casting net in the B'roȯx River, at Cɔɔs, Gua Cha, in 2007. The only fish at that time wdich had survived the pollution were mud-dwelling catfish.

cross it. There is also a spiritual divide that is very apparent to these peoples, arising from the same wild that they confront each day, and this they have also learned to bridge, that they might live peacefully and thereby preserve life.

Ancient trees once dominated the whole forest, their great buttress roots laying claim to the land.

Motionless, a green pit viper sleeps on a plant stem, deep in the forest of the Ragas River valley.

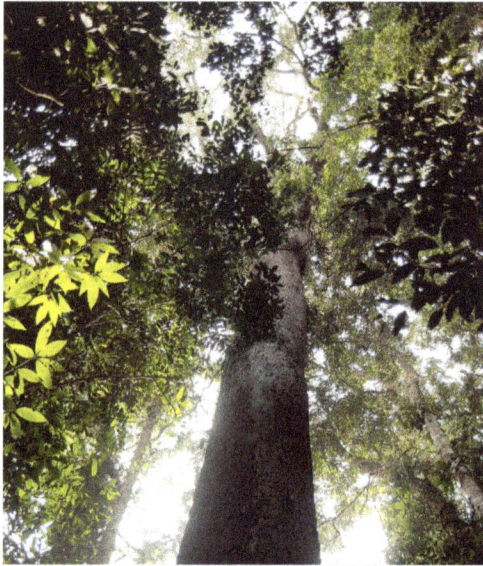

A towering tree on G'maah Ridge, on the boundary between the Píncoʻoŋ and R'koʻob Rivers.

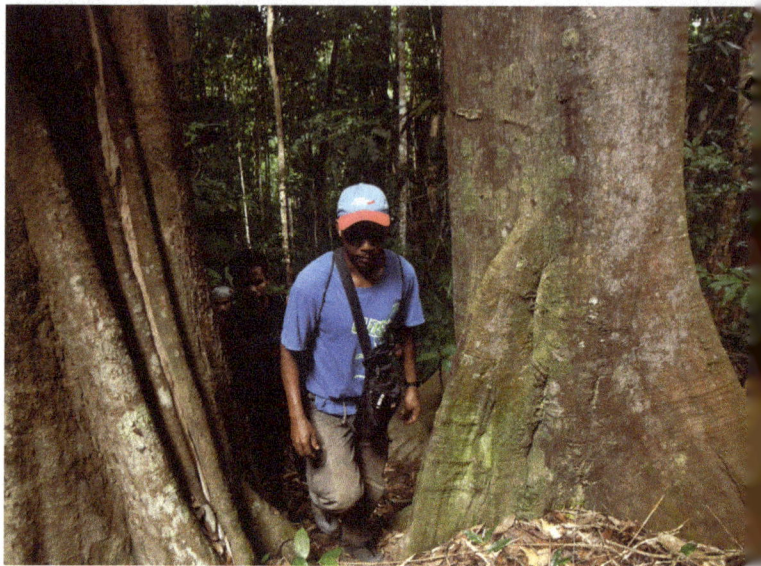

ˀArif Pandaᵏ walks between two trees at S'lipɔɔh hill, before the loggers began operations there in 2013.

The Temiars face a multitude of spiritual entities that are at odds with human activities going on among them, disturbing their realm. According to their belief, the souls of trees, animals, rivers and mountains can all be offended by careless human actions and they may retaliate by causing illness and attacking or stealing people's souls. The great guardian spirit of all living creatures of the wild also replies with thunder and storms when any of his sub-ordinates feel offense as humans encroach on them. While being wholly dependent on the natural realm for their life and sustenance, people do not share the same wild nature, and as the Temiars say, they carry a different odour on them that nature can often sense. The great wild is where they have been put by Nyuᵏ ˀAluj, the Creator, but wisdom is needed to preserve their existence in it and to maintain the balance between cultured human life and the realm of untamed nature. In their own mind they describe themselves as a people of cleared spaces, in the midst of the dense and wild forest, calling their cleared spaces *dɛix*, 'home', and the forest around them, *bɛɛx*, 'the outside'. They must venture out to forage for their needs, and to hunt, so that life at the *dɛix* be sustained. They are not fearful of the *bɛɛx* around them, but they know that it is a wild realm, where they could cause disturbance. Even the fruits, plants and animals that they gather from it can carry risks when they bring them back to the home. The *bɛɛx* provides them an abundance of resources, and yet they must offer respect to that realm, or their lives could become troubled.

In this first chapter, I address all that I have learned about this spiritual divide, and how the Temiars take measures to establish peace with the wild outside, and to placate its displeasure when they have overstepped the boundaries. In the following chapter, I will define the taboos which the Temiars place on committing specific actions and speaking careless words which could cause conflicts with the wild.

A clump of giant bamboo stands immovable, deep in the Ragas River valley, near Rɛnipuy cave.

Elephant foot prints in the mud at the Puyan river-source.

A Temiar cuts a tree to extract the honeycomb of black bees—a sweet life-saver when hungry and weak after a day's trekking without food.

ʔAngah Pandoᵏ at L'moɡ Capɛɛr, a homestead on a swidden located at the Ragas river mouth, on the Upper Puyan.

Tɛmagaaᵏ village; note how all the open space is kept clear of grass, as the Temiars hold that 'home' should be separate from 'forest'.

1.2   SOULS OF NATURE: ANIMALS

All people love to have fun and the Temiars are no different, finding ways to enjoy themselves most of the time, when out foraging for fruits, jumping in rivers, catching newts on the rocks, swinging on liana vines, making models from sticks, painting their faces with colour dots and so forth. But there are some actions that seem fun and harmless, and yet they cross the line into causing interference with the souls of nature. Laughing at creatures that are *nɛ^kcaaᵏ*, caught for food, or are found scurrying or flying about, such as insects, is one activity severely cautioned against as indulging in such frivolity is feared to cause a great storm with crashing thunder. The pig-tailed macaque has one of the most potent of animal souls (and also the easiest to dress up and play with) and the stories tell of numerous occasions where they gathered to play with one and laugh at it, and were then suddenly destroyed by the earth turning over on them or a giant rock falling down and burying them all alive. Of such places where this is known to have happened there can be found a pool of water today as testament to the folly of those fun-makers. Making an animal perform as a human, or a dead animal scratch itself as if still alive, or pretend that anything like a fruit, or even oneself, is an animal, all cross the boundary into offense of souls. Mimicking certain bird calls when out in the forest is another dangerous action that is strictly tabooed. Even laughing too loudly, playing chase too vigorously, and screaming while down at the river are actions that would be asking for a storm to blow over and the elders would in every case order the young ones to quiet down. Reflecting the sun's light upwards toward the sky, with a mirror or by leaving a pot of tea uncovered outside, would be deemed dangerous, as if asking the thunder deity to come and drink, and with him bring his thunder!

Kampuŋ Calɛɛr, a village on the Lower Puyan, with Sakoʾb mountain behind, that borders with the Pos Pasíg territory, to the east.

Mentioning the name of animals, fruits or plants can also prove problematic for daily life, if the attention of the souls of those things are aroused by hearing their names called. It is particularly careless to call the animal's name while preparing or eating its meat and it is feared that to do so would bring on a dangerous bout of diarrhea for whoever eats it, even leading to death. Vegetables, fruits, or inanimate objects, cannot be called *nyam*, or animals, either, as if they were alive. Announcing someone's return from hunting will cause the same kind of trouble for them when they eat the fish or game they have brought home, as well as pointing at or mentioning what animals they caught. Pointing at a hole in standing bamboo, in which bats could be nesting, will cause them to change into a centipede that would jump out and bite the one trying to extract the bats. Naming a rainbow when one is seen is also fearfully avoided, as doing so is said to bring on a storm. Instead, a safer term is used, simply, *na-wȯg*, 'it has risen'.

The actions and speech mentioned above are tabooed for the Temiars and are called, *məsíx*, a term that probably comes from the word, *bísíg*, to whisper under one's breath so that unwanted persons can't hear what is being said. They are actions that would be better not done, or words better said secretively, so that the souls of nature would not hear and take offense and the wrath of the thunder maker not be stirred. Taboos on actions and words are implanted in the minds of children daily, by the adults around them, who will call out, "*Məsíx! ˀAgoᵏ həəy*!" Meddling! Don't do that! whenever a child infringes on something prohibited. And thus they grow up learning to be cautious with their actions, thereby sparing themselves the undesirable consequences of being careless.

There are animals that would create great danger if killed because they dwell in the recesses of the earth, and in deep holes among large boulders. These include two spiny turtle species, the large land tortoise, and the python. One turtle cannot even be approached, for fear of it burning up the forest with fire. A few years back a large python attacked the headman's dog at Kajaax village and he ran for his shotgun and shot it. The dog had already been crushed by the python's coils, but then shortly afterwards a storm blew up and they all had to run for cover. In the 1980s, at Pinaŋ, they caught a large soft-shelled turtle in the main river and a number of people gathered around to have a look, pointing and laughing because it was quite unusual to see. It was in the middle of the dry season and the weather was calm but as they were preparing the turtle to make a meal of it, a huge and sudden gale blew on them and they were frightened for their lives and fled up-river.

Bərcaap village, in 2014, with Tɛmɛnkaaᵏ mountain in the background.

A hunter would never announce he was going out to *siyεᵏ*, or hunt animals, as doing so would cause him to *siyal*, or find nothing to catch. He would keep his intentions hidden by saying he was just going out for a walk, in order to keep his luck intact. A trapper likewise would not say he was going out to set traps, but just that he was tying knots, or running along the trail. The names of *mɛrgəəh*, or dangerous beasts, such as the bear, tiger and elephant, were never mentioned when out in the forest, for fear of bringing their attention on oneself. Avoidance terms would be used to outwit them, such as: *sadaam*, 'menace', or *jɛᵏtuux*, 'feared', for the tiger; *tataaᵏ rayaaᵏ*, 'big old man', for the elephant; *cɛg ʔapoˀs*, 'rips zingiber leaves', for the sun bear; *ludaad*, 'slithering', for snakes. One would never be foolish enough to say that the such and such a beast hadn't been seen in a while, as this would openly remind it to come and call on the house. To call the names of medicinal plants while collecting or applying them would cause them to lose their efficacy. Many other *nɛhtuh julaaᵏ* or secret terms were used, to avoid calling real names or speaking too plainly about one's intentions, as shown in the table below:

Category	Term	Hidden meaning
Animals and foods	*ʔaay*	game in the trees
	nyam	game on the ground
	bəər	vegetables and even bats and rodents
	cōōs	'chirping', birds
	gantɛɛŋ	'bamboo tubes', rats
	boˀh	'fruits', bananas and sweet potatoes
	bɛnhɛd	'sweetness', game
Substances	*kɛndɛg*	'bitterness', blow-dart poison
	bəər	'latex', bird gum
Activities	*dɛhdəəh*	'passing', hunting
	kɛmkap	'tying rattan', trapping
	pɛrpaar	'running', checking traps
	sɛgsūg	'shining', frog hunting
	pɛŋgəp	'sinking a hook', fishing
	ʔis ʔoˀm	tomorrow
	həŋoˀd	nights away
	dɛmdəp	'laying leaves', camping
	kuyoˀw	'wandering', visiting far away
Rituals	*síndul*	'to gather', to hold a ritual dance
	s'gíip	'to wipe', administer ritual healing
	mɛ̄ɛ̄ᵏ	fragrant leaves

Table 1. Julaaᵏ, or secret terms, used by Temiars to hide what they intend to do from animals and souls of the wild

Speaking carelessly, as I have given examples of above, can cause instant dangers to people, even as they strive to maintain an inconspicuous disposition within the wild around them. Making careless promises to someone can also put them in danger and persons should do their best to avoid such flippant assurances. But still, it does often happen and there have been numerous cases of people meeting with beasts of the forest that have set them fleeing. For example, promising to meet someone later on in the forest, to forage or go fishing together, but later on deciding not to go, will cause that person to expect one's company later on, and instead, another somebody will be sure to come and meet them, be it a tiger or a snake, to attack them! Or if one is going on a long walk, or going away and hopes to come back soon, they should say, I cannot promise, I don't know when I'll be back, so that no one will have expectations that will not turn out.

If food or drink is offered, or is made available and has been mentioned by mouth, it is not only polite to take some but it is taboo to refrain from eating or drinking, and doing so would be asking for certain ill fate, such as a centipede running out and biting, or a tree falling on one in the forest, or getting cut with one's own bush knife. So people are careful to take some, even if only a handful, and as they do they say, "*s'lantab*," meaning, I've had a little. In the old days, if anyone teased someone that they should marry a girl or boy, then that person would be ordered to marry her or him as soon as possible, for the suggestion being made was also considered *s'lantab*. If the person who was offered someone as a partner then left without marrying, or their suggested partner procrastinated, then a serious ill fate could happen to them.

Perhaps the most dangerous offense that can be made against animal souls is one that is committed by accident. It happens when one gets scalded while cooking or eating certain meats, either with the hot soup or a hot pan, or an ember from the fire, or else gets cut and spills one's blood. The smell of human flesh or blood becomes mixed with the game causing a conflict of human and animal realms. This mishap falls under a taboo named *pɛlʔax*, also named *məsíx-lòʔot*, blood offense, and its consequences can lead to fatality, be it from a tiger attack or from a calamity out in the forest. A person who commits this offense is said to carry *pɛlʔɛŋ*, the smell of their own blood that has offended, and if they went out to the forest for any reason the avenging tigers, who are an evil kind, would be sure to seek them out in only a short time. They would actually not dare to leave the house if they valued their life and believed that the danger was real, but they would stay at home for at least seven days, until the day of the *c'raŋas* was reached, when the smell of offense on them had ended. It is this *pɛlʔɛŋ* (also referred to as *ŋòʔoy*, smell) that the tigers will seek out on persons to exact their revenge, and it depends on how strong this smell is on someone as to whether they will be sought out quickly or not. Some reptiles are so potent that they can cause a person to *tɛkʰnɔɔk*, or be guilty of the highest offense, if they were careless while eating the meat, and the tigers can seek out the *ŋòʔoy* on them in only one day, so there is reason to fear.

Even pulling off a leech, or squashing a hair louse at the time of preparing food can make one's blood drip and thus cause this blood-offense. It is known to have happened several times in the past, as with one family living at Bɛɛd on the Puyan, in the 1970s, when a woman squashed her daughter's lice the evening they were eating *kaaᵏ kɛnrab*, a sandy-coloured catfish. The next day the girl was out in the forest following after her father (who had warned them not to let her go out) and a tiger attacked her. When her father searched for her he saw the tiger with her body. Another tragic incident happened at the Jɛŋhuŋ River, probably around the 1940s, when ʔAsuh, the young daughter of Taaᵏ ʔAmpís, a great ancestor of the Puyan Temiars, was taken by a tiger in the early

morning as she washed at the river. She also had crushed hair lice the night before. Children are put in great danger if they break the taboo while eating meats such as rats or catfish and they carelessly scald themselves with the food or the hot pan, and thus their parents will often command them to come indoors at dusk, or not to run off anywhere alone, just in case they have any smell of offense, saying, "*Pɛlʔax hāāᵏ!*"—remember your blood offense!

A young boy holds up a kaaᵏ kɛnrab, sandy catfish, that was caught at the Puyan River, a species that carries taboos when caught and eaten.

If the fish is large it must be cut up and shared out with other families, to avoid dangerous ill fate.

Tɛᵏ jɛnrap, or the place of a tiger attack, arouses notable fear in the Temiars, especially as the attacks that happen there are normally linked to the *pɛlʔax* offense. No one would dare venture near such a place (amazingly, even some 70 years after the attack, I discovered) due to the belief that the smell of human blood (and the *pɛlʔɛŋ* that attracted the evil tigers) still remains there. If anyone was to approach the spot, the sky would *s'rɛnyəb*, or darken suddenly, and the dangerous tiger-soul would arise and, without warning, a tiger would emerge and pounce. In the same way, if a person was killed in an accident, it could easily be linked to *pɛlʔax* or another taboo offense and the place would carry their offending smell for generations to come.

The roaming tiger is the most feared of beasts and when they are the evil kind, many times more so. They are known to be able to mimic the chattering of people, the crying of a baby or even call out to people, "*Madoh*!" over here! Thus they are very dangerous to the unsuspecting person who might hear voices and go to see who is coming or go to see whose child was left behind. They also thump the ground or stamp on dry bamboo to make it crack loudly, to announce their presence if they prefer not to have an encounter with humans, or if they wish to intimidate. They might also follow someone along the path, or cut across the hillside above their path, to put fear in them. They can even come under the house, making strange noises, if they want to find someone on whom lingers the smell of *doos*, or sin. Such was their fear of the beast, which abounded in numbers pre-1960, that the Temiars would often build their homes high up in the trees, with a bamboo wall around the base, and a ladder up the trunk to make the way impossible for a big cat to climb up. The tiger was just too powerful a beast to have tugging at the wall or pushing against it in the dark of night, to see if it could be torn down.

An animal carcass (of deer or pig) left by a tiger is also known as a dangerous place to stumble upon, as the tiger will still be nearby, waiting for the carcass to rot, and it will growl and pounce on any intruder. The fruit season and rainy season are particularly dangerous times to walk in the forest as the tiger may think it easy to find someone when they are out fruit picking, or will be waiting to ambush pigs. It is said that the voices of children (especially the sound of their crying) attract the tiger, also of women, whose chatter sounds like that of hens, as the tiger senses they may be weaker prey who can't run far or climb up trees or throw sticks. In the old days, men would always accompany the women when going foraging and the children were kept at home, as they believed there was always much 'smell' on people to attract tigers. In the history of the Puyan River Temiars, there have been a dozen tiger attacks resulting in death, as well as numerous close-encounters and narrow escapes. People with *doos*, or wrong-doings, are believed to be more likely to meet their fate as they will grow weak when the tiger pursues them and be unable to flee, or else they will be pounced on with no warning. Other animals are believed to attack people with *doos* or blood-taboo offense, such as *rɛgrɔɔg*, the yellow-throated marten, and also venomous snakes such as pit vipers and cobras.

The evil kind of tiger is believed to originate from the soul of certain trees and vines, which are classed as *julux*. When the tree is cut down, or the vine is hacked and damaged, the soul of the tree or vine comes down to the ground as a *k'norux* soul, taking the form of a small cat. It then begins to roam the forest, initially seeking the perpetrator of the cutting, and as it roams it grows in size, soon to become a tiger. The Bɛlyans of old dreamed of the *julux* souls and they forbade the people to cut down those trees or vines, warning that anyone who did would soon feel the affects of their actions, and would also increase the danger of attack for everyone else. Until today, people are cautious of disturbing the souls of *julux* trees and most of the fruits of these trees are forbidden for young or susceptible persons. Even palm oil must be avoided in some cases, as the *sawít* palm is a species with a potent *julux* soul. The *manaar* vine, the bud of which blooms into the world's largest flower, the rafflesia, is another *julux* species and camps are never made in areas where it grows, for fear that it may trouble them in their sleep.

Human odour, in general, can cause antagonism in many ways and so the Temiars have certain practices for hiding their odour when they are out walking or to keep it away from the realm of nature when it is thought to be particularly strong. When the Temiars walk in the forest they are quick to spot fragrant leaves growing on the forest floor and they will pick them and stuff them in their loin cloth or waist belt. This hides their body odour with a more pleasant smell of nature. The odour of human blood is believed to cause the greatest conflict with nature, as noted with *pɛlʔax*, above, and women also, must frequently *t'laaᵏ*, stay at home, in order to hide it from souls of the wild. A woman during menstruation and soon after child birth, is not allowed to wash her blood in a river, as doing so would bring on a freak storm, with gale-force wind knocking over trees and causing great rocks to roll down hills. Post-natal mothers and newborns carry the strong smell of *ʔəyɛg*, the afterbirth, on them, for a period of time called *raŋyē̄ᵏ*, that lasts up to a month for the mother and a few months for the child. During that period the mother abstains from bathing at the

1 | **SPIRITUAL HARMONY AMONG THE SOULS OF THE WILD**   11

A lonely place on the Jɛŋhuŋ River, where no one dares venture near. Here a young girl, ʔAsuh ʔAmpís, was killed by a tiger.

river again, as it would cause the weather to *j'ʔaar*, or become stormy, if she did. If her husband helped at delivery and held the child he would also carry the smell of *ʔayɛg* on him, and he should not go out into the forest, for bears are known to attack people with the smell of *ʔayɛg*.

A newly married couple are also not permitted to go out anywhere for a week and a man who has set traps must stay at home until he goes to check on them, so that his smell will not scare away his catch. The trapper cannot prepare his own bait either as it will then have his odour on it, and so another person must assist and dig up the manioc and soak it in water, for two or three days to ferment it. Dropping items that are classed as *dɛix* (or that belong to the human realm) onto the ground can also cause problems in some cases, for example, when soil collects inside an empty food container that was discarded, it will cause trouble for the one who used the item and in severe cases they can suffer breathlessness. Bamboo cooking tubes are always split open after use by hacking at the node and these days even tin cans are punctured on the bottom to prevent them filling with earth. Likewise, old clothing must be burned in a fire, so as not to become covered with *s'moʔr*, biting ants, and cause the owner of it to suffer itching all over the body. Hair clippings are not thrown out either, but are stuffed into the ends of the bamboo wall, to prevent a person suffering hair loss. The reverse is also true in some situations, where humans cannot come close to strong smells from nature. Those who are sick and have received treatment from a soul-medium cannot have smells of animal blood, raw meat or certain raw fruits come near them or they will faint, and may even die.

Many foods from the wild, including numerous species of game animals, birds, fish and fruits, are tabooed for certain persons to eat, as they can cause them to contract serious and life-threatening ailments. The young child and menstrual woman are at most risk of being affected, in both body and soul, as they either haven't grown resilient enough toward the outside *bɛɛx*, or they carry strong odour of the human domain, and they must be prohibited or abstain from eating a great list of wild species. The ill effects they can cause range from physical illnesses such as over-heating, growing thin and having seizures, to behavioural changes believed to be caused by an attack of the animal's soul on the person's soul, such as manifesting the anger of the animal and even acting as an animal, scratching at people and running outside into the bushes. Young people can only start eating wild boar meat, for example, by the age of 16 or even older, depending on their physical development and also whether they feel *lamiid*, or brave enough.

A mother and father will also be prohibited from certain foods during pregnancy, because it is believed that they both contribute to the baby's growth in the womb. Certain foods can cause dangerous complications for the child in the womb and at birth (putting the mother at great risk also) and others will be ingested by the child in the womb and will cause problems for it later on in life, in its childhood especially, but also during adulthood. Mothers generally have to forego eating most wild animals until their last child is weaned off milk, because they are either pregnant

A new home built in 2020, at P̰ɲco̰ŋ village.

at some stage, or else nursing children, and the animals will be ingested by their child through breast milk. There are various species that are only safe for adults to eat and a few that only those in old age can safely consume. Several turtle species are excluded entirely from the dinner menu as they would cause a devastating storm to blow up if they were eaten (described on p7). Some adults have to reap the affects of foods that they ate when they were small, such as a water rat, that can cause them to frequently become breathless. (In the next chapter, in 2.2, I talk more about this taboo called *sabat* and I give a list of all *sabat* species and the effects they can cause).

The elders of any community should be well aware of the species that cause danger to young people and mothers, and would prohibit them from eating harmful foods, while also excluding them from places of preparation of game meat. But some people are careless and allow their children to eat any animal or bird that has been caught and thus they put them at great risk of becoming ill, weak, or abnormal in mental health. Those people who take the matter seriously will keep the bones of any *sabat*-risk animal that has been consumed at the house, by posting them into the tubes of the bamboo wall, or hanging them near the fire place to dry out. The bones are to be kept as a precautionary measure in case anyone in the house becomes ill later on, with symptoms that may indicate a *sabat* animal was to blame. The person who became ill can then be treated with the bones of the animal which they consumed in the hope of curing the illness caused by the animal in the first place. To do this the bones are first baked until blackened, and then they are scraped and ground in a mortar, making a black dust that is then mixed with water and smeared over the person's body.

Another taboo, even more grave than others, is placed on a select number of species of wild animals, that if caught by a hunter or fisherman, must shared out with others at the house. If they do not share out the quarry, as some persons have done in the past by greedily eating the whole thing alone, then the animal will cause *gɛnhaaᵏ*, or misfortune, and either a child in the family, or the hunter himself, will die. There is a case remembered by the Píɲcʊʔʊŋ Temiars, of when a man caught a yellow catfish and was taking it home with him. As he passed by another man on the path he was warned that he should share it, since it had been seen, but instead he disregarded the warning and kept it for himself. He died the day after eating it and the hill where he was warned is now named in remembrance of him, Taŋkʊ́l Kɛnirab, Catfish Hill. The more potent creatures, that are called *gɛnhaaᵏ rayaaᵏ*, great misfortune, would cause everyone present to die if the meat was not shared out and the same fate would also occur if they were carried over to another main river valley. The same goes for anything that is found by good fortune, such as a pool of the river teeming with fish and someone nets them all, or a big turtle in the forest that a dog sniffs out, it must be shared out or it will cause great misfortune to everyone.

1.3 SOULS OF NATURE: TREES AND PLANTS, MOUNTAINS AND RIVERS

The many problems which arise for human life, that I have described so far, are mostly related to human contact with the souls of animals and creatures, and are also caused by these souls, as well as by the thunder god, Karɛiy, who guards over his creatures in many respects. But other souls of nature can cause harm to human life, and these are the souls of trees, mountains and other prominent features of the surrounding landscape. The trees in question are the seasonal fruits that each year give their sweetness, offered in plentiful bunches, that are a welcome source of sustenance to all foragers of the forest. Their souls must be paid proper respect by the eater, as they are the life-givers planted by the Creator, and there are prohibitions that must be heeded during the gathering of fruits. For if these souls are disrespected and their provision taken for granted, or they are given the accidental curse (when falling from a tree, for example) they can steal a person's soul away and cause them to drift into an endless sleep. These souls are also celebrated in ritual dance, to retain their favour and protection, and also to ensure that the seasonal fruits will be plentiful (as some years can be leaner than others). It is believed that if the souls of the fruit trees are not placated with a petition to their guardian spirit before the first fruits are eaten, it would be to tempt ill fate, including the malicious activity of tigers.[1]

1.1 The souls of trees reside in the *jaloˣ*, or canopy, while the *cantɛɛŋ*, or roots, are attached to the souls of the ground, and specifically, the *ˀaam* tigers. Both of these can do harm to the human soul or life; thus in the fruit season one should not do anything to damage the trees. A petition must be made before climbing the most powerful of trees (the *jiyɛɛs* and *soˀic*); the *j'lax*, the towering mahogany, has a powerful *pɑt'rii* soul and thus it is believed that felling them causes serious harm to the land.

P'naŋoˀw Mountain, at centre, as seen from Soˀid, with P'goˀy to the right. (Credit: ˀAri Kɛntoˀn)

Free-standing Sȯid Mountain, with its distinctive four, jagged peaks, as seen from the east side of the Puyan valley, with P'goy, Rɛmŋoȯm and P'naŋoʾw mountains behind it, to the left.

A waterfall on the Pȋ́ncoȯŋ River, where, many years ago, a tiger chased a sambar deer and it fell, and hence it was called Tɛŋkoʾh Kasȋ́ŋ (Deer Waterfall).

Out in the wild, powerful souls are believed to inhabit mountains, boulders, waterfalls and rivers, and these are also capable of stealing away human souls. When visiting such places the Temiars take care not to disturb those souls, and they will never shout or scream at the river, or "woo-hoo" at waterfalls. The flowers on mountain-tops are never shaken about, as they carry the essence of the soul of the mountain, which is called the *pət'rii jɛlmoʾl*, princess of the mountain (likely from the Malay, puteri, princess). The person who offends one of these souls may find his or her eyes closing, being unable to stay awake and falling into a *s'nɛryoʾr*, a sleep from which they cannot be woken. Their only hope is that a soul-medium will help their soul return to them from wherever it has gone. The medium sleeps and searches in his dream for the souls which have stolen that person's soul away, and he says to them, "*Kasaᵏ nyoʾb-siyɛj r'waay-doh? Cacoᵏ yɛiᵏ na-doh*" why have you taken this soul? This is my grandchild. And as soon as they release the soul the person will open their eyes and be able to eat and drink.

To the Temiars, all trees and plants producing food have souls and it is the soul within them that, if treated properly, will produce food and fruits for the tender of crops or nearby inhabitants of the trees. We have seen that the seasonal fruit trees have souls, as do mountains and rivers, and when these are respected and even celebrated in traditional dance, they will never cease to provide their sweetness, each year becoming laden with heavy bunches of delectibles. Planted crops are the same, they have souls that need to be protected in order for them to thrive and provide. These specific souls are called *r'waay canaaᵏ*, food souls. With manioc, for example, those who respect the plants, and are careful to jab the stems back into the ground after harvesting the roots, will see their plants keep growing and producing food for them. Those, on the other hand, who are greedy for today's food and don't care about the life of the plants, and scatter the stems on the ground, will not see more food from the same patch. It is a simple horticultural principle, that to the Temiars is explained by the need to respect the souls of food-bearing plants.[2]

1.2 The breaking of manioc shoots was tabooed (it usually still is today), and only harvesting the roots was allowed, due to the fact that the food soul would be harmed by the breaking of the leaf stems.

A spectacular waterfall on the Kacəŋ River, which flows from Barʔoʼob Mountain, to the east of Gɔɔb.

The clear-flowing waters of the higher Puyan and its tributaries may seem enticing and exotic to us, but to the forest people they are the arteries of life of the land, and they are guarded by powerful souls, which are to be respected.

1.3 Certain plants were always planted on a swidden, including: *moŋlɛɛy*, a medicinal plant (pictured, Vol.2, p13), *buus*, sugar cane, *jaay mas*, sweet bananas, *mantax*, a rattan, *sugih*, a tree, and *gasɛᵏ*, a cotton-bearing palm, to ensure an abundance of crops.

To ensure that the plants keep growing and are not lost because of having no space left to plant the stems, a new patch must be cut and burned while the first patch is still growing. When the plants are still young, only some of the roots are dug up, leaving the plant to keep growing. Diligent planters are called *sɛnʔoʼoy bəjariiᵏ*, or fingered people, as they are constantly working to preserve the life of the crops, that in turn give them life. Such a person will have all kinds of seeds drying around the house, peanuts hanging on cords, and newly woven carry-baskets hung up ready for collecting the swidden's produce. On every visit to the swidden they will come back with seeds, from ripened gourds, squashes and cucumbers, and from aubergines, long beans and spinach plants. Anything edible that grows in the field is enjoyed by them, it is never left unwanted. For if they said, "Those greens are bad, I'm bored of them," then the soul of the plants would disappear and they wouldn't be found again. Their soul, that causes growth of the plants, is the *s'maŋat*, or life-source, of the planter.[3]

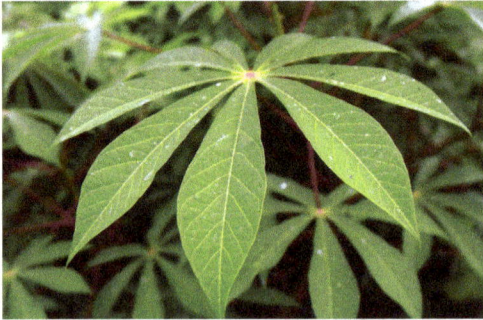

Kayuh, or manioc, is probably the most important staple food of the Temiars.

Any fruits that grow in the rice field, such as these cucumbers, are considered a gift from the swidden and must be enjoyed.

The Temiars' annual crops, millet and rice, are a little different in regard to the life-giving soul of plants and trees. They each have a *r'waay* that guards the swidden. The Taaᵏ Bɛlyans saw them in dreams and learned of their characters, and a *c'naal*, or folktale, was told of them. The *jawaᵏ* or millet soul is known as a *mɛnalɛh*, or young woman, just as the *r'waay tawùn*, or souls of the seasonal fruits. She does not cause harm to people and therefore there are no rules to be followed to avoid arousing punishment. The soul of the rice swidden, however, is an old man, who is called the Tataaᵏ S'laay, old man of the swidden. He is evil-natured, rather like the tigers which are extremely dangerous to any offender, and people must be cautious of him and keep to the rules of the swidden that have been taught by the elders. It is feared that if anyone breaks them, the *Tataaᵏ* will come and torment them in their dreams—*nam-tuh garaŋ*, he will shout angrily at them. Specific rules they must keep include those in the following list:

Stage of the rice swidden	Rules to be followed
After the planting	no one other than the *tuwan s'laay*, or swidden owner, should walk through the field with a bush knife.
Before harvest	the *tɛnrɛɛl* period: people should not pass near the field, they should *t'laaᵏ* or stay away; they cannot cook with spices or wear lipstick (of *sumbaah* flowers, or modern kind).
During harvest	no metal implements should be left behind overnight in the field; persons of another household cannot enter the field to pick shoots or cucumbers (in other words, to steal them), or the *Tataaᵏ* would *dɛndəh*, repay whoever comes down after them to the field, with sickness, and ritual dance and *jamuuᵏ* offerings would be needed to help them recover; young children were not taken down to the rice field for fear that they would scream and pull off rice heads, upsetting the old man of the swidden.
Finishing the harvest	the last work should always be left to the swidden owner; only he can taste of the first rice before the harvest festival is held.
After the harvest	no one should walk through the field to the other side.

Jawaᵏ, a variety of millet, prefers a swidden cut from a forested area. The seed is simply scattered and it grows up among the felled trees and branches.

Another soul that the Temiars fear, which is truly malevolent and can cause terrible grief to any person who comes too close to it, or group which settles nearby, is that of the *bɛrboˀw* tree, the moluccan ironwood. This tree can lie on the ground for half a century before it rots and it is believed to have a powerful soul, alive even in the stump or the old, hardened logs. It is so feared by the Temiars that they actually call it *mɛrgəəh*, a beast, along with the other fearsome beasts of the jungle. When anyone comes too close to the stump or the logs as the sun is going down, they will likely become sick with aches and they may also contract a severe chest pain which is called *pacoˀg*. A soul-medium can give treatment to a sufferer of this condition and can actually extract a splinter of the ironwood tree from a their body, which was causing them such serious grief. Because of its antagonism, homes are never built too close to one of these trees and if one is found to be giving people bad dreams then they will break up their homes and move to a safer location (as happened with the group living at Tɛrsaaŋ, who relocated to Bərcaap, in 2014). Two years ago I found a large ironwood log in the ground just by the house and when I dug it up and started removing and burning it, my wife had a dream of a *tataaᵏ*, or old man, who said to her, "Why are you removing my home?" She had some wit and told him to move on and find somewhere better to live!

Padi, varieties of rice, need to be planted with a dibble stick in a cleared plot of land, preferably where bamboo had grown.

As the rice is growing, no persons other than the swidden owner should enter the field.

Other souls[4] were feared also, that were not attached to creatures of the wild or formations of nature, but took on physical forms of their own. One of these is the *Jaaᵏ Wo'oy*, which has a human female form and a mass of hair which *barwo'oy,* is shaped like an umbrella (hence its name, *Wo'oy*), but it can become invisible if it desires. The creature has a male counterpart, which is less known, the *Taaᵏ Wo'oy,* and they are believed to be *sɛnʔo'oy bɛɛx,* or forest people. They reside in caves, or deep holes in between boulders, and can lure a person into their lair where they will keep them captive indefinitely, closing the rock door behind them to make their escape impossible. It is therefore considered dangerous to be walking alone in the late afternoon in places with many rocks or caves, as one might meet what appears to be a young woman (the creature in a hidden form), stranded but taking shelter in a cave, and when one enters her place she will trap one inside, only afterward revealing her true, ugly form. People are also advised not to stay alone out in the wild for too many days, as the *Jaaᵏ Wo'oy* will take pity on them and come and lure them away. The creature is also feared to steal people's souls and eat their bodies, and it can then take the form of that person's soul, which it swallowed, and return to the village appearing as that person!

1.4 Perhaps these 'souls' would be better described as spirits, not being attached to any physical form to which they would give life to, but in some cases they may have been souls to begin with. To the Temiars they are termed *r'waay,* the same as other souls.

The rice harvest at Píncoʻoŋ, of February, 2019, in full swing after the rainy season.

They will also steal children if they are left alone at home and carry them away atop of their mass of hair. One story is told of a couple traveling on a forest path, and the mother put her child down for a moment, and when she came back it had gone. They searched for it and they could hear its crying coming from the holes in the boulders but they couldn't reach it. If one comes across ferns in the forest which have already had their shoots picked, then it is because this cave creature has been there earlier and if people leave home for a while they may come back and find that squash shoots have been picked from the swidden. The *cɛp woꞋoy*, the black-capped kingfisher, is the pet bird of the *Jaaᵏ WoꞋoy* and it goes out to collect fish for her, and will also report to her about people down at the river (as the folktales tell) and for this reason people are afraid to make too much noise while bathing. If she came to a man alone in the forest and she lured him, and he fell for her and married her, he would then have to forsake the village and live with her in her cave, for if he then tried to leave her she would turn cruel toward him and eat him.

The Bɛlyans of long ago would make petition before entering any cave, to ask the *Jaaᵏ WoꞋoy* to leave them alone and not to close the door on them, and they kept their own souls safe through the *halaaᵏ* power they possessed. Taaᵏ ꞋAti, of the PíɲcoꞋoŋ River, saw the *Jaaᵏ WoꞋoy* in his dreams, or when he walked out in the forest because he could see them even when others couldn't. He said that the young ones were very attractive but the old WoꞋoys were quite the opposite, very horrible. Its name is sometimes mentioned to frighten children so that they quiet down or go to sleep and is also given to the tag person in a game of tag, the *ꞋawoꞋoy*, whom no one wants to be caught by. There is another kind of malicious soul, called *sanuᵏ*, and these can be encountered at graves. When a person comes too close to a grave they can be followed by the *sanuᵏ* residing there, and they will afterward feel very uneasy in their own soul. The Bɛlyans of old would meet these dark, wandering souls in their dreams and cast them out of the place.

To the Temiars, there could be any number of unknown creatures lurking in the river or in the forest, and this gives rise to some strange, mystical creatures that they fear, not to mention the crocodiles that were said to once inhabit deep pools at the river. One of these is known as the *lamboy* (also known as a *biday*), and it is believed to have been formed from a woven mat that blew into the river, long ago. Its body has the appearance of a coloured *Ꞌapííl* or mat, and it can easily swallow a person. It is attracted by the smell of blood and there are still certain places they do not recommend bathing, such as at JoꞋŋ bridge, at TohoꞋy, where it is believed to have eaten a school teacher. It is also known to have caused a calamity once at the Jɛnrol River, when it made a large wave that consumed a group of men who were sleeping on the river bank, leaving only one of them to survive and tell the story. There is another creature called *laꞋoꞋoy*, that is said to be bear-like in appearance, roams the forest in a large pack and would be very dangerous to encounter. It is interesting to note that in the 1950s, the Communists were named after this creature, being called *laŋꞋoꞋoy* by the Temiars, because they roamed about the forest in groups, and seemed dangerous.

1.4   GUARDIAN SPIRITS OF THE CREATION

According to the traditional folktales, there were two spirits that had great prominence in the beginning and were responsible for the creation of the world and all living things. To most Temiars, these two entities, named ʔAlʉj and Karɛiy, are practically deity, as a monotheistic god (called *Tohaat*, Lord, or *Dɔɔ*ᵏ, Father) was not perceived until more recent dream revelations. They are described as *sɛnʔoˈy* or people, but they are not human in the sense of being made of earth and neither are they visible to the human realm. They reside in the atmosphere above the earth and both watch over a multitudes of lesser *rʼwaay*, or souls, placed under their guardianship. To ʔAlʉj, who is good in nature, belong all the souls of the fruit trees, flowers, mountains and so on—the *rʼwaay ʔɛn-balíx*, souls of above—as well as the souls of men who are his *caco*ᵏ or grandchildren. He is the guardian over the created earth, with its rivers and mountains, and also the subterranean cavities beneath the surface. To Karɛiy, who is notably mischievous in nature, belong the souls of all living creatures—the *rʼwaay ʔɛn-tɛ*ᵏ, souls of the earth—who are his *caco*ᵏ. Both are invoked or petitioned by the Temiars during their ongoing endeavor to survive and the need to maintain balance with these two spirits, either to obtain the protection of ʔAlʉj or to prevent the destructive anger of Karɛiy, forms the basis of the ritual dances.

Karɛiy is known by Temiars today as a great tyrant, a fearful being who sends down shattering thunder and devastating storms on those who offend the souls under his watch and is rightly feared for doing so. His proper name, Karɛiy, tends to be reserved for folktales, however, and another name of his, *ʔɛŋkuu*ᵏ, meaning thunder, would not be mentioned at all, for fear of arousing his attention. He is more commonly referred to by some of the following names:

*Taa*ᵏ *Guwaaŋ*	he climbed the *guwaaŋ* fruit tree in the folktale
*Taa*ᵏ *Gorís*	Wicked old man
*Taa*ᵏ *Lʼgaaŋ*	Evil old man
*Taa*ᵏ *Lʼgoˈo*ᵏ	Old liar
*Taa*ᵏ *Luŋgəər*	Old man who booms
*Taa*ᵏ *Tɛŋgoom*	Old man who shouts
*Taa*ᵏ *Roŋgam*	Old man with a bulging body
Hiwəəx	Huge one

He is envisioned as an evil 'King Kong' kind of creature that sends down (or urinates) lightning on the earth, splitting trees asunder and burning them to a cinder. It is widely believed that the crashes and rumblings of thunder must be caused by a physical creature somewhere in the sky above. A soul-medium could make petition to him, with burning of

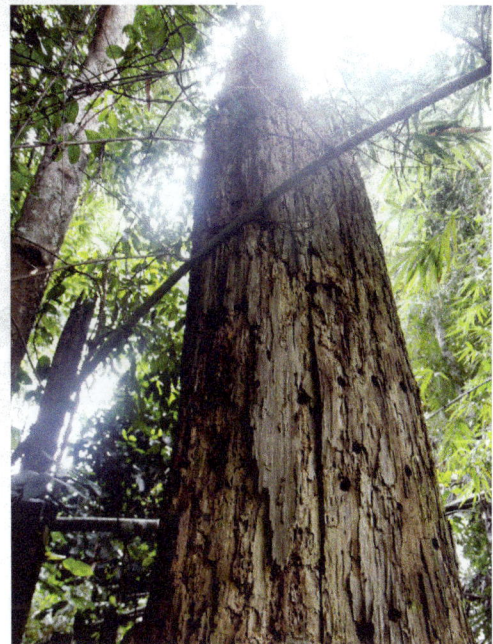

*Kʼnoˈom Guwaaŋ, a tree 'urinated' on by Taa*ᵏ *Guwaaŋ, hit by his lightning, and killed as a result.*

incense, called a *nɛscɔɔs*, in order for the storms to cease. If they knew that the storms were caused by someone's offense, say of *məsíx* taboo, they would make a ritual dance that night and the medium would sit inside a closed booth of leaning palm-branches called a *panoʻoh*, invoking Taaᵏ Guwaaɲ to come and drink of an offering of *cah* tree sap, in order for his anger to be assuaged.

A more drastic measure would be taken if a woman had provoked his anger by washing her child's afterbirth in the river. A huge storm would arise because of this, and they would need to *sumùx*, or make a blood offering, to appease the storm and to preserve their lives. The guilty woman would slash her shin with a sharp bamboo edge and collect some blood in a bamboo dish. The medium would then take it out in the rain and stab a hole in the ground with a rod and pour the blood, mixed with water, into it while beating the ground and calling on Taaᵏ Guwaaɲ to cease his booming thunder. If there was no medium to carry out this ritual then the innocent parties might flee the place, leaving those responsible to their own fate. For if they failed to placate the storm-maker, it was feared that it would *dɛŋdəx*, become even more catastrophic with great rocks from the heavens falling down and killing everyone, and even *yɛlyool*, with the ground where they gathered turning over, burying them all alive. There are pools found today where this kind of disaster is believed to have happened, such as at the old village of Lɛŋraaŋ.

ʔAlɥj is much closer to the human nature and much more considerate than Karɛiy, and therefore he is given the title Nyɥᵏ, meaning uncle (in ritual terms). He is also interceded in many circumstances, but not to send help when Taaᵏ Guwaaɲ has stirred up his wrath, and not with offerings of tree sap or blood to satisfy him, for he does not demand these earthy rituals as Karɛiy does. His power is known to be manifested in multiple entities of the creation, which have been learned of by the *tɛᵏtaaᵏ manah*, the forefathers, in their dreams. Each source of power from ʔAlɥj is known as *bɛlyan* to the Temiars (from the Malay, belian, a polished diamond) and they are able to petition these to obtain the particular kind of power they hold. They are typically invoked by calling on the different names of ʔAlɥj, of which, the most notable ones are as follows:

Nyɥᵏ ʔAlɥj Tampuy: power of the fruit trees, the giver of seasons; invoked when a kin group are about to make the first harvest of fruits of the season or before commencing a ritual dance; the *tampuy* fruit *(Baccaurea macrocarpa) is a julux* species, which means that its soul can cause trouble if disturbed.

Nyɥᵏ ʔAlɥj Lɛnʔoʻoy: power of the *soʻic tree*, giver of long life; invoked when a person is ill or feels close to departing this world; the *soʻic* fruit (*elateriospermum tapos*, perah nut), another *julux* class species, is believed to be the carrier of one's soul in death.

Nyɥᵏ ʔAlɥj Lulɛw: power from the ground, or the layer of the earth from which life comes, the giver of protection; invoked when walking out in the forest, climbing a mountain or making a long journey.

Nyɥᵏ ʔAlɥj Tilɔɔᵏ: power to make things appear near.

There are still more names given to the footprints of ʔAlɥj in creation, such as, *ʔAlɥj d'naᵏ*, *ʔAlɥj ʔɛxʔaax*, *ʔAlɥj məkoʻh*, *ʔAlɥj payɛh*, *ʔAlɥj sɛgiyɛh* and *ʔAlɥj taroʻog*, that are invoked for different purposes.

While making a petition to Nyʉᵏ ʔAlʉj a person will clear the throat frequently, before each sentence, to show that they are only human and are lower and inferior to him. As they speak to him they ask him to look down on them, his *cacoᵏ*, and consider their earthly needs such as their hunger and their need to harvest from the fruit trees, whose souls could become offended by the clumsy activity of climbing them and knocking down fruits. As they approach waterfalls and climb mountains, petitions are made to Nyʉᵏ ʔAlʉj for safety, because the powerful souls of these places were also put there by him. The souls of waterfalls were put there to guard the waters, so that they always flowed, and the souls of mountains were put there to guard the whole life-system that has its source there. It is interesting to note that ritual dances of the present day now involve more petitions and songs to ʔAlʉj than they used to in times past, which is likely due to a new *noŋ* or path that was adopted by the Temiars in the 1990s (see story on p32).

To ʔAlʉj belongs the duty of watching over human life and the Temiars believe that they will return to him in *pantar b'hʉj*, the plateau of heaven (else called *p'yɛɛw*), if they have followed the *noŋ*, or path, and the *hukom*, judgment, that has been given them through the dreams of the forefathers. That judgment is different to the prohibitions placed on foods, and the taboos on actions and words that would stir retributions from Karɛiy, as it regards interaction between humans, not their interaction among the souls of the wild. And whereas the taboos are based on the fear of ill fate falling on one's family and oneself, in terms of calamity and death, the *hukom* of ʔAlʉj is based on a fear that *doos*, or sins made by offending others, will lead to set of uneasy consequences, in this life and in the life to come. The human heart may choose to follow his code and to refrain from anger and cursing, or it may choose to deviate, and reap the consequences of that folly.

And this Karɛiy is not a part of, the relations between humans. He does not reply with his thunder when people offend each other, only when they trespass against the creatures under his sway. In the folktales, Karɛiy did some wicked things to ʔAlʉj and his distaste for mankind, whom ʔAlʉj gave life to, caused him to invent death so that no one would live forever. His animal nature, perhaps, is the basis for this antagonism with mankind, and the set of rules that he watches over involve the animal world, not the human world. Thus the observance of ritual taboos does not constitute a path to better inter-human relations, or good morals, as has been so enthusiastically promoted (Benjamin's 1967 thesis, for example), but it serves only to avoid retributions from entities of the spiritual world.

Three birds, *cɛp biraay*, the oriental magpie-robin, *cɛp tawʉn*, a green dove, and *cɛp hoʔoŋ*, a bird only heard and never seen (probably a cicada, that goes '*hoʔoŋ... hoʔoŋ...*'), are known as '*cɛp ʔAlʉj*' or birds of the Creator, as they have importance in the creation stories. They cannot be eaten and if they were a terrible storm would arise. The magpie-robin, properly called, *Nyʉᵏ ʔAlʉj biraay*, comes by people's homes to tell news of someone coming home or anyone having passed away.

1.5   *C'NAAL NYʉ^k ʔALʉJ*—FOLKTALES OF THE CREATOR

The Temiars keep many *c'naal*, oral folktales, which were learned in dreams by the forefathers and have been passed down from one generation to another. They speak about the origin of animals, birds and plants, that are all believed to have had human forms in the beginning, before they transmogrified into the forms of each species. And also about the trials and vindications of the early humans, who are most often portrayed by a young women and young man (siblings or married) who are always named, ʔAsuh and ʔAlʉj. They tell of giants, called *k'lumbay*, as well as fabled man-eating sub-humans, called the *bata^k*. In accordance with the tradition, the *c'naal* were only recited at night and because they could take hours to tell in their every detail, the recital could continue into the wee hours, if people could stay awake. They also would only be told to an audience of people old enough to ʔaŋgoh, or keep affirming that they were following, by saying 'həə^k', or yes, in response to the tale teller. It was feared (and still is today) that if no one was able to ʔaŋgoh, or if everyone had fallen asleep without the teller knowing, then something else would answer instead from the darkness outside, a *mɛrgəəh*, a beast, the tiger or a dark soul, causing such a fright to those in the house that they would run for their lives. So, in the case that no one could stay awake, the tale-telling would be ended for the night—and thus persons old enough to say they couldn't stay up any longer had to be present, not just children.

The *c'naal* recitals made good evening entertainment, the teller giving detailed description and vivid expressions throughout so that the tale came to life. They also ensured that younger persons learned the tales from their elders, so that they would be able to recite them to their own grandchildren in time to come. Not all children, though, were diligent to stay up long hours in the night, and not all of the older generation were eager to recite either, which means that finding people today who memorised the *c'naal* is not easy.

The primary purpose of the *c'naal*, however, was to teach the *hukom* of Nyʉ^k ʔAlʉj, through episodes of traditional Temiar life and the decisions that the characters made. It is believed that if the *c'naal* were forgotten, or relegated from their place in Temiar society, of teaching the *noŋ* of ʔAlʉj, then the *hukom* would also be lost from their mindset and then life itself would begin to lose meaning. Without the *hukom* of Nyʉ^k ʔAlʉj in their minds, good fortune would not be found, for example, when foraging foods or hunting animals, and consequently their daily existence would become difficult. The *c'naal* also went hand in hand with ritual dance, as the ambiance created by the dances, which were made to celebrate the same entities of nature that were celebrated in the tales, served to invigorate the tale teller and the tales became truly meaningful. As they danced on some nights, and told the tales on others, the life of the forest dwellers was uplifted and hunters would find game easily and their traps would catch animals continually. The bad luck that they always feared would be pushed aside by good fortune.

Here at Pínco'oŋ village we have made audio recordings of some 59 Temiar folktales this year, fifty of them given by one man, ʔAyob Bɛrlɛy (pictured), who had learned them from his father-in-law, Taa^k Ramoy of the Puyan. We collected them as part of this project, aimed at documenting the traditions of the Temiars, and we intend to publish them in the future.

In the Temiar creation tale, Nyᵾk ʔAlᵾj went to cəl, or prod, the ground to see if the mud had dried up enough, after the primordial flood (the Temiars say there were two límbaŋ floods), and when it had dried sufficiently then he made the first man and woman, by putting together bamboo sticks and molding earth around them, first their toes, then their calves, their thighs, their ribs, until their heads were formed. Their blood was given them from the ʔapoʔs haaŋ, a red-stemmed zingiber plant with reddish sap and then he blew on them and they came to life. Everything was made in this way, by blowing it into existence, which in Temiar is to pɛrhíc, to create something without planting it or giving birth to it. The first humans, ʔAsuh and ʔAlᵾj, could also blow things into existence. For example, they could simply blow, with a 'fooᵏ', and a swidden of crops would be planted, without the need to till the earth. Some say that ʔAlᵾj, the first man, would jab a stem of a sugiiᵏ plant into the ground and p'taaᵏ, or petition ʔAlᵾj above, and food would grow for him. There was no need to work and sweat in the beginning. But Taaᵏ Karɛiy interfered with human life from the start—and I am still in the process of discovering the tales which tell of what he did, which is no short adventure—and he dissuaded ʔAlᵾj from petitioning for help from above and encouraged him to use natural means to aid his survival.

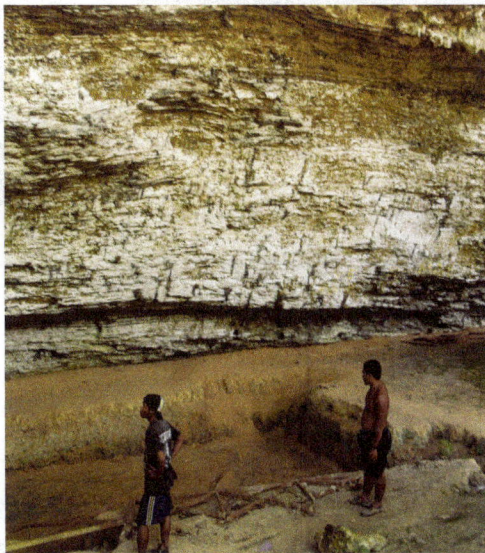

Guwɔɔᵏ Cɔɔs, an ancient rock overhang that was used as a natural shelter by Temiars several times in their history. It was excavated twice in the last century by archaeologists.

There is a tale of a catastrophic flood—which would be the second límbaŋ—that covered the whole earth with raging water. The first humans lived at Guwɔɔᵏ Cɔɔs (so named due to the cɔɔs, or petition made with burning incense, that was made for the flooding to cease, but otherwise known by its Malay name of Gua Cha), on the Nenggiri River. Two youths, also named ʔAsuh and ʔAlᵾj, fled from there up the Pɛriyas River valley and reached the Perak border, although there were no great mountains at that time. The two reached Cɛŋkɛy mountain on the seventh day of walking, while the flood arose and waters poured from out of the earth with great waves, and they remained there to await their death. They survived on that outcrop of land for three years, eating only fern shoots. They were sad to be alone there and decided they should marry. They bore a child and then ʔAlᵾj dreamed of a spirit that told him he must sacrifice the child and cast its blood on the water to make the flood abate. While doubting whether this was right, the baby itself spoke and told him he must do it. On sacrificing his child the flood abated and the next day they saw all kinds of crops growing that they could eat, from millet to manioc. Afterwards they had twelve children, six sons and six daughters. These were married off, pair by pair, and in turn they produced the Temiar, Jehai, Bateq, Menriq, Semai and Temuan people groups. The Temiar group moved to the B'rɔʼɔx river source and from them came the Temiar, Lanoh, Jahut and Semelai groups and each were taught their own language and the taboos and rituals to be held.[5]

1.5 This story may have some variations, especially the names of the people groups mentioned.

1.6   THE *HUKOM* CODE OF LIFE

The *hukɔm* of the Temiars teaches the way of being *mɛnhaar* (generous) over being *kariyɛd* (stingy), and having *kaloʾn* (pity) on others instead of having *tɛnruuᵏ* (anger) and *kɛnʾíís* (hate). It is a code full of sound value, and has been passed down by the forefathers to their descendants, being taught orally whenever situations arose that required guidance. Through adherence to it a social fabric of patience and self-constraint has been nurtured and rooted in minds. Those who pay attention to its path find that they have peace with other people, even when friction and strife arise.

The Temiars have been labeled a "peaceable people" in the past, and the description is true to the degree that the Temiars almost always desist from causing physical harm to others. But the reason why they were called this was largely based on a poor observation of Temiar culture, as well as a fabricated theory of dream control.[6] It was claimed that the Temiars could dissipate violence in their dream experiences, so that in conscious life they were always found non-violent. The *hukɔm* that lies at the heart of the Temiars (especially those of old) seems to have been missed by many researchers, a code which guides their actions and is much more likely to be the cause of their non-violent lifestyle. In their heart they know that striking out against another will cause them to have *doos* and that *doos* will be required of them at some later date by Nyʉᵏ ʾAlʉj.

Men from different villages gather at the balɛɣ ʾadat hall, at Tɛmagaaᵏ, in preparation for a formal discussion

1.6 It has been claimed that the "Senoi people" (referring to both the Semais and Temiars, whose languages both use the word sɛnʾóʾɣ for 'person') are able to cultivate psychological health and social happiness through control of their dreams (Kilton Stewart, in his 1951 article, Dream Theory in Malaya, and Patricia Garfield, in her book, Creative Dreaming, 1974). This theory made the basis for the "dreamwork movement" that began in the 1960s, but it carries little truth in regard to the customs of the Orang Asli. For one, the Temiars do not actively control their dreams, or see what they want to see in them, but they use them to interact with other wandering souls. Secondly, contrary to the claims that they spend much time telling their dreams to one another, it is really only the adepts, or mediums, who describe their dream experiences to their people, to share knowledge of the spiritual realm and to pɛryad, or give guidance.

The discussion in progress, each man present can take turn and have a say on the issues at hand.

The Temiars believe that only those who have followed this code will be allowed into the abode of the souls of the fruit trees when they *p'lo͘ow*, or make the journey of the soul. On passing away, a person who has done good is taken by ʔAlʉj Lɛnʔo͘oy, the soul of the *so͘ic* tree, to a beautiful place among the souls of the seasonal fruits, called *pantar r'duuᵏ*, the shaded plateau. This is the place of *tɛmɛlʔo͘oy*, where nothing ill or harmful is found, only good. Those who are full of *doos*, however, will be taken down into the *rɛŋho͘oŋ ʔo͘os-jùx*, or the glowing fire beneath our feet!

The most prominent *hukom*, or moral code, that the Temiars hold concerns having respect for others, as each person is considered a *caco͘ᵏ*, or grandchild, of ʔAlʉj, their great guardian. Persons must always be addressed with their proper relational term and personal names are never used to address someone once they grow past childhood (perhaps so that their soul is not put in danger by those souls that may hear their name mentioned). Relations are addressed by their status, such as, grandmother, uncle older than parent, uncle younger than parent, older sister, older brother's wife, older brother's child, and so on. Non-related persons are addressed according to age, relative to the speaker, such as, little girl, young man, older man, grandfather, great-great-grandparent, friend between sisters, friend between men, newly married, newly married who was married before, widowed man, childless woman, mother whose first child is a boy, father whose first child is a girl, son-in-law's parent, and so on (the list is extensive). A mother-in-law cannot be addressed by a son-in-law and a father-in-law cannot be addressed by a daughter-in-law, as it is practically a taboo (but really it's due to shyness) for opposite sex in-laws to speak to one another. The siblings of a parent-in-laws are addressed and respected equally as they are. There are many other codes that are followed when interacting with people, especially those older than oneself, such as not walking behind someone's back without telling them, or walking between people who are conversing, unless one crouches low and parts the way with one's hand. When one passes by someone's home they should make it known that they are there, either with a cough or by making a remark about something like the work at the swidden, and not creep past silently. Persons who show no respect or do *ragam* or disorderly things are said to be *to^k barhukom*, or to have no morals.

Temiars believe it is important to share with others when they have need, whether it be tubers from the swidden, rice from the sack or money from a sale of produce, or even a benefits payout. It is feared that neglecting to show hospitality to a traveler or visitor will cause the hosts *gɛnhaa^k*, or some kind of misfortune, such as a crop failure or even a death. Causing any harm to anyone would be a *doos*, or sin. Another kind of wrong-doing is called *tulah* and this can typically be described as committing an act of profaning someone who deserves proper respect, whether by belittling them, cursing or slandering them behind their back or stealing their possessions. Those who deserve this respect include one's immediate family as well as one's spouse's family, with respect for one's father-in-law and mother-in-law playing an important part in upholding the social framework. One's parents-in-law are deserving of much respect because they have been good enough in the first place to provide one with a spouse and also a share in the inherited land with its fruits and whatever resources it holds. A son-in-law or daughter-in-law is equally respected by his or her parents-in-law, if he or she acts with proper respect toward them, and thus they are accepted as valuable new members of the family.

In-laws must be addressed appropriately with their respective titles and never be spoken to rashly or vulgarly, as if they were on an equal or lower level. They should be given help with chores such as food and firewood gathering, swidden-cutting and planting. Parents-in-law of the opposite sex cannot be addressed directly, or even looked in the face, or laughed with or smiled at, and one may not pass nearby them, sit close to them or block their path to the doorway or anywhere else either, such as a river crossing. A parent-in-law will not address their child's spouse of the opposite sex either, but they will provide for them through the channel of their child. Causing in-laws any harm, such as slandering them, stealing from them or forsaking them when they are in need would be serious *tulah*, as would speaking badly of other close relatives, such as a brother- or sister-in-law. This custom would extend further than one's direct parents-in-law, as their siblings, cousins, second cousins and third cousins (considered also their siblings), are also to be treated as parents-in-law through one's marriage, and should be addressed, or not addressed directly, as appropriate.

Committing incest is another serious act of tulah, and communities where marriage with close relatives frequently occurs are believed to bring many misfortunes on themselves. Disrespecting people's rights to their inherited land and evicting them, or stealing from the resources in their land, is also considered tulah. For example, non-heirs build homes on the land without any right (such as they would have through marriage), or non-natives arrive and say to the present-day heirs whose ancestors have been in the land a thousand years, "Because we are so kind, we will allow you a small piece of land to dwell in." In doing this they completely negate the inheritance rights of the existing community, achieving only strife and uncertainty about the future, as well as making their own lack of morals clearly apparent.

Having such a mindset, believing that wrong-doers will meet their own fate in due time, allows the Temiars to react passively in many adverse situations, for example, when people become impatient with them, accusing them of neglect, or cheat them for profits and steal from their orchards when they drive by. They believe that the perpetrators will soon receive their just recompense. And indeed, it has been reported many times over, that bad-natured traders and logging bosses alike have ended up in an accident, in the forest or down on the main road, or else their workers have paid the price, instead, for their boss's flare of temper against the natives.

In Temiar society, all important activities or problems are discussed openly in the long-house, where the elders gather to *ciwaaᵏ*, or exchange dialogue, in order to come to an agreement on any matter at hand. Sometimes elders from neighbouring valleys are called over, to hear and give guidance. These discussions can go on for hours, even through the night, and are only closed when a decision has been agreed on by all parties, whether it be the issue of marriage, where to cut a new swidden or any other difficulty. Marriages are usually easier to arrange and an elder will *kiraaᵏ*, or speak to the couple, stipulating all that is expected of them, and ask each in turn if they agree to the conditions. As soon as there are no barriers then the couple are considered married and they can move into the same long-house compartment or the girl's house. No dowry was required in the old Temiar tradition, and this is still so in the Puyan Valley and most other valleys in Kelantan. Sometimes, if there were enough youths ready for marriage, five or six couples would be wedded at the same time, after holding a feast and a dance.[7]

Dream revelation is not limited entirely to the wise men of old, as in recent times also, certain Temiars have learned of the being and nature of Nyuᵏ ʔAluj through their dream experiences. From what I have learned, however, most people who have had such experiences tend to keep the dreams and their implications much to themselves. This is because, even with the level of enlightenment that the dreamer may have received, possibly elevating his or her knowledge of the unseen, and even of the Creator, Nyuᵏ ʔAluj, they would not want to appear as a preacher of new knowledge and seem to challenge those who maintain a position in society with their own dream revelations, having their own ideas of the unseen. One man's dream journeys, in the 1990s, had such an impact on the Temiars that a vibrant resurgence of soul invocation through dance came about that continues until today in many villages. He was Taaᵏ ʔUsop, of Laloᵏ village, on the Panɛɛs River, on the Yaay.

Around the years 1991-1992, he began to have Around the years 1991-1992, he began to have dreams which changed his way of life and gave him some extraordinary powers, which he considered were given due to a closeness he had with Nyuᵏ ʔAluj. ʔUsop's wife was flown out by 'med-evac' to deliver her child at hospital. Tragically, she didn't survive, even though the child was saved, and her body was returned to Laloᵏ. ʔUsop was shocked at this, because his wife had been healthy. After the burial he told his children not to enter or disturb him, until they saw smoke from the house, because he wanted to seek the soul of their mother. For seven days he lay in his house, while his soul traveled.

1.7 To court a girl, a boy would begin to provide for her from his hunting and fishing, to show her his skills and to earn the approval of her father. In Temiar culture males and females were largely segregated in the home and in their activities, and also the behaviour of adolescents was watched over by the elders, so a boy would never socialise with a girl alone but always in the presence of her family. If any of the boys were too playful with the girls, say, down at the river while casting a net and picking fern shoots, it would be reported by the younger ones and disciplinary action would be taken. Promiscuity was not permitted in the slightest, as the youths still had duties to fulfill (especially toward their grandparents, who may have brought them up since their childhood) before they could think about marriage. And also, having pregnancies among unmarried girls was far from beneficial to the kin group, which needed every person to do their own duty, to enable survival of the whole.

ʔAini P'diᵏ of Tɛmagaaᵏ village hits a maŋsiiᵏ cane on its end, to mash it into fibers, ready for use as a tɛmpuŋ, or cooling medication.

The tɛmpuŋ is hung up at the centre of the dance hall so that the dance participants can squeeze its water on their heads to obtain its health properties.

Fragrant leaves, called cɛnlaay, are hung from cords all around the hall, to infuse the place with their aroma.

He searched among the souls of the *boʾod*, the fragrant plants, looking for her face, but he didn't see her. The souls told him to look underground and so he went below to search there, and there he met ʾAlʉj Lulɛw. But he told him to search above, so he then went above, to ʾAlʉj Tampuy, and implored him to show him his wife. Eventually he saw her there, among the souls of the fruit trees, and she implored him to follow the *hukom* of ʾAlʉj and do only good. She also showed him that the *maŋsii^k* cane was for his healing, as ʾUsop was born with clubbed feet and couldn't walk.

Due to the visions he had he became something of a prophet to the Temiars at Laloᵏ, and to many others who traveled to hear him, including a crowd of people from the Puyan region. He began to *pɛryad*, or show the way that he had learned from ʾAlʉj. He had seen that it was dark and frightening with ʾAlʉj Lulɛw below (who is identified as being the *ndaŋgaaᵏ*, or subterranean serpent, by some), but with ʾAlʉj Tampuy above it was *b'yoʾog*, light, and he was the *dɔɔ^k*, or father, the Creator. He thus called Nyʉᵏ ʾAlʉj by the term of ʾAhaat, which is the term of address for a *tohaat*, 'healer'. His wife had given him a black vine in the dream, and this he would put in water and cover with leaves, and the water would rise, enough to baptise the people and make them clean of their sins. When he washed with the *maŋsii^k* cane he was able to stand up, to everyone's amazement, and his face was changed and he became handsome. Some, however, did not receive his message about ʾAlʉj being the Father (and they conspired to end his life because of it) while at the same time many others began holding ritual dances to celebrate Nyʉ^k ʔAlʉj, which the Temiars had never done previously (only souls of nature had been invoked in their rituals).[8]

To confirm the validity of his revelations, Taa^k ʔUso̓p performed certain miracles, and he could *tɛrbíd* or provide food for the people. For example, in that time they couldn't catch any fish at the river, so he told them to make a big *bubuu^k* fish-trap and put it in the river with the mouth facing upstream, and one more facing downstream. Then he prayed and the river level dropped and all the fish fled into the two traps. Then once again, he petitioned for wild boars, because many people were there and they needed food. In the morning, *taʔo̓ŋ bado̓o̓t*, bearded pig, came into the village and they speared them. Another time he petitioned for langurs and they were found too, in the nearby forest. In his dreams, he saw where a certain manioc plant was growing, that was good for food, and finding it the next day he told people to take stems of the plant and plant it at their own homes because it was *mɛj*, good. This strain of manioc is still planted in many villages today and they call it, 'kayuh ʔasal', original manioc. It is also the preferred variety, because its roots are soft and starchy when cooked, therefore filling, and it has no hardness or bitterness like other varieties.

He also received new strains of millet, sweetcorn and yams and everything that he received in this way was believed to be from ʔAlʉj and was called ʔasal, original, because it grew of itself and wasn't planted by anyone. Also, ʔAlʉj showed him in his dreams what was of the *rɛhŋah*, or darkness, and that he should refuse those things. He had power to close the path to the house so that people could not find a way through, or he could cause them to walk around in circles so that they would wear themselves out trying to find the way.

He entertained many people at his village and taught them to do good, to stop their wrong-doings, commanding them not to hit their children or shout at them. They sang to celebrate ʔAlʉj at night and also in the day time. They had lamps burning during the dance and didn't put them out (this was changed later on, because they found that darkness was necessary for invoking their other soul guides, in order to obtain their powers). He used the *maŋsii^k* cane at the dance, beaten to make a *tɛmpuŋ* pulp, to bathe people with its water for their health. Through his teaching a vibrant new branch of Temiar ritual practice emerged, that is found in many villages until today, where the community assembles to dance three times a month. But as is often the fate of popular people among the Temiars, who say they have dreamed and heard a message from Nyʉ^k ʔAlʉj, others sought him harm and the mediums of B'ro̓o̓x, Tuwɛl, Haw and B'latim gathered, to use their magic against him. But their efforts were futile initially, as no matter how many five-inch nails they made fly at him, he stopped them all by his power from ʔAlʉj. Eventually, as the attacks continued, he dreamed of his wife, who called him to leave this world and join her where she was. He told them that the next day he would return to ʔAlʉj in *b'hʉj* above. When they attacked him again, with flying glass this time, he succumbed to their magic and died that day, and they saw blood coming from his mouth.

1.8 Geoffrey Benjamin describes this new wave of ritual dance and invocation as a resurgence of ritual practice (*Temiar Religion, 1964-2012*, 2014, p370), even calling it a re-enchantment of Temiar spiritual life (as if the Temiars had ever become dis-enchanted with their spiritual beliefs!) It was in fact a new path that the Temiars received through the dream encounters of one man, and which they have adapted in recent times with more dream revelations, whether as sincere as ʔUsop's, or not.

1.7   THE HUMAN SOUL

The Temiars believe that the life of every living thing, including trees and flowers, and even mountains, is its *r'waay*, or soul. In humans, the *r'waay* resides in the *hup*, or heart, the life-beating organ of the body (which some may describe as the liver, and is also called *h'nom*, from *hom*, to breathe). Just as with English, the Temiars say that a person is *mɛj-hup*, good-hearted, or *laʔəs-hup*, evil-hearted, due to the fact that a person's *r'waay* is perceived to be tied to their *hup* or heart. But for the Temiars, the *r'waay* can wander away from the *hup* and the body at certain times, and this can be both useful and dangerous. During deep sleep and dreaming, a person's *r'waay* is said to leave their body, exiting by the top of the head, and then, wandering free of physical constraint, is able to meet other wandering souls, whether they be of people, animals trees and plants, mountains, or even other kinds from above or below. On the other hand, if a person's soul is made vulnerable to a powerful soul of nature, it can be stolen away, leaving them in a state of perpetual sleep, unable to be wakened, until they died from dehydration. It is considered dangerous to disturb someone who is in a deep sleep because of the fact that their *r'waay* has wandered away (they are said to *rɛywaay*, be 'soul-drifting') and if they were to wake up too suddenly, their soul would not return to them in time and they would be left in a dazed state, unable to recollect anything, until washed with water.[9]

Studies claim that the Temiars hold to a belief that multiple souls belong to living beings,[10] be it human, animal, plant or even a geophysical object, such as a mountain. I interviewed Temiars from several different valleys, trying to find proof of this theory, but in every case they described to me the concept of singular *r'waay*, and I was actually told that humans cannot have multiple souls. Anthropologists have inferred from Temiar descriptions of *r'waay*, especially of its ability to wander away from the physical body during dreams, or in trance-state, that a duality of soul must be involved, with humans having one soul that remains resident in their heart (a so-called 'heart-soul'), and another soul that has the ability to wander (a 'head-soul'). But this idea contradicts Temiar belief that the *r'waay* of any being is its life,[11] for how could a human or other creature have more than one life within?

Other aspects of *r'waay* that were supposed by researchers to be additional souls are also found not actually souls. Take the *wəəg*, or soul shadow. When a person passes away, their *wəəg*, also called the *yəəl*, *ləə*ᵏ or *j'rəəx*, is said to remain near the house or at their grave for seven days, while the

1.9 During burial, a person would be laid with their head facing the sunset, to enable their soul to leave in the right direction. Being hit on the head with fruit peels poses danger for a person's soul, which could be made to wander away by the soul of the fruit tree.

1.10 Especially Benjamin's thesis on 'Temiar religion', published in his aforementioned book (pp34, 114-117 etc.).

1.11 The life they refer to must mean consciousness, as the physical body can still breathe and remain alive when the soul wanders. However, the wandering of the soul for an extended period is considered dangerous.

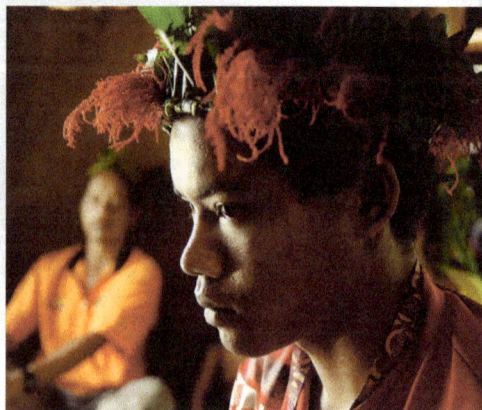

*Temiars gather for the ceremony, to send away the soul of ʔAndo*ᵏ *ʔAti, by making a ritual petition. After the ceremony there will be a pati, or feast, with plenty of game meat.*

New headbands are arranged, tied with soul-guide flowers, for a soul-sending ceremony.

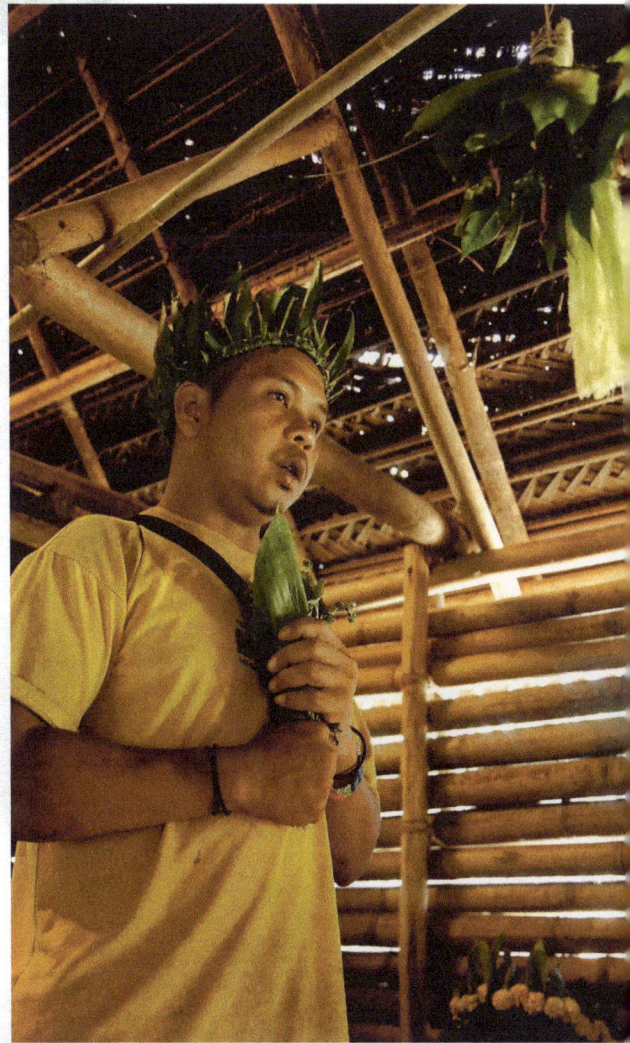

Yusman ?Ando^k. son of the deceased, petitions the soul of his father to leave in peace and not to return and disturb anyone.

grave is watched over by a little bird, the *cεp c'riyεj*, or dark-necked tailor bird. After seven days, when the ceremony is held to *tεrsε^k*, or release, the deceased person's soul, the bird flies off and the *wəəg* also departs. The *wəəg* can only be seen by a spiritual adept or medium but its voice can be heard by others, for example, a deceased person's *wəəg* can be heard calling for its child. A deceased soul can make known its departure to people in other villages, such as to relatives, making a sound like the hum of a cicada, in order for them to make petition and pray *s'lamad*, or peace on that soul.

The *wəəg* is the shadow of the soul and is only seen or heard when a person's soul departs, but in life it can also be feared as it can be cast by the soul even as a shadow is cast by a physical body. When someone is lying sick, and has most likely been blown on ritually for healing, it is prohibited to walk by them and cast one's shadow over them as one's *wəəg* will also be cast over them and interfere with the essence of the dream-guide (about which I describe below) that was invoked to bring healing. A sick person's soul is also left in a vulnerable state and there are many normal activities that others should abstain from, such as cutting down bananas or playing games outside the house, that if undertaken might affect them, or even cause their death.

1.8 DREAM LIFE AND *HALAA^k* POWER

Dreaming is an integral part of Temiar life, giving them knowledge of the wild, of the dangers that lie in wait, and spiritual vitality, through dream guides that taught them to invoke souls of nature and obtain help from them. But such knowledge would normally be learned by adepts, or those who had soul-guides that they followed in their dreams. The more common kind of dream, which the less adept could also have, might tell of events that were about to happen. For example, dreaming of a person would mean that the person was on their way to the house; of a new house, or weaving roofing palms, it would indicate that a death had occurred; of a pool of water, it would mean rain was coming, or of many birds flying about, it would be windy; of something on fire, such as the swidden, it meant that there would be dry weather; of a wild animal, such as a snake, or of getting attacked and cut, with blood, or a tree falling on oneself, it meant there was danger for oneself in the forest, or of a wild boar or bear pouncing, it would mean that one was likely to fall on a stump and shouldn't go out; a dream of the *ndaŋgaa^k* serpent rising would mean there is danger at the river, one should not go down there.

As well as dreams, certain circumstances were also believed to give signs of current events: if one choked on a drink, swallowing the wrong way, it meant that somebody somewhere had mentioned one's name, and thus one would think of them too (after choking). If one tripped up, or felt lethargic, or dropped the food on the floor, it meant that someone was on their way back or coming to visit. Catching nothing when out fishing, gathering only bad fruits, feeling faint, being restless at night, unable to sleep, or if the cooking turned bad, meant that there had been a death in another village, and it had caused *gɛnhaa^k*, or misfortune.

Those who were brave enough to approach souls in their dreams could converse with them and discover if they were good or evil, whether they would share knowledge and protect them or would try to kill them. Many kinds of souls could be met in dreams, including the souls of mountains and fruit trees that appeared in the form of *lɛwtoˀw-mˈnɛhlɛh*, young men and women, and sometimes *tataa^k-jajaa^k*, old men or women, with wonderful bodies and faces (the *rˈwaay balíx*, souls of above). The souls of animals and birds (the *rˈwaay ˀɛn-tɛ^k*, souls of the ground), appeared in dreams with their natural forms. All souls, if good, could share spiritual essence with the dreamer which would enable them to counteract negative forces in the natural world such as sickness. This essence, called *kahyɛx*, would *cˈroboh*, or flow to the dreamer like a stream of water, and remain with them in their *hup*, from where they would call on its efficacy in daily life. Its presence gave them a degree of *halaa^k*, or spiritual power (a person with such power was also called a *halaa^k*).

The great ancestors of the Temiars met the souls of the mountains and rivers in their dreams and sometimes these would *soroˀŋ*, bestow their power on them, such as with Taa^k ˀAmpís, who met the soul of the Puyan River. But in order to guarantee a steady flow or possession of this power-infusing *kahyɛx*, a *halaa^k* would seek to take a *kahyɛx*-issuing soul as his or her *guníg*, or dream-guide. When a good soul came in a dream it would say to the *kahyɛx*-seeker, "*Yi-cɛn ma-hāā^k, yím-guruu^k ma-hāā^k*," I desire you, I want to call you master. Then the dreamer would obtain a token from that soul, normally a stone called a *batu^k tˈgas*, or in some cases a tooth or claw, if from a beast, and then the soul would become the person's *cōˀō^k*, or pet, and the person would become its *kɨɨl*, or keeper. The *tˈgas* stone was kept in their *ˀapoˀ^k* pouch and no one would dare to steal it for fear that its issuing *guníg* would soon come after them. The keeper would endeavor to maintain a union with the *guníg*, following it in dreams and gaining knowledge from it of the souls found in nature around.

The *guníg* could protect its keeper from evil *guníg*, and give him or her the songs that would bring the *kahyɛx* up in his or her *hup*, at times when it was needed. Only the souls of animals and birds would be made *guníg*s as they could roam the forest and come to their keeper whenever he or she called them. Those animals typically included the *kasíŋ* sambar deer, *jɛɛd* barking deer, *kawííb* sun bear, *bawaaj* pig-tailed macaque, *rɛgrɔɔg* yellow-throated marten, the *cɛp biraay* magpie-robin, and even the *ʔalaaj* elephant and *r'laay* python. The *guníg*'s keeper would call them in time of need, such as when sick, and the *guníg* would appear at the house and enable their master to get up and recover. A keeper would send their *guníg* away if it was in danger of being hunted by others, or caught in a trap, or in order to keep his crops from being grazed. He might even send it to trample on someone else's manioc field if they had mocked him. If someone met a person's *guníg* it would disappear quickly to avoid any harm to itself (as it is too valuable to its keeper). The *halaak* may say to the people, "Don't go out there at this time," because he knew that his *guníg* was resting or feeding there.

A person could keep up to three or four *guníg*s, but never a multitude of them because it would be impossible to tame so many, let alone sing to them all. Most often a person only kept one *guníg* unless they were more spiritually adept. The *towaak*, or headman, of Jadɛɛr village, is perhaps more unusual in that he keeps Taak Guwaaɲ as his *guníg*, as well as a tiger, and when a storm brews up because the children have misbehaved or broken taboos, he can petition his thunder *guníg* to cease his storm-making. It is said that a storm can blow up suddenly if he has passed by a place on his way somewhere. Jaak ʔAbơơɲ of Tohơy village is said to keep a *biday* as her *guníg*, the mysterious river creature mentioned above (see 1.3). She can petition it so that it leaves her grandchildren alone when they are down at the river.

Keepers of *guníg* soul-guides shared this *kahyɛx* with them, infusing it into each-other's *hup* in dreams by the action of *p'rɛnlùb*, blowing through the hand onto the head or heart. Thus they became a *s'lantɛɛs*, or joined in the power of their *guníg*, and had this power available to them in daily life. They were also a guide to the people in their valley and could *pɛryad*, or show the way forward for their *k'mơơm*, or kin group. In times of uncertainty, such as happened when a solar eclipse darkened the midday sun and everyone ran outside into the open, the *halaak* was implored to go and sleep and dream. When he awoke he could give his assurance of safety because his *guníg* had told him that no ill fate would fall on them. At other times he could direct what activities should be done, such as going hunting upriver, or where to cut a new swidden, because he had seen the rivers and the land in his dream, and the places which were ideal for finding food.[12] A *guníg* animal that roamed the forest was also called a *kɛnlơơx sɛnʔơơy*, someone's eyeball (or else, *mad sɛnʔơơy*, someone's eye), as it belonged to a master and it saw for him or her as it wandered about. When the master passed away, the stone or tooth that he kept would return to the *guníg* and the animal would be set free. This was exemplified at the passing of Busu Loŋ, who lived at the Tabơh River, on the Puyan, when his *guníg* yellow-throated marten, a black, dog-sized mammal with a long tail, came bounding about in clear view, to show that it had been freed.

The most powerful of *guníg* was the tiger, and not any normal tiger but a roaming soul of the *julux* trees, that had become a wandering *k'norux* soul, taking the form of a tiger. This soul was actually evil, in that its nature was to hunt down people with the smell of blood offense on them, being sent out by the tiger lords, Mɛŋkah and G'nacəb, who reside one to the East and the other to the West. But a brave adept could meet a *k'norux* soul in his dream and make it his *guníg*, if the tiger requested that he become his *guruuk*, *or* master. By taking its tooth or claw he would make the tiger *l'mɔɔn*, or tame, so that it would not attack him but would respond to his call when bid, and

1.12 The *halaak* dreams of the souls above, to keep the rain off while the swidden cuttings dry out, and then, when they are ready to burn, he dreams of the rain, to allow it to fall the day after, to prepare the for land planting.

1.7 I was also told that a person's *kɛnlơơx* can remain wandering about after the person's death, and cause problems for the living, bringing them sickness and so forth. Hence the reason for sending off the souls of the deceased properly, so that they do not have these soul attachments that remain in this world, looking for them or for others. In which case, the *kɛnlơơx* is not so simply defined, as being the actual dream guide animal, but it is more like a spirit force that attaches to the dream guide keeper and his/her dream guide animal. They also refer to it as a *b'ndəah tɛkruuk*, 'thing of anger', meaning something that rose up in that person's *hup* during their life.

would become relaxed by his *g'nabag*, or singing. The keeper of a tiger *guníg* was called a *halaaᵏ rayaaᵏ*, or great medium, and the power available to him was also of a much greater degree than that available from other *guníg*. Because of such power that they held in the realm of souls, there was normally only one great medium per river valley, to whom people went in times of trouble or to participate in the ritual dances that he led. Women never became great mediums because they were not *lamiid*, or brave enough to walk with a tiger, in dreams perhaps but not in life.

The great medium was also called a *Taaᵏ Bɛlyan*, because of the token he held from his *guníg*, the symbol of having *guníg*-union and the power at his disposal through it. They would say that the old man held a *bɛlyan*, and he was rightly respected because of it. For example, he could visit places in his dreams and see what people had in their homes, to check if they were hiding anything stolen or if they had any poison that they might use on someone! He could *bacax*, or recite magic, and send people speedily along the path, or make them wander around in endless circles trying to find the house, if he did not want them arriving to see him. A powerful *halaaᵏ* could *p'laaw*, or fly off without his physical form being seen, and reappear elsewhere, which was a useful tactic when circumstances were threatening. It is told that a Temiar in Perak, when apprehended by the police and locked up, being accused of aiding the Communists, disappeared from his cell in the night and was later found back at his home doing his work.

His *guníg* taught him what would offend the forest souls, the things that are taboo, of foods or actions that are forbidden, and it would protect him from other tigers and show him in dreams where they were roaming. In their dreams the Taaᵏ Bɛlyans of old would walk or fly with their *guníg* up on the mountains, and from there they viewed the rivers and valleys below, and thus they became well acquainted with the land. Many of the mountains were also named from their dream experiences. A Taaᵏ Bɛlyan might see in a dream that the tigers were looking for someone in particular and he would warn them not to go out at that time. He might dream of a bear chasing someone and order them not to go out anywhere—and if they did they would be likely to meet with ill fate such as falling with their rear-end on a sharp stump.[13]

A great medium could call his *guníg* to come at any time, to his aid or perhaps to *pɛgyɔɔx*, scare people, who might have mocked his status. For example, if they say, "You have no *halaaᵏ*!" or they revile him, he will send his *guníg* to meet them when they walk in the forest, to make them fear for their lives and flee without managing to collect what they went looking for. Thus he would *bɛᵏcoᵏ* or tease people and they would soon learn not to disrespect him. When somebody did something that was distasteful to him, or against the tradition he taught, he would lay a *mayaŋ* on them, a fine, and they would surely pay up[14] for fear that his *kɛnloʼox* would constantly tease them when out foraging. That said, the *halaaᵏ* would keep his *guníg* away from the village so that people were not put in danger and so that it wouldn't run into a spear trap set for deer or wild boars. When the *caŋwoʼoj*, the brown wood-owl, was heard cooing at night, it was the sign that the *guníg* tiger was prowling in the forest nearby, causing people to fear leaving the house too early in the morning. The the owl is said to ride on the tiger's back and it is called the *woʼog sɛnʔoʼoy*, the face of the tiger's master. Its call is also believed to usher in the *tawùn*, or fruit season. Another bird, *cɛp t'ranɛᵏ*, the chequer-throated woodpecker, that lives in the hollows of trees, signals the presence of the tiger in the daytime with its call, 'wɛɛh-wɛɛh,' or of other animals such as boars if it calls, 'rɛh-rɛh'. One other bird, *cɛp yooc*, which is never seen, calls when the tiger has made an attack on a wild boar, or on a person.

1.13 A medium would burn *kasay* root at the year's beginning to determine how the year would turn out: if he saw *m'naŋ*, or cords, rising in the smoke, straight up, things will be good, but if falling to the side, there would be problems. If there were cords of birds and animals, the year would have plenty of game and food; if of a *dɛŋdəx* storm, the year would have a lack of food; if of the tiger, there would be danger, as a tiger may seek to take one of them and they should always go out in safe numbers (tigers from elsewhere, and not their own, were more feared).

1.14 In the old days, people would keep rings in their pouch, in case they needed to pay a fine, because the punishment for not paying was too fearful.

A great medium's soul did not *p'loʿw* as others, when he died, but it became a tiger itself and wandered away down-river, to a great rock, called, Batu^k B'ralo^k, where it abode with other tiger souls. His tiger *guníg* would then be freed and would look for another master to keep it. The *halaa^k* would normally introduce the *guníg* to his son at the ritual dances, so that he would be familiar with it and less afraid to take its token in a dream and tame it himself. This practice has not continued to the present generation however, and tiger mediumship has practically disappeared. The great medium of the Píncoʿoŋ River, ʔAti Kabɛl, showed his *guníg* to his daughter, ʔAsuh, probably over 60 years ago, and after his death she dreamed of the tiger and took its claw, which she still keeps. But this was just to keep a remembrance of her father's spiritual power, she did not acquire that same *halaa^k* power—she would have needed to entertain it with vine water in a darkened booth, in order to have possessed its real power. She was never afraid when she walked in the forest because she knew that the tiger looked to her, although she never invoked its help. The tiger was known to roam near the village and it never harmed anyone, even though it showed itself to several people. But a formerly kept tiger *guníg*, roaming without a keeper, is thought to be a very dangerous animal to meet with, as no one is taming it with songs to calm its soul.

The *ʔaam*, or tiger, would request of its *guruu^k* in a dream that the people sing to it the following night, saying, "*Jawah ma-yɛi^k,*" play for me, and prepare *jamuu^k*, or special offerings for it. The offerings would include *boʿod l'bag*, a smooth-leafed plant that grows on the forest floor abundantly, and *c'boʿoh cɛŋcoʿox*, the water from a certain liana, as well as other fragrant plants that it might prescribe. The leaves would be cut up and laid on the floor inside a *panoʿoh* booth, and the water would be contained in a bamboo flask. The *halaa^k* would sit inside the booth of palms and sing a slow and sad song, of a wavering voice style called *pɛnʔəəy*, to music made by the stumping of bamboo tubes. Incense of *kasay* root burning on hot embers was carried around the outside. At a certain stage in the song the medium would begin to *lāās*, jump about, and *k'roox*, to shake, and then he would *wəl*, forget himself and enter a trance (and some say he would also levitate into the top of the booth). Then he would begin to *hilad*, tell

S'laa^k l'bag, a plant from the forest floor which was required by a dream-guide tiger to be laid out in the dance hall.

of the past and the future. As the medium called on the tiger to come in from the dark outside, he would say: "*samon b'lantɛɛy,*" petition him with the drink offering; "*ʔíntɛy gɛlg'lɛɛl,*" coming from the mountains, he jumps on the booth; "*gabaŋ tɛrman,*" sing to please him; "*samon s'naŋ caloon,*" petition well with the leaf bunch. At a certain moment he would call out, "*Tataa^k nam-huwal,*" the old man will come out of hiding, implying that the *ʔacoʿog*, or tiger in song language, was entering the booth.

The medium's song would *tɛrh'wal* the tiger, or bring it out of the darkness and into the booth, and then the top of the booth would begin to *l'pɥd*, or rustle as the tiger landed on the palm leaves. It then came down, with a 's'luuh' sound, to the leaves on the floor and at that moment the medium requested the liana water to be passed to him, saying "p'saar b'lantɛɛy," send forward the offering, and this he gave to the tiger to drink. The tiger was said to be physically present in the booth but no one would see it, unless the halaaᵏ permitted them to enter or to put their hand in and feel its fur. The late great medium of Píⁿcơóŋ took certain persons into the booth so that they could touch the tiger, which was placid as a cat they say, and his daughter (mentioned above) was also shown the tiger in this way. The villagers had to comply with each of the tiger's requests and prepare each dance correctly, laying out a specific kind of leaf or flower, for example. Thus doing, they would keep it l'mɔɔn, or tame, and prevent it becoming evil, and liable to attack any of them at any time. It would even be dangerous for the halaaᵏ if it was not entertained properly. So the halaaᵏ courted trouble when he became a tiger-keeper, and surely he was aware of that, as in reality the tiger kept him. But there were good advantages to be shared by the whole group through such a soul union and their survival in the realm of wild souls became much more feasible.

A halaaᵏ could use his guníg's power to sɔɔᵏ (Malay, jampi), or administer healing to sick persons or those suffering from ailments or soul-loss caused by souls of the wild. This he would do during a dance, but also at other times, in whatever house he was called to. Women could also sɔɔᵏ others, but only for other womenfolk or for their own husbands. When performing such a ritual, he would k'tup, tap the chest to find the kahyɛx, and then s'rơóp, kneel down next to the person with the illness, and garr or shake a bunch of fragrant leaves over their body. He may also rapơr, hit the air with the leaf bunch, or pɛgpơg, hit two bunches together. Then he would t'hool, or blow through his clenched hand on the person's heart, to pɛrlùb, or infuse his guníg's essence, and after some reciting and more blowing on their body he would be able to extract the sickness through his hand and throw it aside.[15] But one session may not be adequate and he would need to return later to infuse more kahyɛx on the patient. In the meantime, he would prescribe taboos on certain foods that could interfere with the ritual's power, and even cause the person's death. The patient would not be allowed to go out in the sun or to eat chili, which would make them hot and give them the shakes.

He may also blow on items for the patient to use such as drinking water and tobacco, and herbal medicines such as moŋlɛɛy (see Vol. 2, pp12-13), for them to bathe with, or dyes such r'mɛɛd (turmeric) and ʔulơx (a yellow root) to paint on their face, and also amulets for them to wear around the neck. This was in case the halaaᵏ couldn't attend to them for a few days, so that when they felt they would sɛlwah, or faint, they could touch the item infused with the guníg's kahyɛx and feel well again. The halaaᵏ would also pɛrlùb or infuse kahyɛx on those willing to follow his lead and become an adept or on the one chosen to succeed him as the next great medium.

The nɛᵏsɔɔᵏ, or healing ritual, is known by the Temiars as the only cure for many kinds of illness that are believed to be incurable by other methods. Those would include problems caused by eating tabooed foods and also some other illnesses that are believed to be jungle-born. One such illness, called bahyaaᵏ, gives a person acute pain in the stomach or back and is caused by bathing in cold river or stream water. Infant children are most susceptible and for that reason they would always be bathed with warm water.[16] Another is called taníg, a gout of the knees that is caused by kicking taníg rocks (exact identity still not known to me) down a slope. The halaaᵏ could also tɛrmaaᵏ, or return, someone's soul if it had wandered away and couldn't come back or if the souls of nature had stolen it. He would be able to find their soul in a dream and bring it back, and the person would awake from their dangerous slumber. Another illness they prefer to avoid is mamɛɛŋ, a migraine that comes on with the midday heat. It is believed to be caused by the cold air, the mist, or the

1.15 The medium sucks out the illness through a clenched hand. In some cases, depending on his or her qualification as a medium, a solid object will be removed, that was the cause of the ailment.

1.16 This is not to be confused with baad, a long black worm which is sometimes found in the gut of grasshoppers, and also fish. Small children are not permitted to touch raw fish due to the possibility of coming in contact with one, and also, they are not bathed with fresh, cold river water, which they call ʔơóx baad, or water with baad worms.

dew dripping from leaves, having contact with one's head during the early morning. Children are susceptible because they may run straight out in the morning without first washing their face.[17] The remedy for this is more simple, however, as it can be relieved by pulling a clump of hair on the head to 'crack' the scalp. A more serious condition that a medium would be sought for was *gɛɛs*, the inflammation of the genitals or abdomen, believed to be caused by committing incest (or resulting from close marriages). But only a qualified medium would know how to extract the disease (they would find and remove a small rag) and be able bring relief to the sufferer.

Some people followed dark souls in their dreams and obtained token stones from them, called *batuᵏ t'lag*, in order to retain power from them. This was deemed useful to them in the same way as *kahyɛx*, but it was a dark power and could be unleashed to cause serious harm to other people. A *t'lag* stone could be buried in the ground in order to inflict a deathly illness on anyone passing that way and if it was buried near a home it could cause chaos. Some practiced *pɛnsuuᵏ*, the sending of sharp objects. First the object would be blown on to give it power and then it would be sent off, liquidizing in mid air and solidifying again once it lodged in the flesh of the target person, to cause them serious pain or death. It might not be flying objects that were sent to their victim but debilitating diseases such as arthritis or swelling of the abdomen, that would make their life extremely difficult or even end it. One woman I heard of, who lived at Kajaax, was targeted by someone's magic and she became sick, with a burning feeling inside her. After two months of suffering she died and a witness said that ants came out of her mouth and ears.

Another dangerous type was called *sɛnpug*, whereby someone would *s'pug*, or pull away another person's soul, causing their inevitable death. A less harmful type, but very manipulative one, was *cɛnwoʹoy*, the love charm. A person was given something that had the water of a charm dripped on it, in order to *cɛrwoʹoy* them, or put them under a spell, so that they would become desperate to marry the charm's holder, crying for them, even if that person was old-aged and ugly. Only to find out after a year or so that they had been charmed, but then be too afraid to say anything as the charm holder may well cause them a premature death!

Temiar sorcery is said to be less potent than that of Jehai, Semai or Indonesian origin, but to the Temiars it is still powerful except that they choose to keep it hidden. They don't readily use it to inflict harm on others (as just described) but it is used to procure long life for them in other ways. It is said that keepers of these magic charms die miserably, being tormented, unable to depart this world, sometimes going crazy and climbing up in the roof rafters. It would depend on how far somebody had strayed from the light of ʔAlʉj into the realm of the *sɛnʔoʹoy rɛhŋah*, or dark souls. Persons who possess forms of *halaaᵏ* power often appear quiet and thoughtful, as opposed to those with loud and humorous character, and when they see another person of quiet demeanor they may search that person to see if they have any *halaaᵏ* and they may also try to *taroʹŋ*, or contest them, to prove which *halaaᵏ* is the stronger. It is believed that many persons with *halaaᵏ* who die sudden deaths were challenged by other *halaaᵏs*. The late Rtd. Sgt. ʔUda Siyam, of Kacəŋ village, was believed to have been challenged by an Indonesian builder working there, without his knowledge. His level of *halaaᵏ* proved far inferior to the foreigner's and the result was he became incurably ill, and died soon after.

Other stones were obtained in dreams also, to aid one's hunting and gathering in the forest, or for protection from beasts. These included the *batuᵏ t'gas*, from the tiger, to keep one safe from them, or a larger one from an elephant to make it a *guníg* and to keep them away from the swidden.

The *batuᵏ manoˇw* from manau rattan, was kept to enable finding rattan easily. Those found in animals, such as langurs, siamang, certain fish (*ʔayoˇm, t'ŋɔ̄ɔs, bawuh*), large rats, bull frogs and the porcupine, were all used for finding and hunting these creatures easily. The adept first blew on the stone to give it *halaaᵏ* power and then kept it with him. But stones of the python, millipede and centipede were not taken as these creatures wriggled and no one would want to meet any of them!

In recent years, there have been many cases of persons affected by dark spirits, causing them different forms of psychological disturbance, leading to insanity and even demonised behaviour. The Temiars of the past always had the occasional *ʔayɛɛŋ*, or crazy person, to bear with, like an old man who talking nonsense, but not the kind of cases that I describe here. The affected person first loses his or her human feelings, and then their sense of cleanliness, not bathing for weeks, eating things in the dirt and sleeping under the house. They may start interacting with a 'person' that keeps appearing to them, but is invisible to others (except for an adept person). Their 'companion' spirit will either terrify them, or make them laugh, and even lead them out into the bushes at night. It is often called their *toˇw*, husband, or *lɛh*, wife, even if they have a real spouse, because they are always observed responding or talking to it.

Because of their detachment with real life, which puts fear in other people, this person will be labeled a *sombiy*, or zombie. Ultimately, such a person will *sɛdsiid*, or become possessed by the spirit, often in the evenings, and will gain super-human strength, so that no one can restrain them. They will disappear or fly away so that no one can catch them and they will lust for blood and catch chickens to bite their heads off. *Nɛᵏsɔɔᵏ* ritual blowing may have no effect at dislodging the spirit from them and after attempts have failed they will be left to themselves, while people shut their doors for fear of being bitten by them. It is also feared that their presence in the village causes everyone to be frequently sick. Sometimes they can be washed with *maŋsiiᵏ*, the water of spiral ginger cane, to restore their sanity. To my knowledge, in the last few years there have been around a dozen such cases at Pos Gɔɔb, out of some 300 adults from a dozen villages, with half of them coming from one village.

It is believed this kind of spirit-possession occurs due to a person's *doos*, their miss-deeds, or to a person's exposure to something that shocks their psyche. For example, a person is startled by seeing a jet aeroplane (this caused insanity for one Semai man I know of) or they have seen movies that are way outside their norm and the scenes were believed to be real life. Perhaps, also, they were introduced to narcotics and had hallucinations. One man, of B'roˇg village, a retired Sergeant, had seen someone in a bloody state while serving in the Army (based at Bidor, Perak), and this caused him to go insane. He was retired early because of his condition and since his return he has become a danger to the other villagers. In January 2021, he was flown out for medical care, but they soon returned him, unable to find a cure for him.

A more sinister cause of insanity among the Temiars is linked to malicious spells. Indonesian loggers or labourers who have been in the area, who possess *halaaᵏ síhíír*, or dark magic, have been known to *pukoˇw*, or cast spells on objects and then bury them near a village, in order to infect people who pass by. One is believed to have been buried at the loggers' yard opposite B'roˇg village, causing at least two persons to be affected, and become insane. There are two other places where charms were buried in this way, and both places were named Habog, which means 'ash', because when a charm is buried it is wrapped up in a packet filled with ash. One was buried near Cɛnantəl, by a Semai working at the Fort at Gɔɔb, many years ago, and until today no one dares to live there.

The other was buried more recently, near Bɛɛd, and this caused trouble when a group tried to settle there in 2014. After a few weeks, they awoke one morning to find all their chickens headless and blood scattered around. They had to abandon the site because they feared a dark spirit possessed the place which was hungry for blood.

Temiar children residing at the boarding school of J'rɛɛg (also more recently, in 2023, children at the Pos Tohoʻy school) have been affected by the sɛdsiid type of demon-possession several times, which was believed to be caused by malicious spells, as these problems have never occurred before among children.

Habog, a small settlement not far from Píɲcoʻoŋ, that was abandoned after 'dark spirits' disturbed the people.

1.9 RITUAL DANCE AND INVOCATION

Already mentioned above are two types of ritual dance that are made in order to appease and pacify two powerful entities, those being Taaᵏ Guwaaŋ, the thunder-maker, and the great medium's tiger *guníg*, which is a dangerous *k'norux* tiger soul. During both these rituals the *halaaᵏ* would sit inside a booth made of palm branches, chanting in total darkness so that his invocation was not interrupted. The rituals were solemn gatherings without room for excitement or pleasurable singing and the people were probably somewhat stricken with fear anyhow. The medium entreated these powerful entities so that he could lure them into a state of calmness and thus procure safety for everyone in the kin group. Once he succeeded in his petitions, then the dance could change pace and more vibrant songs be sung, with enthusiastic beating of bamboo tubes as they began to celebrate the souls that gave life. This faster style, *nɛhpɔɔh tawùn*, the dance to the seasonal fruit souls, was by far the most practiced of dances.[18]

Its main purpose was to invoke the souls of the *bɛɛx*, and to seduce them into approaching the hall where they could meet with the soul-medium. When they arrived he would speak with them, to secure their favour on all the people, and also be their mouthpiece and tell about things from their perspective. Failing to celebrate them would also cause them to withhold their fruits, which are a vital life-support of the Temiars, and for that reason the dance was typically held before the fruit season begins and as the first harvests are made so that the trees would yield their sweet bounties in plenty. It is believed that the *cɛndoʾoy tawùn*, the souls of the fruit trees and givers of a healing water in the dance, are more active during the fruit season. Also, if traveling far from the home valley, a dance would be held before departing to seek harmony with these souls, and especially so that they would not meet with the two *ʔaam rayaaᵏ*, the great tiger souls, Mɛŋkah and G'nacəb, on their travels.

The dances were performed in the *dɛix tagoʾd*, the communal long-house, and this was first decorated all around with *cɛnlaay*, fragrant leaves hung from cords by their stalks. The aroma of these plants, together with bunches of more fragrant leaves mixed with flowers in the hands of dancers, and the beautiful flowers adorned by the women, infused the place with an aroma normally never experienced in such constant intensity, even when walking near flowering trees in bloom or when picking these leaves to stuff in the waist. This infusion of scent in the house was necessary to make the visiting souls of the forest feel a homely, perhaps intoxicating, atmosphere on their arrival. The men *t'pɔɔᵏ*, crown their heads with woven bands made of palm leaf and flowers, and the women *cadùg*, adorn the hair with beautiful flowers and *coʾod*, or dab dots on their faces with sticks dipped in colours. All these decorations helped to create unity of soul between the dancers and the visiting souls which descended from their forest abodes.

The women-folk would enter and sit alongside a smooth log, on which they to beat their two lengths of bamboo tube, one long, the male, and one short, the female, closed ends down, to create a resonant and deep, bi-tonal music. The men stood in the middle of the hall under the hanging leaves and moved about slightly to the rhythm of the bamboo high-low 'huuŋ-hooŋ'. A song leader among them performed his best recitals, line by line, as the female percussionists sung in reply, overlapping the end of the lead and maintaining a constant flow of vocals. The men waved their *caloon*, or tied bunches of fragrant leaves, to infuse the air with a powerful fragrance, sometimes holding them in their own faces while breathing in deeply. Then they would start shifting from one foot to another in small hops, and, as the tempo increased and the songs become excited, they would start to *pɔɔh*, or jump to the rhythm of the bamboo music, while still maintaining the shifting

1.18 This dance is also called the dance of *ʔadoʾot p'rɛnhíc*, the great-grandfather who created life, and it is held to protect the *r'waay canaaᵏ*, or food souls of the forest.

of feet. And as they jumped, they made a percussion on the bamboo floor (and hence the dance was designated the term *nɛhpɔɔh,* jumping about).

This song style is called *taŋʔəəy,* and it involves the sheer enjoyment of good voice and skilled, but often improvised, lyrics. The songs include stanzas about the rivers and hills around, life in the forest and the plea for ʔAlʉj to protect it, as well as spiritual ideas about *pantar r'duuᵏ,* the abode of the deceased. The *halaaᵏ* would invoke the souls of mountains in his song, calling on the names of the high peaks all around the valley, such as P'naŋʊ̆w, Síríŋ, Lírís, Sʊ̆id or Bərlɛɛy, and then the souls of the seasonal fruits, calling them *mɛn-ʔalat b'rəx,* the hands of the fruits, from *s'galaaᵏ menwaaᵏ,* all over the land. When the *cɛndʊ̆ʊ̆y tawùn* (also called *cɛndʊ̆ʊ̆y b'riix*), the visiting souls, arrived near the hall, they wouldn't enter but their presence caused the *halaaᵏ* to *lāās,* jump about, and to *hilad,* speak things that he heard of them. Then he would request them, "Yaah, ham-ʔʊ̆ʊ̆x c'bʊ̆ʊ̆h," give me the cool water, "yím-tɛrmuh ʔomnaᵏ" I will bathe them with it. This water would travel down *p'rɛmjɛɛm* or silken cords dangling from the roof (else called, *m'naŋ tawùn,* threads of the seasonal fruits), which were only visible to the *halaaᵏ,* down onto the *tamuuᵏ,* a ring of hanging leaves at the centre of the hall. The medium then collected this water with his leaf bunch, or in a dish on the floor, and with it he would *ramus,* or sprinkle all the people present.

In today's form of the dance, the participants squeeze water on their heads at the end of the dance, from a bunch of beaten *maŋsiiᵏ* canes hanging at the *tamuuᵏ*—the same cane that Taaᵏ ʔUsop, the Temiar prophet from the Panɛɛs River, saw was good for healing. Once the ritual was completed, the song was ended with a sudden and loud, "Hoo!" from the medium, and with that the *cɛndʊ̆ʊ̆y* were sent back to their abodes of nature. In the dance he would speak with them to obtain an assurance of safety for his people, and for the next few days a peace lingered, and all who had been present would feel *mɛj,* or well, in soul and body. When walking out among the trees they

Latíf ʔAson of Gawíín village, recites a pɛntaaᵏ with burning of incense, before a dance.

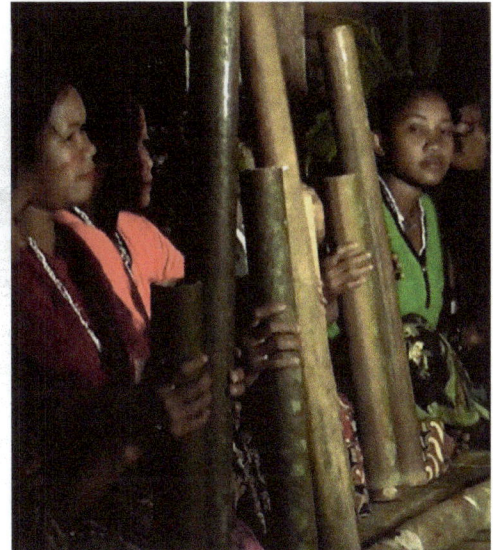

Women stump their bamboo tubes on the log while singing the repeat of the lead gabag.

felt safe from molesting souls and animal dangers. The dance was so beneficial to health that it would be held whenever the sense of peace with nature had dimmed, as well as those times when persons had overtly offended and brought troubling retributions on themselves. Through the dance, the outside realm was brought into the human realm and the two met, in a celebration of souls, and a unity was established, thanks to the spiritual adeptness of the medium.

Certain flowers were planted around the house, such as purple *tahoñ (Gomphrena globosa)*, red *carax (Celosia argentea spicata)* and yellow or orange *tambus* (marigolds, *Tageties erecta*) which were not only used for women's hair decoration, or stuffing in men's head bands, but they were ritually important and couldn't be picked for fun or have their petals torn off. Their souls were believed to aid dreamers in learning the songs of spirit invocation. When a spiritual adept met them in dreams they gave the songs that would enchant the souls of the seasonal fruit trees and cause them to come down to the dance hall and give their blessing. A *guníg*, a proper dream-guide, on the other hand, taught the songs that invoked the souls of the mountains, for the *guníg* was familiar with them, always wandering far and ascending the high peaks, where it felt fresh, and it would also take his keeper there in his dreams. The songs of the Taaᵏ Bɛlyans often reflected on the occurrences they had seen in their dreams and many of these have been passed down as well-known songs until today. The dances were held on a monthly basis or on special occasions such as during a good millet harvest or for the sending away of a deceased person's soul.

The current celebration of Nyʉᵏ Lʉj Juwɛl (the more reverent term for Nyʉᵏ ʔAlʉj, used by today's adherents) sprang from a resurgence of dedication toward ʔAlʉj, that began in the 1990s with a Temiar prophet from the Panɛɛs River (see 1.6 above). Perhaps half of the Temiar villages in Kelantan follow this new *hukom*, where they observe 'hariᵏ jadiᵏ ʔAlʉj' or the birthday of ʔAlʉj, three times each month, by holding dances with much fragrant foliage hanging all over, and some stringent rules of participation for the villagers. The men call each other "*nyʉᵏ*", instead of the age-old Temiar term "*yaah*", to profess their brotherhood under Nyʉᵏ ʔAlʉj. They no longer celebrate the tiger *guníg*s and there are no great mediums who keep them, but their *guruuᵏ*, or teacher, seeks *bɛlyan* power from the sources of ʔAlʉj and they also still celebrate the seasonal fruits. In times past, Temiars did not celebrate ʔAlʉj with their *g'nabag* songs, it was only the souls of the creation under him who were invoked in this way. But the adherents now believe that ʔAlʉj requires complete darkness, as did their *guníg*s, in order for *bɛlyan* power to be given. They also hold that once they have begun this cycle of monthly dances, they cannot cease from it, as they would then become poorly and sick. Most of all, they aim to obtain *bɛlyan* so that they may have the ability to perform healing rituals on their family members.

Some *halaaᵏs* still keep tiger *guníg*s (the headmen of Jadɛɛr and R'koʼob for example), even when most of the last great mediums have already passed away, but they don't practice the ritual with a booth of palm branches in the darkness, they sing to their *guníg* out in the forest by themselves. It is said that nowadays people are less supportive of the great mediums and their tiger *guníg*s due to the advent of modern conveniences, such as smart phones and motorbikes, that seem to have given people new freedoms.

Another ritual dance practiced by the Temiars is *s'lombaŋ*, a form of mediumship performed to placate the great Ndaŋgaaᵏ serpent spirit, which abides in the subterranean realm (also called the *s'lombaŋ*) and is held today at Kampuŋ Wʉʉd, a village down on the ʔUyas River. It is characterised by a song style reminiscent to the *taŋʔəəy* monotone, but with a faster rhythm of

Tambus

Carax

Tambus *(Credit: ʔAnɛl)*

Ritual flowers: tahoˈn, carax and tambus. The flowers are planted near the house and are important for enhancing the dream-life of Temiars, as their souls will teach how to enchant the souls of the wild.

Tahoˈn

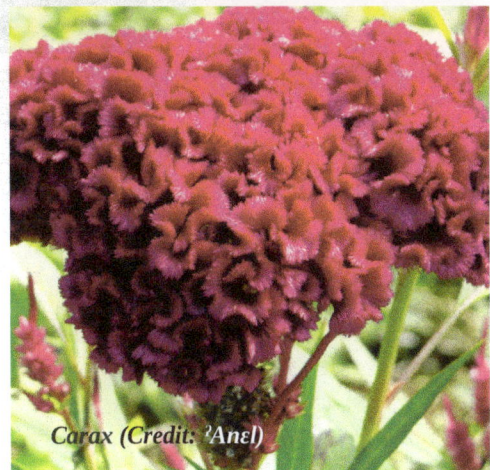
Carax *(Credit: ʔAnɛl)*

music, and with trance-like swaying of the head and beating of the body with split palm leaves and other plants. Sweet *k'mínam* tree resin is burned, and their headbands and leaf whisks are made of *k'waar* palm—and the medium's power is held in the whisk, which he hits in the air. The language of the ritual was received from *goʾb gayíp*, or foreign spirit beings,[19] which only the medium, who is called the *Toᵏ Pawaŋ*,[20] can understand. The dance is said to have been held ever since the great *límbaŋ*, the catastrophic flood that covered the whole earth with raging waters, and there have been 25 generations of mediums, who have entreated the serpent. To *jamuuᵏ*, or make their entreaty, they enter a cave in the limestone stacks, called Guwɔɔᵏ Jaŋɔɔd, and pass through a narrow opening, by candle-light, into chambers filled with turtles and centipedes (it is only for the brave). Some say that they come out on Mount P'naŋɔ́w, or Camaah, the home of the serpent, but I was told that this doesn't happen in the ritual and thus such transportation probably takes place only in the medium's dreams. As they perform the ritual, a boom can be heard in places afar off. The ritual would be necessary whenever they felt that the world had become unstable, such as

Gool buhyaaᵏ, the deep 'crocodile pool' at the Palɛɛs River confluence, into which Taaᵏ ʔAmpís threw seven coins, to placate the Ndaŋgaaᵏ

1.19 This source of influence has been confused with the Malays (also called *goʾb*). Note also that the *tataaᵏ s'laay*, soul of the padi swidden, and the *bɛrbów*, or ironwood tree soul, are also called *goʾb*, or foreign spirits.

1.20 Toᵏ Pawaŋ is a term borrowed from Malay; the medium is properly called a Taaᵏ Bɛlyan.

when the earth quaked, as they believed that the dragon had been disturbed. It was Taaᵏ ʔAmpís, the great medium of the Puyan River, in the early 20th Century,[21] who entreated the Ndaŋgaaᵏ during the 'red flood' of 1926. He saw it in a ritual dance and it ordered him to throw seven coins in the deep pool at the Palɛɛs River mouth, which flows from Pʼnaŋŏw mountain, and when he did this the flood abated.

It is said by today's practitioners of *sʼlombaŋ* that if they did not continue their entreaties of the serpent it would arise from its depths to destroy the earth. The earth has a number of layers, they say—those being: *tɛᵏ* (the upper soil layer) – *sʼlombaŋ* – *ʔudŏŏx* – *rʼmɛɛy* (a place of living people below)—and with each of man's exploitation of resources, such as logging and mining, a deeper layer is disturbed, causing the Ndaŋgaaᵏ to awaken from its abode. The *mʼnaŋ sawuh*, the cords keeping the earth in place, could even be damaged and then earth itself would disintegrate! When the Ndaŋgaaᵏ was seen traveling from downriver toward the mountains, there was no danger, but if from the river source toward the sea, then real danger was posed. It is believed to swim up the Puyan River when it floods and some people claim to have seen a huge, long creature in the billowing and raging waters. Those without *bɛlyan* powers would not dare to mention its name, however, and would call it *ludaad*, the avoidance term used for snakes. Two persons were believed to have been bitten by the serpent in the past, one at Sɛrpŏŏr, on the Bərtax River and one at Pʼlad, on the Puyan, and they both died from their wounds. In the second incident, a woman went to bathe while the river was in flood, and she had been warned not to because the odour of childbirth was still strong on her. She stepped in the water and felt a sharp pain go through her foot, as if she had been bitten. It caused a chill to run up her body, to her head, and she died shortly afterwards. Her father, ʔAti Kabɛl, a great medium, dreamed and saw the soul of the serpent.

Even with the disappearance of the great mediums who practiced ritual dances to their tiger *guníg*s, the beliefs in souls and caution of over-stepping the lines of offense are just as strong today. The keeping of taboos is just as rigid now as it ever has been, even among those Temiars who call themselves by the name of new religions. Prohibitions on foods and activities, actions and words are still taught to the young and stringently held to. Small mediums still abound and they regularly practice *nɛᵏsɔɔᵏ*, the blowing on the sick to procure healing and most Temiars prefer that treatment to making a long and arduous journey down to a clinic, where they receive non-natural medicines.

It is questionable whether the Temiars could have survived for millennia in their isolated environment, if they had not learned the codes and rites of the souls that inhabit the land and the deities which reside over them, being more powerful than anything human. Anyone who says they have been here that long must know something about the spiritual environment as well as how to be resourceful in the natural realm, not to mention a great deal about the hills and rivers of the land. Without such knowledge it is almost certain they never would have prolonged life to succeeding generations. There are no supermarkets here, nor are there other religious rituals to practice, one must comprehend the customs required by the guardians of the wild *bɛɛx* to be a dweller within it. The Temiars call the dense forest *sʼrŏx*, and themselves, they call the *sɛnʔŏŏy sɛŋrŏx*, or the people of the deep forest. This label is testament to the fact that their life is completely contained by the forest, by its resources and by its spiritual code and that they were put there by ʔNyʉᵏ ʔAlʉj.

1.21 Taaᵏ ʔAmpís was also known as Taaᵏ Jaan, because he had a butterfly dream-guide that flapped its wings, with a '*jaan, jaan*' sound; he is known today as Taaᵏ Ranal, because of the fact that he was laid to rest on Ranal Hill, near the Bərtax River. It is said that he also held *ʔAmɛɛᵏ Cɛnhɛɛr*, the sun, as a dream guide, and thus people could not look into his eyes, which shone. He was certainly one of the greatest and most revered Bɛlyans of the Temiars.

1.10 SUMMARY OF SOUL TYPES ORIGINATING FROM THE WILD

The table below simplifies the types of soul found in nature, that are encountered in dreams or in real life, which the Temiars fear in certain ways and follow measures to avoid having confrontation. If there is contact made with them and they cause trouble, in physical or mental health, then there are often ways in which the trouble can be remedied. Remedies would often involve *nɛᵏsɔɔk*, a ritual whereby an adept would kneel next to the patient and, calling on his/her guníg, locate the cause of the illness in their body and then suck it out through the hand and discard it (see p40).

Soul type feared	Taboo or cause of trouble	Consequences of offense	Remedies

R'WAAY ʔɛN-BALÍX – SOULS OF ABOVE

Soul type feared	Taboo or cause of trouble	Consequences of offense	Remedies
Taaᵏ Guwaaŋ, the thunder deity	*məsíx* – interference with nature	storms, floods and destruction	*cɔɔs* petitions, *jamuuᵏ* offering at ritual dance
Tawùn – souls of the seasonal fruits	*r'waay* – cause offense by cursing or throwing fruits	soul stealing	*nɛᵏsɔɔk* sucking
Pət'rii – souls of mountains, waterfalls, rivers, mahogany	*r'waay* – cause disturbance	soul stealing	*nɛᵏsɔɔk* sucking
Tataaᵏ bɛrboˊw – soul of the Moluccan ironwood tree	live too close to a tree or come too close to its logs	bad dreams and severe chest pains called *pacoˊg*	*nɛᵏsɔɔk* sucking
Tataaᵏ s'laay – the rice field soul	breaking the rules of the rice field	tormenting dreams	*nɛᵏsɔɔk* sucking

R'WAAY ʔɛN-Tɛᵏ – SOULS OF THE GROUND

Soul type feared	Taboo or cause of trouble	Consequences of offense	Remedies
Of wild animals that are eaten	*sabat, tɛᵏruuᵏ, gɛnhaaᵏ*	on-going illness, spirit-possession, death	*nɛᵏsɔɔk*, treatment with crushed animal bones
K'norux – souls of evil tigers	*pɛlʔax, doos* or sins against others	tiger attack	stay home at least seven days for *pɛlʔax*
Ndaŋgaaᵏ – subterranean dragon	disturbing the earth	great floods and earth destruction	*jamuuᵏ* ritual entreaty

Table 2. Types of soul to be feared in the framework of the Temiar belief system.

Soul type feared	Taboo or cause of trouble	Consequences of offense	Remedies

R′WAAY RƐHŊAH – DARK SOULS

Soul type feared	Taboo or cause of trouble	Consequences of offense	Remedies
Jaa^k Wơơy – cave soul	come too close to its lair, stay alone in the forest	holding captive in its cave	petitions made by the Taa^k bɛlyans on entering a cave
Sanu^k – grave souls	come too close to a grave	unease, sickness	*nɛ^{k}sɔɔ^k* sucking

Table 2. Types of soul to be feared in the framework of the Temiar belief system.

Temiars are fearful of building their homes close to the stump or logs of the bɛrbơw, the Moluccan ironwood tree, for fear that its dark soul would trouble them, causing sickness and even death.

2 | TEMIAR TABOOS

Integral to the daily life of the Temiars is their stringent adherence to a complex web of prohibitions, which were taught first by their ancestors, the Tataaᵏ Bɛlyans. Precaution is vital, and avoidance of taboo actions, words and foods is essential, in order to guard against ill fate that could be caused by disturbing the many rʼwaay or souls of the forest. The constant fear of an accident, a tiger attack, a devastating storm blowing up, or ill health, is enough to ensure that the people are taught what is disallowed from very young. By keeping themselves from acting without care, the spiritual balance between man and nature is maintained, and thus life can be better preserved.

In my research over the last eight years I have been able to categorise thirteen[1] main classes of taboos. I can further divide these into three main areas of human activity that is associated with them, those being: taboos that concern actions and speech, taboos that concern foods from the wild, and taboos that concern human and nature odours.

2.1 TABOOS CONCERNING ACTIONS AND SPEECH

Məsíx

This is a class of prohibitions that pertain to behaviour and speech, and largely concerns the disturbing of souls in the animal world, which will be seen and punished by the thunder deity, Karɛiy, who watches over them. It is taboo to call the name of any animal or food during its preparation or while eating it, or to play with food and pretend it was another object (a vegetable becomes an animal, or a human object, e.g. a phone or car) or it was still alive when dead. Such utterances or actions will cause the eater to rʼwaac tʼnaaᵏ, to have bloody diarrhea, and waste away until death. A similar fate will come upon a hunter or fisherman, if someone thinks to cɛᵏrɛɛᵏ, or point at him on his return from the forest or river and then he eats the game or fish he brought home. Playing with and laughing together at animals that are caught for food, which is especially easy to do with a pig-tailed macaque or gibbon monkey, is the most dangerous offense and it will bring on a storm with the earth collapsing and turning over with rocks falling down, killing every one involved. Likewise, laughing together at small creatures that go about collecting their food, such as the dragonfly, butterflies, caterpillars, spiders, ants, cicadas, the carpenter bee, millipedes, scorpions, preying mantis, cicadas, skinks, and possibly others, is prohibited as it would surely bring on a storm.

Certain birds are called cɛp məsíx, taboo birds, and mimicking their calls when they are heard is feared a dangerous preoccupation. These include cɛp tɛŋtoˈox (greater racket-tailed drongo), cɛp wɛdwāād (white-throated fantail), cɛp hoˈldox (black-naped oriole), cɛp sɛŋʼn̄ēd (Asian paradise-flycatcher), cɛp cíntaap (white-rumped shama), cɛp cɛdcad (little spiderhunter) and cɛp sʼmɛrloŋ (white-winged black jay), as well as cɛp hoˈoŋ, a so-called bird that is never seen, only heard. Reflecting the sun's light upwards is another taboo, which will invite a storm from the thunder deity, Taaᵏ Guwaaɲ (he will see a drink shining up at him and come to drink it!). Laughing loudly

2.1 As of 2023, this count now stands at 15 and there are likely many more minor taboos one could add (see footnote 2.2). The updated list can be found in the document, The Temiar Ritual Belief System, at my Figshare pages.

while playing chase or chasing a dog around are also likely to usher a storm, and children are often told to play more quietly. A sudden thunder storm is often blamed on people copulating outside in the day-time, in full view of Taa[k] Guwaaɲ (who in the folktales copulated with many young women who were really stinging ants and they did him serious damage!). Calling a rainbow by its name when seen is also refrained from and a name-avoidance term is always used, *na-woɡ*, it's risen.[2]

2.2 We can add here, *pacoɡ*, the taboo on certain activities that would disturb the malicious soul of the ironwood tree stump, such as being too playful in the evening, or, more specifically, during *s'rimaay*, when the sky turns yellow: children are given warnings like, *"Ham-gəl, pacoɡ hãã[k]!"* sit down, your chest pain! It is also a taboo to *b'ranii[k]*, or to mention the ill fate of anyone, e.g. by saying, *"Ham-k'bəs!"* you'll die!, or anything inferring that someone might snuff it soon or fall into a calamity, as the fate may well come on that person later. It is likewise taboo to do any action that would make a newborn child seem unwanted, as it then might not survive long. The action of kicking certain *taníɡ* rocks down a slope is another taboo, and those actions that would disturb the 'old man of the padi field' (listed on p18), are also tabooed.

2.3 When a person enters a deep sleep, it is believed that their soul wanders away, and it takes time for it to return to its place when they wake up. Thus, a person should not be startled in their sleep by any sudden noise, as their soul would not have time to return to them, leaving them in a dazed state. It is particularly serious for young infants as their soul might not return to them at all. Other activities also could dislodge a newborn child's soul, which is still insecure and vulnerable: the child cannot be bathed at evening, as the sun goes down (so either earlier on or after...

Small creatures such as these, with fascinating appearance and motion, would be tempting to interfere with, especially for children, but to do so is to break a taboo and to welcome a thunder storm. Creatures of the animal world should not be hampered as they go about their work of finding food and they also should not be 'made human' by playing with them. (Credit, carpenter bee and ant: ˀAnɛl)

R'waay

This is the taboo on actions that would cause a person's soul to *r'waay*, or drift away and not return.[3] Disrespecting the seasonal fruit trees, which have souls that are seen in dreams and are celebrated in the traditional dance, is one such prohibited action. It is believed they have power to cause a person's soul to wander away, so that the person enters an endless sleep, which leads eventually to death. These fruits include *jiyɛɛs*, a green fruit with orange pips, *kabaax*, jungle rambutan, *l'cax*, today's rambutan (imported from downriver), and similar small fruits that grow in bunches, such as *tampuy*, *raro'h*, and *rambɛy*. One may not utter profanities at them, or throw their fruits around, because hitting a person on the head with them would cause the person to *r'waay*. Neither should anyone go climbing the trees to pick fruits toward the end of the day, when light begins to fail. Powerful souls also inhabit the prominent places in nature such as mountains, waterfalls, caves and rivers, and shouting or yelling in those places, or shaking the flowers on a mountain-top, would endanger someone's soul. Petitions are made while walking in the forest and especially when ascending a mountain, for the souls inhabiting there to forego causing harm to anyone. Persons who have not been on the mountain before are considered to carry new 'smell' on them and may cause bad weather or a storm to blow up. They will cut a piece of hair and burn it in order to hide their smell from the souls that live there, making petitions for the sky to open up.

Jahruu^k

Certain actions are tabooed that will disturb the medium during a ritual dance, his singing to invoke the souls of the forest or his trance when they arrive to converse with him in the dance hall. Shining a light in the hall or taking photos, passing nearby him, or leaving the hall before the closure of the ritual are all deemed to disturb the ritual and thereby may cause consequences in the days ahead if the souls have not given their peace at the dance.

P'rɛnhɔɔd

To *pɛrhɔɔd* someone is to cause them to want or expect something, whether it be one's company going somewhere, in the forest or down to town, or perhaps a gift that one promises to give. It is different from making an arrangement to go and carry out some work, such as cutting a swidden or going trapping, which is to *pakad* together, because the thing suggested will not be done immediately, and later on one may not be able to fulfill it. The person who is expecting to have one's company somewhere out in the forest will be put in danger, when one forgets to meet up with them or one takes a different path and doesn't find them. They are likely to hear voices and chattering on the path behind them, and thinking it is the one who promised to catch up with them, they will have a sorry encounter with the 'striped old man', the tiger, the one that was mimicking people's voices!

Also, when a person goes on a long walk, hunting or fishing for example, and promises to be back later, but he walks too far to return or the sky turns dark with rain and he must sleep in a shelter somewhere and return only the next day—he puts people at home in grave danger because he spoke, making them anticipate his return, but then he couldn't return. While they are still expecting his return in the evening, instead, the tiger will come by for them, prowling under the house. The more careful procedure is to say, "*To^k yi-pɛrhɔɔd*," I can't promise you, I may stay the night up there. And the same danger will occur if one makes others expect someone's return, who has gone hunting or down-river, by saying, "So-and-so will be back soon!" and he or she doesn't come back that day.

dark); people must not crowd around the newborn in the house, as they will *hawul* or cast their shadows over it while it is still oblivious to those around it. The parents or grandparents *t'hool* or blow through the hand on the head of the child to help secure its soul. They also will not cut an infant's hair until it is old enough to sit up, as it is believed that its soul will easily drift away without hair on its head to stop it. There is no "soul-sharing" between the child and its parents, as was suggested before (Benjamin, 2014), but it enters the world in complete vulnerability to the souls around it.

S'lantab

This is the case where something has been offered to someone, food or drink in most cases, and usually while paying a visit to another house, and this provision must be accepted, if only to taste a little and even if feeling full already. Even if the hosts of the house mention that they have something available, like tea on the boil, one must wait for them to serve it and take some. While tasting someone would say, "*S'lantab*," I've satisfied my thirst and there won't be anything else coming to take it instead of me. If one refuses and leaves without eating or drinking, a centipede will surely run out of somewhere and bite, or a tree will fall on one in the forest, or an accident will happen in the swidden. It can also cause the same danger if one asks for something to eat and it's not available, or even craves for something that is not possible to obtain. It can even apply to something being shared out among everyone, like some delicious fruit or a bowl of meat, and one comes late or from another village—one would need to find a little piece of it to taste, and say, "*Na^k, s'lantab!*" In the old days, they wouldn't even say that someone should marry a girl, as that would be offering them something that they would need to take, and if they didn't then marry, an ill fate could come on them.

The bite or sting of these creatures could prove fatal. It is believed that when one doesn't s'lantab, or take something when offered, one of these will run out of nowhere, or slither out of the brush, and bite. (Credit, scorpion: ˀAnɛl)

2.2   TABOOS CONCERNING FOODS FROM THE WILD

Julux

This is a class of certain tree and vine species, including many fruit trees, that in Temiar tradition are taboo to bring carelessly into the house, because they contain powerful souls that cannot be brought into the human domain without asking permission of their guardian-creator. Most of these fruits are also classed under a food taboo (see *tɛᵏruuᵏ* below) and cannot be eaten by post-natal or nursing mothers, young children or menstrual women or they would cause dangerous side-effects to their health. These include several species of seasonal fruits as well as other fruits that are eaten by birds and rodents, including *sawít*, oil palm nuts, and thus to eat animals that have consumed these fruits may also cause problems.[4] The julux species that is eaten by a child is said to *r'gɛᵏ*, or cling onto them tightly, constricting growth and causing them to be thin and weak.

When the first fruits of the year are to be harvested, such as *jiyɛɛs* (a variety of breadfruit similar to the keledang that is known to Malays, *Artocarpus lanceifolius,* which is called *pɛrgəəs* in Temiar), *tampuy* (tampoi fruit), *sɛmpaaᵏ* (varieties of jungle durian), or *soʿic* (perah nuts), they are gathered only after the annual petition is made to Nyʉᵏ ʔAlʉj Tampuy, the guardian over the souls of the fruit trees, with burning of incense. This is normally conducted at the first *jiyɛɛs* tree to be harvested in the fruit season and at the first *soʿic* tree where the nuts are gathered a month later. Back at the house, the group gather round with a great heap of all kinds of delicious fruits at the centre, to *kahyax*, or celebrate, the provision of the *b'riix*, or seasonal fruits. After this, traditionally, the men must go down to the river and *ruuy s'laaᵏ*, cast leaves in the water to float away as an offering to the souls of the seasonal fruits.

2.4 Langur meat (normally a safe meat) is avoided by women and children during the hot months of the year (April-June) for fear that the primates are eating fruits of the *p'latow* tree.

Roslan ʔAŋah, of Pĩ́ncoʿoŋ, makes a petition at the foot of the first jiyɛɛs tree of the fruit season to be harvested. After the petition is made, no harm will come to the people as they climb the trees, harvest with hook-poles and collect the fruits that fall to the ground below.

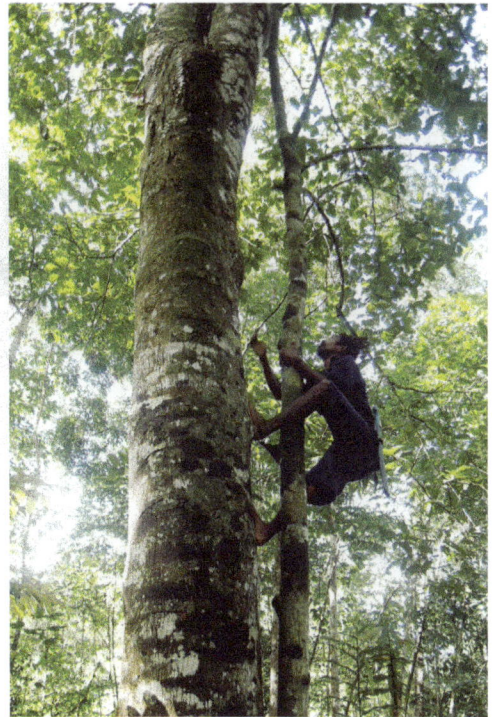

Julux trees and vines, which include *k'bəə^k ^{ʔ}ajɛɛl*, a fruiting vine, *manaar*, the vine of the rafflesia, *hariyuw*, a palm with broad fan-shaped leaves, and *^{ʔ}awɛn gantaaŋ*, giant bamboo, must not be cut down or damaged, as they have potent souls that can descend to the ground and take on new form if their plant life is killed. They will become an evil *k'norux* soul, and take the form of a tiger, small initially, but growing larger as they roam. These tigers are more feared than any, especially by persons with taboo offense (see *pɛl^{ʔ}ax* above). It is said that the soul of the *sawít* palm often comes down as a small cat and it is also known to cause anger in women and children if they consume any palm oil during menstruation or the *raŋyɛ̄^{k}* period. The *manaar* vine is quite feared and Temiars never camp in areas where it grows, and its bud, a medicinal herb used for treating post-natal mothers, cannot be collected by the father during the pregnancy.

Jungle durian trees. such as this bagan variety, grow massive in size and can produce a thousand fruits each year. (Credit: Rapi)

The extracted pips of ripened jiyɛɛs, a delicious treat the Temiars relish, that comes every year.

Jungle durians are more fragrant than durian, and can become alcoholic if they lie two days on the ground.

The bud of the manaar vine (Malay, pakma, a rafflesia), which is known as a herbal medicine, for treating post-natal mothers.

Soᵓic nuts can be grated and cooked into a hot, nutty paste.

The manaar blooms. Temiars will not pitch camp in areas where the vine grows, for fear its soul will disturb them.

The hariyuw palm, the trunk of which can grow as large as sawít, or oil palm.

ʔAwɛn gantaŋ, or giant bamboo, is found only in the cooler montane forest.

A soˀic tree that was planted a hundred years ago by Taaᵏ Ramoy, at Maŋgəs, in the Ragas River area.

Sabat

This is a category of animals and fruits from the wild that can cause severe problems and illnesses to persons who are susceptible to soul-attack, especially children (even in the womb) and young people, if ingested by them or anyone who can directly affect them. These foods are taboo for mothers and fathers during pregnancy, for children, and for women during menstruation, as well as the *raŋyɛ̃ᵏ* period (the month after child-birth). A breach of the taboo by a mother or father will result in complications during pregnancy, if they are *tɛᵏnɔɔᵏ*, or the 'right kind', meaning susceptible, such as the unborn child tangling up or becoming lifeless in the womb. And also at birth, the child may not deliver, the umbilical cord may tangle around the neck, thus also greatly endangering the mother's life, or it could be born with deformity. It could also cause the child to be born weak and sickly (i.e. not surviving long), and other illnesses for it in later years (depending on the species of animal or plant that was eaten).

Likewise, if children or young persons eat any *sabat* food they will put themselves in danger of whatever illness it can cause. Such illnesses include: wasting away and becoming thin (leading, ultimately, to premature death), having high temperatures, having fits or becoming deranged or stupid, having breathlessness, dizziness, vomiting or cutting pain in the stomach. And some of these effects, such as breathlessness, are believed to hit them later on in life, in their adulthood. It is also not surprising that seizures are a possible effect caused by *sabat* foods, as the word *sabat* is closely related to the Malay word for epilepsy, sawan.

Bawaaj

Taʼoŋ

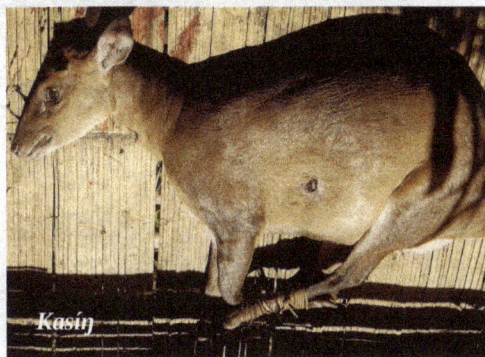
Kasiŋ

ʔɛsʼoʼos

Hayom

Tapəər

Kayiix

Tawɛl

Gɛriyɛx

Tɛnyuᵏ

Səəl

J'kuus

Deddut

Hɘlaŋ

B'rawɛl

ˀAyoˀm

Some sabat species (pig-tailed macaque, wild boar, sambar deer, slow loris, bear cat, palm civet, bat, flying fox, rough-necked monitor, tortoise, brush-tailed porcupine, bamboo rat, greater coucal, rhinoceros hornbill, green-pigeon, mahseer) that are taboo for certain persons to eat. The magnificent hornbill was found fallen, dead, after it had succumbed to a fight with another. (Credit, monitor and hornbill: ˀAnɛl)

Sabat animals include the pig-tailed macaque, siamang and gibbon monkeys, slow-loris, sambar deer, barking-deer, mouse-deer, bear cat, civets, mongoose, squirrels, bats and flying fox, tortoises and turtles, monitor lizards, porcupines, bamboo rat and other rats, pheasants, most hornbills, doves, swallows and some fish. I have listed over a hundred species in total, including 28 fruit and plant varieties. Those animals which men may eat and mothers who are still nursing children may not, are cut up and fur-singed on a fire outside the village or in the forest, and the meat is usually cooked outside the house and eaten from dishes separate from those used by women and children, as even touching or smelling the raw odour of the meat is considered dangerous for them. Youths must be physically grown enough before they can start eating *sabat* meat safely, which is usually only by the age of 16 years or older.

Certain fruits must be abstained from by both parents during pregnancy, such as pineapple, which is believed to cause elongation of the child's head in the womb, and twinned banana, which is believed to cause deformity of the child. *Ndaŋkaaᵏ*, or jack fruit, is also avoided as it would cause problems during delivery of the child. Certain ferns are also risk-prone if eaten during the pregnancy,[5] such as *bayas* and *bəər pakuᵏ* (Malay, pucuk paku), and the pithes of palms, as they have latex and can cause the womb to stiffen. Three fruits which have a strong smell, *b'taar* (petai), *sọ́ic* (perah) and *ʔaŋrəəy* (niring), cannot be eaten during pregnancy or by women during menstruation, as they would cause a person to go *ʔayɛɛŋ*, or lose their mind and run off alone into the forest, possibly even getting lost for days until others found them and brought them home.[6]

2.5 There are many *sabat* dangers for pregnant women: fish caught with a bought casting net, i.e. made by machine (it has a different kind of overlapping at the outside edge) or one newly-made or a one with a new chain, will cause dangers for an expectant mother and so she must avoid eating any. She also must not eat any fish caught with the fish trap with two funnels inside (*bubuuᵏ gəət*), but only from the egg-shaped trap (*pacōōᵏ*), and if fish caught by a hook, the hook must not be lost but kept safe. When a mother begins labour, any casting nets in the house (or any in the village from which she has eaten fish caught in it) must have their pull ropes untied immediately, and all the bottles must have the caps removed, to enable a safe delivery.

2.6 Even the flowers of the perah tree that drop in the rivers can cause people dizziness.

Temiar children from the different villages in the Puyan Valley. They will be kept rigorously away from sabat foods, as well as taught to avoid other taboos, in order for them to grow up healthy, safe from physical or mental problems

Tɛᵏruuᵏ

(A sub-division of the *Sabat* taboo)

This is a more serious form of soul-attack, of a class of certain animals and fruits that are forbidden for children to eat and also women during menstruation. If they did eat them, they would *hāāw*, or waste away and become skin and bones, and also manifest animal-like behaviour. These animals include *taʔoŋ*, the wild boar, *kaaᵏ ʔayoᵈm*, the Malay mahseer (*Tor tambroides*, Malay, ikan kelah; a pinkish carp with large scales), *tabɛɛg*, the bullfrog and all the *sɛnʔoᵈoʸy rayaaᵏ* or 'big people' animals, including tapir and gaur, rhinoceros and elephant. All these animals are ferocious in nature and eating their meat would cause the child's *hup*, or heart, to become possessed by the soul of that animal and the child would then also *t'ruuᵏ*, or begin to manifest the animal's anger. It is believed that the animal's soul rises up inside the person, causing them to *hɛrmaar*, become ferocious and start behaving as the animal itself, growing long nails and scratching at the fire-mound or at people, climbing up in the roof or running outside into the bushes. Eventually, the animal will start to emerge from their *hup*, which can result in their death.

The bullfrog is quite a potent creature and it can cause women and children to *hɛrmaar* seriously. A few days after they eat it they will feel a chill and start growling and scratching, and even have dreams of the frog, which will say, "I hate the menstrual woman touching me, but the others I don't mind." The *sabat* animal will *j'hɨɨd*, or suck on, the blood of the woman who eats it when she is vulnerable, causing her to waste away and be weak the rest of her life.

Many fruits are also classed *tɛᵏruuᵏ* and they include all forest fruits from the *julux* class of trees, such as, *kabaax* (wild rambutan, with longer hairs), *k'naraᵏ*, *kɛdkoᵈij*, *kuriiᵏ*, *lɛɛg*, *p'latow*, *rɛmmaŋ*, *s'taar*, *tampuy*, *tɛrhiᵏ*, *mancaŋ* (sour mango), *s'poᵈoʸy* (wild mango), *sɛmpaaᵏ*, *pɛrgəəs* (similar to *jiyɛɛs*), *sawít* (oil palm) and even some well-known fruits such as watermelon, winter melon, dragon fruit and terap. Although *jiyɛɛs* and *dɛriyan* (durian) are listed as *julux* species as well, they can be safely eaten by women and children after the petition to *ʔAlɨj* is made at the beginning of the fruit season.

Lɛɛg

Gɛnhaaᵏ

This is the misfortune caused by offending another soul, be it of animal or person. Some kinds of wild meat are classed as *gɛnhaaᵏ* because they must be shared out when caught, they cannot be eaten by oneself alone. The consequence of doing so would result in death, either for a child in the family or for the one who withheld it, if the animal was a potent one. For example, the pangolin, monitor lizards, tortoises, bear cat, gibbon, certain frogs and catfish (if two-hands wide) are all classed as *gɛnhaaᵏ*. Certain animals are *gɛnhaaᵏ rayaaᵏ*, extremely potent, and cannot be carried over to another river valley, including the *wɛjwooj* (the pangolin again), and the Malay mahseer. There are still more prohibitions they must follow with these animals, such as not breaking the intestinal tract, or the hip joints, and the bones must be put tidily in one place after they have eaten the meat.

When something is found by good fortune, such as a net full of fish, or a giant tortoise, it is called *jurūūh*. The catch must be shared out or else it will cause *gɛnhaaᵏ* to the one who found it. Other things can cause misfortune also, such as dropping coins through the floor (ash or water must be poured down the hole before going to retrieve them) or pointing at someone with the middle finger! Forgetting to show hospitality to visitors will also cause *gɛnhaaᵏ* to the household.[7]

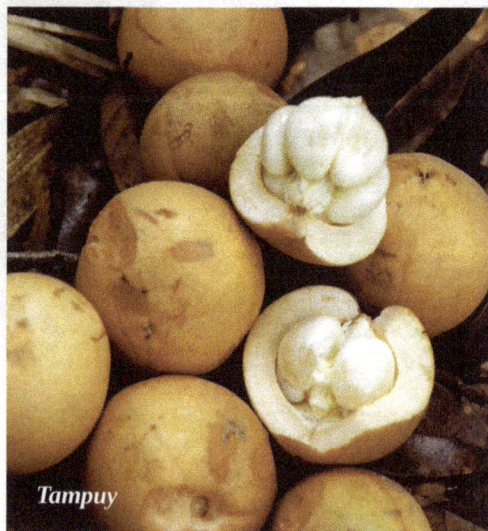

S'po'oy

Pɛrgəəs

Tampuy

2.7 *Gɛnhaaᵏ dɛix*, or misfortune of a house, is caused when the home's soul is dislodged. A new house is believed to have a *k'norux* soul, and the Temiars *juul*, or wave smoke, in the rafters in order for it to stay and keep the house at peace.

Kuriiᵏ (Credit: ²Anɛl)

Wild fruits such as these are taboo for young persons to eat. Many are either sour or they can burn the lips (like s'pɔ́ɔ́y, wild mango), and they are also found in the deep forest, away from the home, so they are not enticing for children to eat.

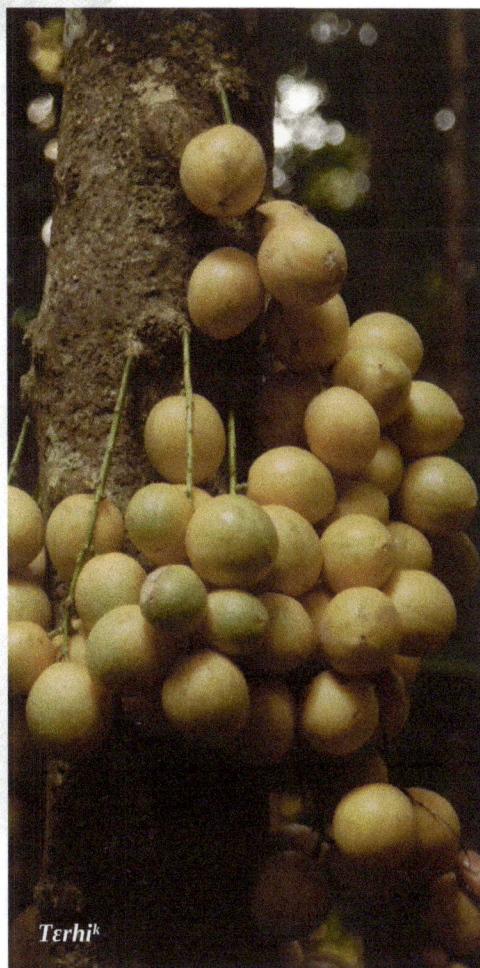

Tɛrhiᵏ

2.3   TABOOS CONCERNING HUMAN AND NATURE ODOURS

Pɛl²ax

This taboo is also called *məsíx-lɔ́ɔ́t*, blood taboo. It is the case of mixing one's own flesh or blood with the meat of certain animals, such as by scalding oneself with the hot soup of game, or by cutting oneself while eating the meat. Even a leech spilling one's blood, or squashing a hair louse full of one's blood while eating meat can cause trouble. A particularly dangerous fate will come on the offender if they go out soon afterward into the forest, as they will carry *pɛl²ɛŋ* on them, the *ŋɔ́ɔ́y*, or smell, of their blood mixed with meat, which evil roaming tigers will seek out! These tigers are *k'norux* souls in tiger form, sent out by Mɛŋkah, the tiger lord, to catch those who have offended. Many have already met with this fate, as the stories testify. A person who commits the offense would need to *t'laaᵏ*, stay at home for a number of days, until the *c'raŋas*, or day of release, came. They might find a great *Toᵏ halaaᵏ* to help them by petitioning his soul-guide tiger to hold back the evil tigers.

Most game meat can cause *pɛlˀɛŋ*, and are classed *pɛlˀax*, but a large number of fish are exempt because there have been no cases of tiger attacks after eating them and being cut or scalded. The greatest *pɛlˀɛŋ* is caused by the *kˈnoɡ*, the large land tortoise, and one would need to stay home for a year if one was careless while preparing or eating its meat! The *ɡɛriyɛx*, or rough-necked monitor, could cause one to stay put for a month in the house, for fear of being pounced on soon after leaving its safety. Also, as a new, modern category of the taboo, when canned food has been consumed in the morning those who ate any should not sharpen their bush knives afterwards, but should go to work with it blunt. The reason for this, I am told, is the sharpening stone will be cut into by the knife and make *ŋoˈoy*, but it is not obvious how this is connected to the tinned food.

T'racɔɔg

This is the condition caused when certain items from the *dɛix* or home are discarded on the ground after their use, where they would become soiled with earth, such as bamboo cooking tubes or modern tin cans. It is feared that the person who used the containers will become breathless, and so bamboo tubes must always be split in half after their use and tins punctured on the bottom. Hair clippings are another item of the human domain that should not reach the earth, as this would cause a person hair-loss, a danger for the soul which might drift away through the head if there is no hair to prevent it. Used garments also cannot be thrown outside as they will become soiled or covered with swarming ants, and this would cause a person to suffer itching all over. Hair clippings are stuffed inside the wall or a pouch or bag to prevent them falling under the house and old clothing is always burned to prevent it rotting on the ground. A more severe case can be caused by a child spilling drinking water, or urinating, down a house post into the ground, resulting in the child becoming *sɛdlɔɔd*, breathless, or even dying.[8]

When a new fire-log is placed on the fire mound, whether in the house or outside, it must be put with its top end toward the fire, to be burned first, and not with its base end—the end nearest the ground—toward the fire. Failure to follow this rule will cause illness to anyone in the family, or worse, if a mother is expecting it will cause her baby to be born feet-first. A tree with a closed fork between two branches, or a tree that has grown up touching another tree is said to *t'rɛgcoˈoɡ*, or be causing odour, and cannot be used for anything at the home, such as a house pillar, and its fruits cannot be collected. Likewise, the mushrooms that grow on a log of a tree, if the tree has fallen and any part of its trunk has *c'rəd*, or stumped the ground with the upper end, are called *bəər cɛnrəd* and cannot be collected, or they would cause those who consumed them to become breathless.

Raŋyɛ̄ᵏ

Pre-natal and post-natal mothers with their newborns carry great risk of harm due to the strong odour of *ˀəyɛɡ*, the afterbirth, and cervical fluids that are associated with childbirth.[9] The period after childbirth is called *raŋyɛ̄ᵏ*, and it lasts two weeks to a month for the mother, and two to three months for the child. Washing the afterbirth into the river would be calling for disaster to strike, as it would cause a *dɛŋdəx*, a terrible storm, and if the mother bathed or washed her clothes in the river during the *raŋyɛ̄ᵏ* period it would also cause *jˈˀaar*, or stormy weather. Such storms could go on for weeks until they reached the stage of *rɛŋrɛɛx*, the earth flooding and collapsing, and in that case a ritual dance would be held to invoke Taaᵏ Guwaaɲ, to petition him to cease making his

2.8 Nothing that a young infant uses, such as food, or diapers, should be thrown out, but burned if necessary. A newborn's bathwater should not be thrown out carelessly, either, for example into rubbish, but poured out somewhere safe.

2.9 As this smell is so strong and carries so much risk, anything contaminated with it (clothes) would later be burned. The placenta was traditionally washed and hung up somewhere to dry out, but because these days there are so many people about who could chance upon it and be affected by its odour, it is now buried, and the ground on top is burned with fire to prevent ants reaching it.

storms. Infants are not taken to the river during this period, as it is feared their soul would be taken away with the flow. The mother must also abstain from food with salt or oil, in order to protect the child, who can be affected by it through her milk and suffer *k'laab*, or 'gall pain'. When the period ends for the mother she will eat salt again and then she will go to the river and *ruuy s'laaᵏ*, cast fern leaves in the water, to float away as an offering to the *r'waay* of the river.

I was told that the blood of females and the afterbirth, if it reaches flowing water, will cause the Ndaŋgaaᵏ's anger to arise, the serpent which resides in the subterranean cavities of the earth and also rides in the flooding waters of the rivers. The Ndaŋgaaᵏ then appeals to Taaᵏ Guwaaɲ for him to make his storms, in retribution on this offense, which it finds detestable. If anyone else held the child at birth, such as the midwife, or during the said short period of blood-odour, then they also would need to abstain from food in much the same way as the mother. The lingering smell (especially in the days before they had soap) would *tɛg*, or hit, anyone who touched the newborn child. The father would only touch or hold the baby when the odour had safely passed, for if he had this smell on him and he went out to the forest, a bear would likely attack him, because the smell causes it great anger. Also, if a father ate *sabat* game during this period, he would have to abstain from holding the child, as the child would likely be harmed by illness caused by the *sabat* animal.

Tɛnlaaᵏ

This is the abstinence of normal activities that certain persons must observe for a period of time, generally to avoid ill fate, bad luck or the loss of efficacy of herbal medicines. Persons who must *t'laaᵏ*, or stay at home, include women during menstruation, or in late pregnancy and after childbirth, a newly wedded couple, a man after setting traps or someone who has broken the *pɛlʔax* taboo. They must not go out anywhere, especially into the forest where fate could meet them, because of the human 'odour' they carry on them. Mothers and new-born children must *t'laaᵏ* and not go to the river, due to the smell of the afterbirth that they still have on them.[10]

Women during menstruation are described as *tiiᵏ ma-moẏ*, or being out of normal activities. They must abstain from foods which would be harmful to them, including some common fruits such as pineapple, and foods with palm oil or salt, and even glutenous rice. They also cannot eat together with other people, as it would endanger everyone else if they did. When their period has ended they will *jamah*, or break their fast, with a little of the food that they had abstained from, such as fish or chicken cooked with oil. Palm oil is particularly risk-prone because it comes from the *sawít* palm which has a malicious *julux* soul. They must also abstain from planting manioc during menstruation, as if they did the manioc would grow rotten.

In the case of persons who have had ritual healing administered to them by a soul-medium, they must refrain from foods with a hot taste (notably, *soẏc*, the perah nut, chili or curry) and certain smells, such as of earth, manioc shoots, raw meat or blood, as these would cause them to faint or even die. The medium may prescribe for them further abstentions they should keep, that he was told to give them by his dream-guide.

Animal calls in the forest can also signal the need to *t'laaᵏ* at home. The *cɛp cicarr*, black-eared shrike-babbler, is a small bird which has a shrilling call and is known as the *cɛp t'laaᵏ*, because when many of them call together people must stay home and not go out to plant their crops.[11]

2.10 I am told that an expectant mother carries this smell on her even before childbirth, and thus she must take care of herself, especially when going out into the forest.

2.11 When a *g'cɛᵏ gɛnwaaɲ*, or full moon with ring around it, is seen, one also cannot cut a swidden the next day. When cutting a new swidden, they make the *tɛnkɛɛd*, or test cutting, on the first day, and on the next day they rest, in order to see if there are any malicious souls (whether *bɛrbòw* or *pət'rii*) on the land that they should avoid disturbing.

2.4   *SABAT* ANIMAL SPECIES AND ASSOCIATED DANGERS

Of the above defined taboos, *sabat* is probably the most complex of them all, involving a large list of wild animal and fruit species and with various different complications tied to each one. The danger of *sabat* species is also one of the most serious that the Temiars must guard against, along with those associated with *məsíx, pɛlˀax* and *gɛnhaaᵏ*. It is imperative that the elders of the community teach which species are tabooed, and prohibit those persons who could be easily affected from eating them.

Looking at the effects of *sabat* naturally, it might appear that allergies to the animal's meat are to be blamed for these troubles. If so, the allergic affect must become less and less harmful with age, as the danger is much greater for infants and children than it is for adults (see the chart below). But there are indications that this is not the case all the time. For one, an unborn or infant child would be put in danger by its mother or father consuming tabooed meat as it is believed that they both contribute to its growth—the mother through the womb and breast-feeding, the father through semen during pregnancy. It may also appear to be an attack by the soul of the wild animal because in some cases there is mental derangement caused and, at other times, behaviour described as spirit-possession.

Women are prohibited from eating *sabat* foods throughout their child-bearing years as they could so easily endanger their children, as well as themselves. Only when they have stopped bearing children and have reached menopause are they entirely safe to eat game. Otherwise they are affected by all *sabat* species, including those that endanger pregnancy (category A on the chart below) and their child in infancy (category B), as well as those that endanger themselves at other times (category C), including during menstruation and the *raŋyɛ̄ᵏ* period (the month after child-birth) as they will be highly susceptible to attack. Fathers are only prohibited from eating them (categories A and B) during the pregnancy and they can resume eating them after the child is born. They could easily put their child's life at risk by being careless about what kind of game they eat during the gestation period.[12]

The womenfolk of Tɛmagaaᵏ village gather in the afternoon to socialise.

2.12 Every small health issue of children seems to be blamed on a *sabat* taboo breach, by some or other animal that was consumed by the parents. Vomiting is blamed on *sabat ˀaŋkuuy*, them having eaten frogs with poisonous skin. The swelling of a foot is blamed on *sabat ˀudaŋ/sùmboŋ*, eating shrimps. Dizziness is blamed on *sabat cɛp*, eating bats, or *sabat kayuh*, eating manioc shoots, or other strong-smelling shoots, such as *bəər l'haaw*, a plant eaten by older folks (pictured Vol. 2, p16). Redness of an infant's eyes is blamed on *sabat ladaᵏ*, eating chili during the pregnancy. A child always burying its head in its mother's armpit is blamed on *sabat ˀayam*, eating jungle fowl and a child crying constantly is blamed on *sabat tagùt*, eating the yellow-crowned barbet. Cures can be made for some of these, such as with burnt shrimp shells, or heated chili leaves or with the beak of the barbet.

Women of child-bearing age must observe numerous taboos, in order to guard against ill health, for themselves and their nursing children.

A large, male wild boar on a pole. These days, the wild boar makes the most frequent of animals caught by traps as they are so populous. And yet their meat can't be shared out with all as it is feared as an anger-causing animal. (Credit: ʔAnɛl)

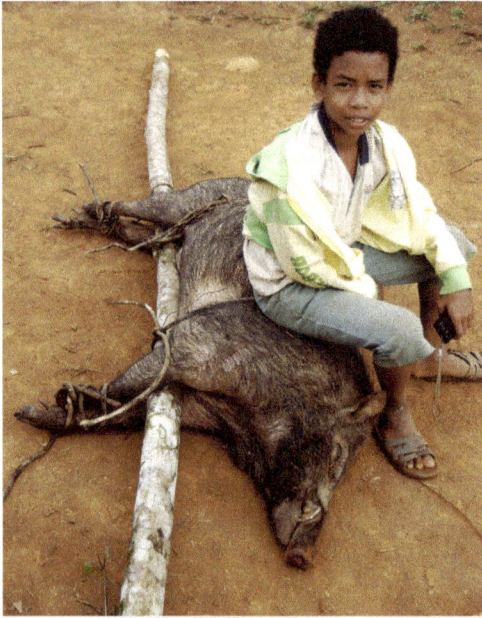

A Temiar boy sits on a wild boar that was speared by a hunter. He is probably just old enough to begin eating the meat with the other men.

If a woman eats *sabat* meat during her menstruation, she will endanger her own health, and if she actually began to menstruate while eating *sabat* food, she would *j'roh*, or cause *sabat* danger for anyone eating the same food with her, who was also susceptible to attack. She would cause them to *t'ruu^k*, or manifest anger in them due to the animal's or fruit's soul interfering with their own. When this happens, the food they were eating would be discarded to avoid risking any health attack from the animal. A woman could only safely eat if she knew her period was over recently and wasn't about to suddenly come on her. If they were eating *so'ic* nuts at the time, which are delicious when roasted or baked into a cake in bamboo, a susceptible person, such as a child, could be affected by its pungent smell. They might seem to lose their mind at times, needing the family to watch out for them so that they don't run away, with spirits calling them to follow. In another case, if she eats

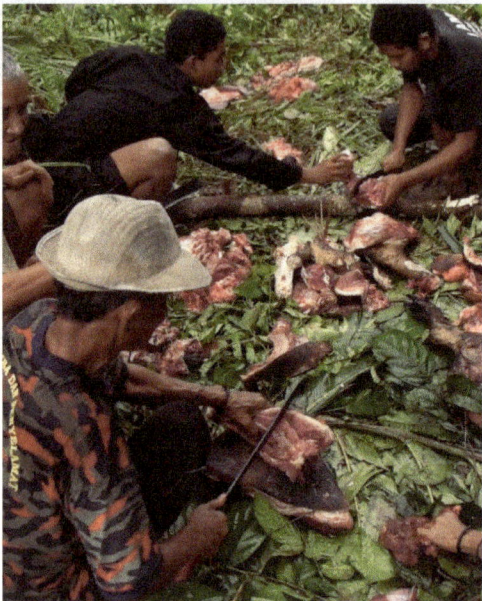

The animal is butchered outside and its meat is cut up with bush knives. Then it is shared out equally between the number of homes.

A wild boar is fur-singed on a fire, outside the village. Such work must be done away from women and children so that they don't come in contact with the blood or its smell.

food with any salt, MSG, palm oil, sugar or milk added and begins to menstruate, she will get an itching cough (or gooey, depending on the food additive), along with anyone else who was eating the same food with her.

Sabat meats are prohibited for children because they are growing up, and either their soul is infantile and vulnerable to attack, or because they are not yet physically developed enough to consume it properly. A child may not *cāmpāā*ᵏ, or touch, the meat or even come near the *p'ʔiih* or raw smell of its blood. Young people can only start eating *sabat* meat at the age of 16 or 17 by the earliest, when they have grown up enough, but some animals, such as the siamang, gibbon and slow loris, are so potent that they are not even safe for adults to eat, and only old-aged people would venture to eat them. Three turtle species are not eaten at all as they would cause an immediate storm to blow up if they were killed. Of these the *ʔawaa*ᵏ, a flat, spiny turtle, cannot even be approached where it dwells in the mountains, as doing so would bring on a catastrophic storm, or even a forest fire—it is said to be repulsed by human odour (therefore the fear of it follows more the *mɔsíx* taboo).

Young men roast some ribs on the fire, to taste the meat before taking their share home.

2.4.1 *Sabat* Danger Charts

The chart below illustrates the degree of danger that *sabat* animals pose to humans, depending on their age.

Red shades indicate the most vulnerable stages of human life, and Green shades the less vulnerable stages.

A-D are categories of *sabat* species that pose danger to each stage of life, when eaten (even touched and smelled in the case of children) by the persons on each label.

	BIRTH	3 – 4 YEARS		16 – 20 YEARS		80 YEARS	

Pregnancy	Infancy	Childhood – Youth	Adulthood	Old Age
A, B, C, D. Mother/Father	B, C, D. Mother/ MW/Child	B, C, D. MW/Child/Youth	C, D. MW/Adult	D. Old-Aged

Fig. 2. Sabat danger through the stages of life.

Category A: *Gestation danger*

Prohibited for a mother and father to eat, will endanger the pregnancy and also the life of the mother. Non-child-bearing persons may freely eat them but a married woman should not as she may become pregnant.

Category B: *Infancy, childhood and menstruation danger*

Prohibited for both parents during pregnancy, nursing mothers, children and menstrual women to eat; they will affect the child in later years if eaten by the parents during pregnancy. Even though a woman may have reached adulthood, she is brought into high-risk due to menstruation.

The 3-4 years mark is the end of a child's infancy or breast-feeding (which might come sooner than this), at which time a mother may start eating class B animals again, but she would still be at risk.

Category C: *Adulthood danger*

The more potent animals that are dangerous from pregnancy through childhood to adulthood, which only the old-aged may safely eat.

Category D: *Danger to all!*

Animals that can't be eaten at all or they will cause a storm.

MW stands for menstrual women: a woman endangers herself if she eats during menstruation and she can endanger children, youths and adults if she begins to menstruate while eating tabooed food together with them.

The chart below shows the number of *sabat* species belonging to each category of danger (A-D), totaling more than a hundred (that I have discovered to date—see the list of *sabat* species, in Table 3, below), including several generic and 28 fruit and plant varieties. There is notably less danger of animals causing illness during adulthood (excluding women in menstruation) and old-age stages of life.

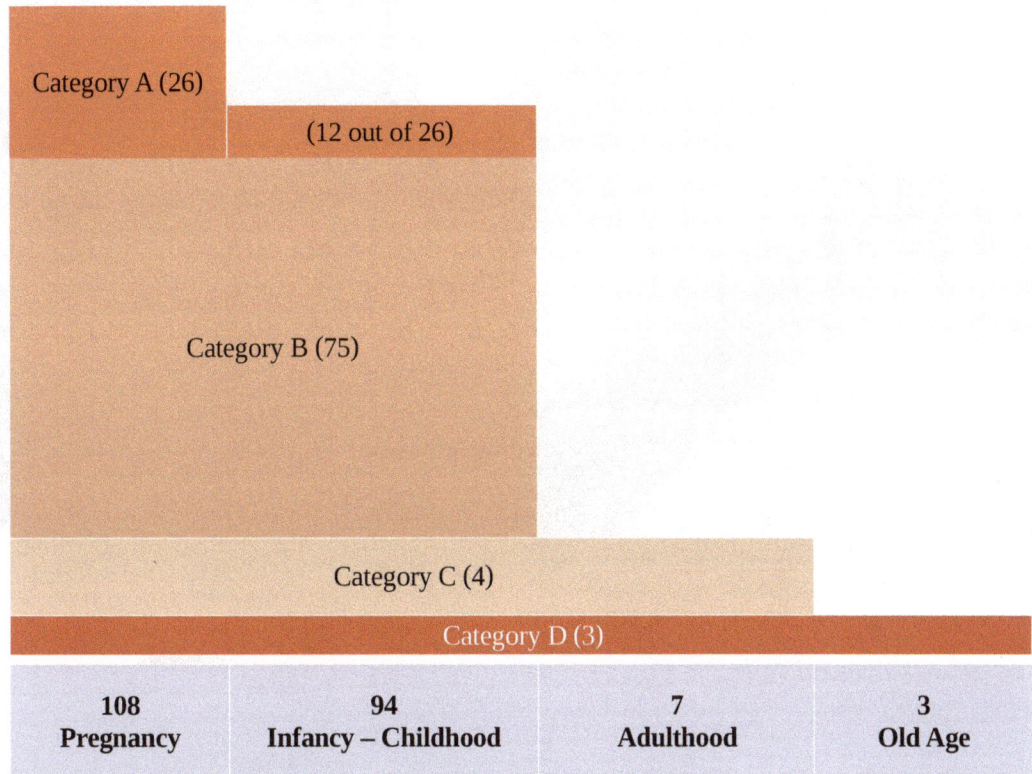

Category A (26)			
(12 out of 26)			
Category B (75)			
Category C (4)			
Category D (3)			
108 **Pregnancy**	94 **Infancy – Childhood**	7 **Adulthood**	3 **Old Age**

Fig. 3. Total number of sabat animal and fruit species (not to scale).

Sabat meat is always cooked in separate pans and eaten away from women and children.

2.4.2 List Of *Sabat* Animal And Fruit Species

The list below has been created after careful research was made with the Temiars of Píŋcoʻoŋ village, in 2019. There may be additional species to add and also the allocations of certain species to particular categories of danger may differ with Temiars of other regions, but it is close to accurate for Temiars of the Puyan, Jɛnroʻl and Pɛriyas Rivers.

CLASS A

Description of Danger	Culpable Species	Nature of Cause
lipad, tangled up in the womb	*bagɛɛt* – rough-necked monitor lizard*	monitors wriggle as they go
	gɛriyɛx – water monitor lizard*	
	wɛjwooj – pangolin*	curls up in a ball
cɛggɛg, strangulation of child in the womb [13]	*sab b'sii^k* – animals caught with a wire noose	because the wire cuts the flesh
	jaloʻo^k k'dɛy – fish caught in a machine-made cast-net	the net is woven differently to hand-made nets
sɛgsoʻg, not delivering	*k'noʻg* – large land tortoise*	lives in caves and holes
	labii^k – river turtle*	turtles burrow in the mud
	pɛlɛd – soft-shelled turtle*	
	kaa^k palo^k – 'log' fish	doesn't move
	kaa^k kɛnrab rayaa^k – sandy catfish (if large)	swims in the rapids, not moving
	k'rɛdlaad – giant squirrel	makes a nest
	k'dííg hayoʻm – bamboo rat*	lives in the ground
	k'dííg dɛndut – a ground rat*	lives in a burrow
	cɛp tapəər – all bat species	roost in caves or in bamboo cavities
	cɛp kawēēd, cɛp lasar – giant bats*	hang from high trees
	k'bəə^k ndaŋkaa^k – jack fruit	the fruit has sticky latex
c'goʻd soʻop, hardened embryonic sack	*bəər bayas, bəər ta'oʻo, bəər paku^k* – wild ferns*	have bitter properties
	c'kəər – edible piths	

*Species marked * above, also come under Class B, Infancy-Childhood-MW, causing danger of breathlessness, among others.*

2.13 We can add here to *cɛggɛg*, strangulation in the womb, fish caught with the *bubuu^k gəət*, a long fish trap with two funnels inside.

cacat, deformity	jaay k'maar – twinned banana	doubled, will cause deformed parts
	k'bəə^k k'nas – pineapple	long-shaped, will elongate the head
hayuur, chills	kaa^k p'rɛd – a sleek fish	full of bones
bɛnboʈ hí^k, always feeding at the breast	k'luboʈŋ, ca^{ʔ}ɛɛ^k – mice	live inside bamboo

CLASS B

Description of Danger	Culpable Species	Nature of Cause
b'lɛɦŋēh, weak and sickly*	dɛddud – greater coucal	makes a nest
bʉd t'naa^k, body heating; na-giyɛg, fits; bəs'ram, become demonised	jɛɛd – muntjac	many of these animals have dark meat that causes heating of body
	b'co^k – mousedeer	
	kasíŋ – sambar deer	
	j'lɛɛw – long-tailed macaque	
	kawííb – sun bear	
	tɛnyux – bear cat	
	taŋlín – banded linsang	
	rɛgrɔɔg – yellow-throated marten	
	coŋ hadaa^k – crab-eating mongoose	
	k'dííg s'koʈl – variable squirrel (white)	
	k'dííg ca^{k}lɛ^k – variable squirrel (brown)	
	k'dííg, ^{ʔ}aŋaaŋ – plantain squirrel	
	kayiix – flying fox	
	^{ʔ}ampax, l'jùx, gɛnhooŋ – flying squirrels	
	^{ʔ}ancōh – flying lemur	
	k'dííg səlaman – moonrat	
	h'nwaaŋ – great hornbill	hornbills make loud calls
	d'kug – a white hornbill	
	kahkuuh, kahkōōh – white-crested hornbills	

* This means not surviving long, of a newborn infant.

	k'wɔɔx – great argus (if red)	
	c'kum – crested fireback	
	d'na^k – junglve fowl	
	cɛp pugaa^k – a pheasant	
	j'koŋ – brown boobook	
	cɛp bɛrkooh – mountain imperial-pigeon	
	cɛp b'rawɔl – green-pigeon	
	rɛgwoog – little cuckoo-dove	
	j'rɛgpaag – a dove	
	c'mog – red-billed malkoha	
	sɛgduwag – chestnut-breasted malkoha	
na-hāāw, wasting away; *tɛ^kruu^k*, anger; *hɛrmaar*, animal-like behaviour	*ta²oŋ* – wild boar	fierce animals
	s'lada^k – gaur	the *sɛn²oóy rayaa^k* 'large people' animals
	barɛɛw – tapir	
	hagaab – rhinoceros	
	²alaaj – elephant	
	kaa^k ²ayom – Malay mahseer	reddish meat
	tabɛɛg – bull frog	has claws
	²apoós haaŋ – a zingiber variety	has red juice like blood
na-hāāw, wasting away; *tɛ^kruu^k*, anger;	*kabaax, kurii^k, lɛɛg, p'latow, s'taar, tɛrhi^k, tampuy, mancaŋ, s'poóy, sɛmpaa^k, pɛrgəəs, ndaŋkaa^k, tɛmbikay, kundur, sawít, tarap*	all *julux* fruits (some are imported, i.e. dragon fruit, water melon, winter melon, oil palm, terap)
na-lut kɛɛd, extruding of the anus	*lɛdlɛɛd* – masked palm civet (red)	the meat causes diarrhea
	h'laŋ – rhinoceros hornbill	
sɛdlɔɔd, breathlessness	*j'kəəs* – East Asian porcupine	porcupines live in rock holes
	tood – brush-tailed porcupine	
	karāāc – Malayan box turtle	turtles sleep in water
	kajēē^k – a mud-dwelling turtle	
	k'dííg ²ɛn²oóx – bandicoot rat	swims under water
	cɛp rəx – a flying fox	lives in a high *r'guul* tree
	sɛgnug pɛnpon – a small river-side frog	

gayaar, a child bites people or acts stupidly	*bawaaj* – pig-tailed macaque	travels far and eats many wild/tabooed fruits
na-gəd ʔɛij, cutting pain in the gut	*kaaᵏ bɛgbaag* – an eel	long, like a knife
kɛᵏkoᵏ, vomiting	*k'dííg tukaŋ* – a giant squirrel	poisonous meat
loyyɛc, dizziness	*cɛp layaŋ* – swallows	fly about like aeroplanes
na-kag, stopping of breath	*ʔapoʼos k'rag* – a zingiber variety	has hard skin
ʔayɛɛɲ, crazy[14]	*b'taar, soʼic, ʔaŋrəəy* – petai, perah, niring	have a hot smell

CLASS C

Description of Danger	Culpable Species		Nature of Cause
gɛgyɛg, fits	*ʔamaŋ* – siamang		these primates hang from branches
	tawɔɔh – gibbons		
	ʔɛgʔaag – crow		eat snakes
	sɛmpəl – grey-faced buzzard		
butaᵏ mad, causes blindness	*tampɛl* – slow loris		has poison glands behind its eyes

CLASS D

Description of Danger	Culpable Species		Nature of Cause
na-dəx, causes a storm	*koʼoh, ʔawaaᵏ* – spiny turtles		live in the mountains, cannot be disturbed
	səəl – large land tortoise		

Table 3. Sabat animal and fruit species.

2.14 We can add here to Class B, *sùmboŋ*, river shrimps (live in mud), which cause *nɛshĩĩs jùx*, or inflammation of the feet, and *ladaᵏ/kari*, chili and curry (both spicy), which cause *mad cɛŋləx*, or redness of a child's eyes when consumed by the parents.

The 'red palm civet' may cause outward growing of the anus of children if the parents eat it during pregnancy and they are 'tɛᵏnɔɔᵏ', or 'allergic' to it. The condition can be treated by burning some civet bones and applying the ash to the child's body, in a similar way that treatment is made using other animal bones when those animals have caused illness. Other conditions listed above can be treated by nɛᵏsɔɔᵏ, the ritual blowing on a person by a soul-medium.

Animals that are termed *pɛᵏraaᵏ*, meaning that they are not eaten by the Temiars, include: cats, dogs, dhole, otter, eagles, owls and many non-fruit-eating birds, snakes, grubs and insects. *K'maay k'laad*, the small grubs found inside giant bamboo, may have been eaten in the old days, as well as the python. The Semais don't hesitate to eat snakes but to the Temiars they are detested as slithering, wriggling creatures. I have heard from one source that the *tɛᵏtaaᵏ manah*, or ancestors, may have prohibited most of the animals and birds in the list of *sabat* species above, from consumption by any persons, no matter their age. It is possible that only in recent generations the Temiars have become either brave, more reckless or disregarding of the *hukom* of the forefathers, in choosing to hunt and eat all these kinds. In comparison, the Bateqs, a nomadic tribe, will not eat any animals that roam about on the ground, but only those that dwell in the trees.

Grubs and snakes such as these are eaten by the Semais, but the Temiars find them repulsive creatures.

2.4.3 NON-*SABAT* ANIMALS

With such a full list of animal species designated dangerous for parents and infants, young people and adult females to consume (see Part 2.4.2), it would seem there would hardly be any animals left in the wild that were considered safe to eat by the Temiars. And this is almost the case, as, with mammals and primates, there are only three species, including two langurs and the serow, which are classed non-*sabat* or *məl*, normal. The serow, or mountain goat is considered a healthy animal, whereas goats (as well as cows) would be classed *sabat*, because they eat grass with their own dung! While langurs are considered *məl*, if they are hunted up in the mountains they would not be safe for for infants and vulnerable persons due to the fact that they would be feeding on wild *julux* fruits. The giant squirrel, *k'rɛdlaad*, which is classed as *sabat* in the table above, is considered safe if it is all black, not the variety with a white front, but Temiars further south may call this variety *sabat* also. The plantain squirrel, *s'koʾr*, may also eat *julux* fruits at certain times of the year and thus it would become unsafe for children to eat.

Of birds and fish, there are a fair number of species considered *məl* (note that the list in the table below is not exhaustive in regards to these two groups). These are given ardently to young children to eat, as soon as they are old enough to consume meat (by one year of age) and they may be eaten by women and parents without any complications. But care must still be taken not to cook the *məl* animals with *sabat* ones, for example when they are brought back in the same basket or leaf packet together. Those in charge of cooking must sort out the *sabat* from *məl*, such as the water rat, the bandicoot, from the white-bellied rats, or the *sabat* fish, such as the mahseer, from the others, to make sure that they are cooked separately and children are given only what is safe for them to eat.

Some animals that are classed as dangerous for parents to eat (Class A, above), such as bats, giant squirrel and sandy catfish, would be considered safe for children and women to eat. But other species (of Class A) , such as monitor lizards, turtles, bamboo rat and some wild ferns, still carry danger for children and women and must be avoided.

K'dííg ʾaŋaaŋ, which is red-breasted, is a sabat species. K'dííg s'koʾr, a non-sabat species, is similar but with white on its front.

Class of Safe Species	Species
ʔAay məl, safe game	*ʔamɔɔ^k* – serow
	raŋkuu^k – banded langur
	tabəəx – dusky langur
K'díɡ məl, safe rodents	*ʔabíír, ʔajo'or b'rawaaŋ* – tree shrews
	cadɛ^k – red-cheeked squirrel
	cɛŋko'b d'ko'h – a yellow rat
	j'nalɛ^k – a brown rat
	k'díɡ man – white-bellied rats
	k'rɛdlaad – giant squirrel (black)
	s'ko'or – plantain squirrel (white)
	s'laa^k liyaax – red spiny rat
	siroŋ – himalayan striped squirrel
Cɛp məl, safe birds	*dɛŋdo'oŋ* – a red partridge
	ʔɛsʔɛɛs – ocraceous bulbul
	jagrɛɛg – golden-naped barbet (lowland)
	k'wɔɔx rɛŋah – great argus (black)
	p'dlaaj – asian fairy-bluebird
	sɛŋuwɛɛŋ – sunbirds
	t'raad – fire-tufted barbet
	tagùt – yellow-crowned barbet
	tambooj – whitehead's broadbill
	to'gro'h – golden-naped barbet (montane)
Kaa^k məl, safe fish	*bataŋ, bawu^k, bɛɛl, b'lɛmbad, daro^k bidín, daro^k c'mp'raas, gaho^k, jawa^k, kɛnrab rɛŋah, lampəə^k, lɛ^k, nip-t'luuy, p'ridoŋ, s'baraw, sɛlwooj, sikaŋ, siyɔɔ^k, s'laa^k, t'ŋə̄əs.*
Sɛgnug məl, safe frogs	*ʔaŋkuuy* – a pimpled river frog
	bəj'rù^k – a slender green river frog
	dɛmdup – river newts
	barhɛj – a burrowing river frog
	sɛɛŋ – a small river frog with dappled skin

Table 4. Animal species classed as non-tabooed to the Temiars.

Sɛgnug ʔaŋkuuy, an edible river frog that has toxic skin, which must be removed. Even so, the meat can cause one to vomit if improperly cooked.

Tabɛɛg, the bull frog, is a sabat creature particularly dangerous for women and children to eat.

Cɛp bajaw, blyth's hawk eagle. Birds of prey are not hunted by the Temiars.

Dɛmdup, newts, can be found sucking to the rocks at waterfalls. They are ardently hunted by women and children, and are a good source of meat.

3 | THE OLD HOMELAND (PRE-1950s)

3.1 EARLY LIFE IN THE PUYAN VALLEY

The Puyan River begins its journey as a small, sandy brook, flowing out of a mud bog called L'baax Sɛnduŋ, situated at the mountain pass facing Perak. It grows into a gentle-flowing and rocky river, shrouded by cool forest, before it passes over hard granite rock outcrops making some thundering waterfalls. Further down, after some rocky gorges, it meets with the Bərtax, the main river from the north-western region, and there it becomes wide and flat. As it meanders, it is joined by other rivers, including the Gɔɔb, Kacəŋ, Pɛrloŋ, Bɛɛd, Píɲcoɵŋ, Taboʰh, B'la²əər, Waaj, Bagəd and Ləəŋ, flowing past Sakoʰb mountain with flat water and rapids. Finally it meets the Jɛnrol, a larger river from the neighbouring region of today's Pos Pasíg, to the east, which itself flows into the B'roʊx, not far downstream. The distinctive and carefree hoo-hoos of gibbons were heard all along the Puyan, in the mornings, and later on the low tones of siamang calls from the hills. In the foothills, the persistent call of the golden-naped barbet was heard, *toʰg-toʰg-toʰg-toʰg-g'roʊh*. At the higher and cooler river sources, the mocking call of the great Argus pheasant was heard, *woʰh-wah, woʰh-wooh*, resounding through the stillness of the forest. In the old days, the Puyan was shaded by tall trees leaning over its sides and its water was crystal-clear with deep pools, which could appear black because of depth, and especially at the waterfalls, which were said to be *gool buhyaaᵏ*, or crocodile pools. Hundreds of small river valleys connect with the main artery, which was also the main valley-descent route for the inhabitants in the region. It enabled them to reach the lowland, with their wares, by punting and steering large rafts made of bamboo poles. The return journey would take a few days on foot, along a path that crossed back and forth over the B'roʊx, up the Jɛnrol and finally back to the Puyan and its upriver homesteads.

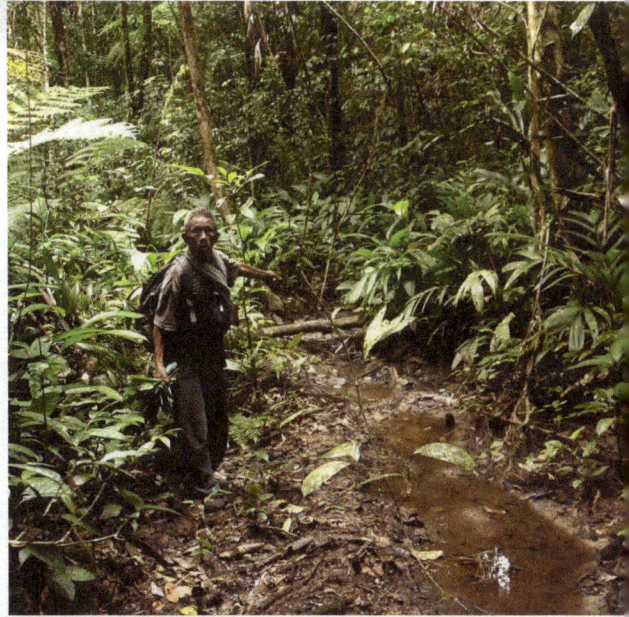

The mud bog from where two rivers begin, the Taloŋ, which flows into Perak, and the Puyan, which both begin with quiet water covered by cool forest.

The deeper waters of the Puyan before it merges with the Bərtax River.

Looking northward up the Puyan valley from J'nɛɛs; deep forest still covers the sides of the river.

Lower down on the Puyan, where once there were deep river pools, and the rocky sides of the river at its mouth. (Credit: Wahab ʔAlʉj)

Ancient paths led all over the region, following the main rivers and ascending the ridge lines up to the surrounding mountains and over into the neighbouring river valleys. Generation after generation of Temiars and Jehais had walked them, and the hack marks made in the trees along them bear witness to their journeys. Heavy hooves of rhinoceros, elephant and tapir had also trodden them down, and kept them clear. The sun bear and the tiger prowled along them, one hunting fruits and the other hunting deer and boars! They were the primary routes of the natives, making for communication lines between long-houses and escape routes whenever dangers arose. Each Temiar had a mental map of the paths and knew which would be the most direct to a hunting camp, or a swidden up the valley. Men walked bare-foot, with blowpipes rested on the shoulder, silently up their chosen route under towering canopies of *j'lax* mahogany. The family group would embark on a journey together, walking single-file with their young in slings on the back. But finding their way about was only a part of the knowledge of the inland forest that they held, for they knew of a myriad of plant species, those edible and those poisonous, the feeding and nesting habits of animals and birds, the kinds of materials to build with and where they could source herbal remedies. They possessed vital tying, weaving and trapping skills, all which aided them in daily survival. Their millennia-old knowledge of the forest was passed down to them from the generations that trod the paths before them.

A path up the Puyan, made muddy after recent manau rattan collection.

A group takes a rest after reaching Ɖulŋaal Ridge, on the path leading to the Perak border.

Kapoʻoᵗᵏ hayom

ʔUup

K'rag

K'rag

Gapəd

To the Temiars, many forest plants are recognised for their usefulness. The ʔapoʻós plants, or zingibers, give zesty fruits and each variety can be identified by its own flower.

Haaŋ

Tapix

Gancɛɛr

ʔUup

Gancɛɛr

Gapəd

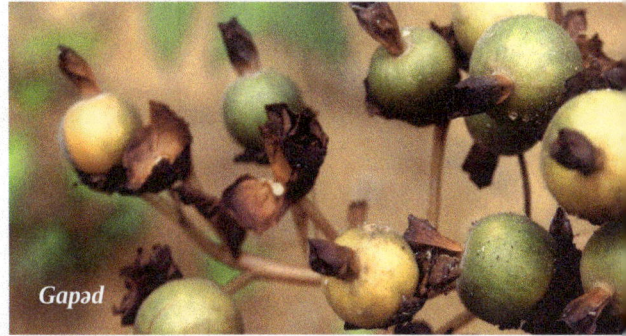

T'hoɽ

Different zingiber fruits, which are sweet and zesty when ripe. Some are picked and eaten when encountered, and some, like ʔapóʼs ʔuup, are foraged by the basket-full.

Tapɪx

Gapəd

Kapóˀoᵏ hayom

Haaŋ

There were hundreds, if not thousands, of natural species that the Temiars were familiar with, many of which were important to their daily needs. In their inventory of fauna, they have close to 300 tree species (refer to Appendix I, for a complete list), including 80 wood species, 130 wild fruiting trees and creepers (with fruits eaten by birds and animals) and 70 fruiting species (with edible fruits). Identification of trees was made in several ways, firstly at ground-level, by observing the colour of the tree trunk and its wood under the bark, and by looking for fallen flowers and fruits. Then by looking upwards, to observe the density and splay of the branches and also the shape of the leaves. They also had 26 varieties of rattan and 20 varieties of bamboo to choose from, while of food plants, 11 varieties of sugar cane, 14 varieties of yam, 25 varieties of banana and 20 varieties of manioc and sweet potato. Equally impressive to their botanical knowledge, they could identify over a hundred species of bird and almost fifty species of fish. Practically all other creatures native to the forest were known to them also, and were even told of in their folktales, be they of reptiles, snakes, frogs, bees, wasps, leeches, grubs, ants and cicadas, as well as rats, squirrels, civets or other mammals.

The gooc tree is identified by its secretion of whitish resin.

Gɛrhaar, a wild fruiting tree, has a globular trunk and white sap.

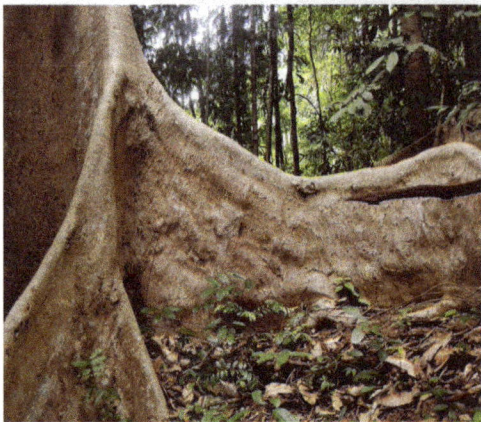

The kijax tree has distinctive, board-like buttresses.

The fruits of the cabol tree are similar to kolím, but larger, and are eaten by porcupines.

In the early days, they lived entirely on wild fruits and tubers. They dug yams such as the white *k'waay ʔakíís* and the similar, but slippery, *k'waay c'ŋəəl*, or the large, round *k'waay gɛnsuul*, found only in highland areas. The tubers of the *k'waay c'ʔaag*, were found above ground, growing from a thick trunk, but it was bitter-tasting and had to be soaked several days to reduce the strength (it was also used as a fish poison). Digging up these yams carried certain taboos, especially when digging them in mountain areas, as anything living in the ground there was believed attached to the soul of the mountain. They couldn't *cɛᵏrɛɛᵏ*, or call their name, when finding them, and they couldn't dig downward from the vine, on top of the tubers, they had to dig the ground from the side (thus a steep slope was preferred). Once a yam vine was located (they take good eyes and knowledge of the right colour to find) and they began unearthing the tubers, the whole root system had to be excavated, they couldn't leave any tubers in the ground. Failing to observe these codes would result in the earth *yɛlyool*, or turning over on them. But a few hours of digging with pointed sticks would procure food, and after the work they could bake the tubers and rest. Even more recently, the Temiars found themselves dependent on wild yams, when they fled into the forest during times of Communist and army activity and couldn't collect or plant their manioc.

Digging k'waay ʔakíís, the tubers produced by a small, thorny vine. A hundred years ago, such tubers were the staple food of the Temiars.

The tubers baked in the fire, had a crunchy texture inside.

Other forest plants were eaten such as *cɔɔg jaay*, the flower-bud of wild banana, and *c'kəər*, the pith of certain palm trees such as *bayas, pacɛy*, and *t'ʔơơ*. They also lived on *k'bəək d'koh*, an autumnal fruit and a variety of cempadak (but with no sweetness), the stones of which were cut out and cooked. There was also *k'bəək ʔajɛɛl*, a vine fruit with hard stones that had to be cracked open and roasted, but it had a pungent taste and was not safe for young people to eat due to the *julux* taboo. *K'bəək k'laat*, a large bean-pod that grew on a tree and turned dark red when ripe, was baked in a fire to make its beans edible. They picked wild fern shoots and ate them raw as they walked, because to cook them required a fire to be made which wasn't a simple affair. Lighting a fire involved pulling back and forth on a cord wound around a pole, set in a socket of a log. With enough friction the socket would heat up until the wood smoked, and then a wad of ultra dry *saməl*, or palm cotton, would catch light and a pile of bamboo shavings would be held to the cotton.

D'koh (Credit: ʔAnɛl)

ʔAjɛɛl (Credit: ʔAnɛl)

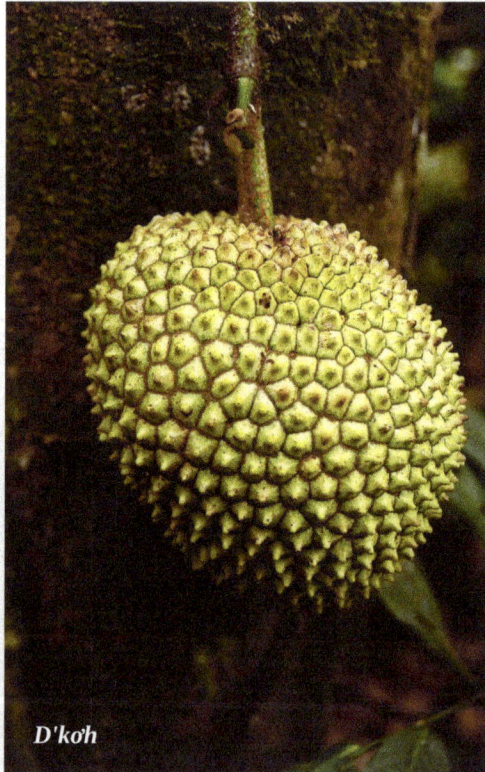
D'koh

With no fabric clothing in the old days, the original dress of the Temiars was a loin cloth made of tree bark, which the men would *cawɛ̄ɛ̄d*, or wrap around the waist and between the legs, pulling it tight by a tail at the rear. For the women, they made a long wrap-around called the *ʔawɛ̄ɛ̄d sơơg*. Both were made of the bark of certain trees, such as the *s'waŋ, haʔoog* or *dơơg*, beaten soft with a hard rod, and the bark cloth was also made into blankets for cold nights. When the cloth had been used a while it would become too itchy to wear and needed replacing. While sleeping they would rest the head on their arm, with *ʔabaag*, or bamboo halves, underneath it. Or they made a *karơx*, a woven pouch stuffed with *sanơơx k'lơơj*, the shavings of rattan vines. Men pierced the septum of the nose with a *k'lɛg*, a porcupine quill, and wore it wherever they walked, as a sign of being Temiar.

Mamoᵏ

The Temiars of old were dependent on many fruits of the forest for their nourishment, even though some of them were bitter, such as ʔajɛɛl, or were full of pips, like the wild banana.

L'ʔɛɛg

Caŋo'o'd

K'laat

G'woʼm

Jantaal

Kɛlpoʼŋ

Many other fruits were eaten whenever found ripe in the forest.

Baay

B'rɛgnoʼʼg

Bɛltoʼp

Baloʼŋ

C'kəər, the pith of certain palms was cut out and eaten raw.

ʔAbus Sɛnawɛɛŋ shows an ʔabat soʼog, a cloth made of tree bark. (Credit: Jadɛɛr)

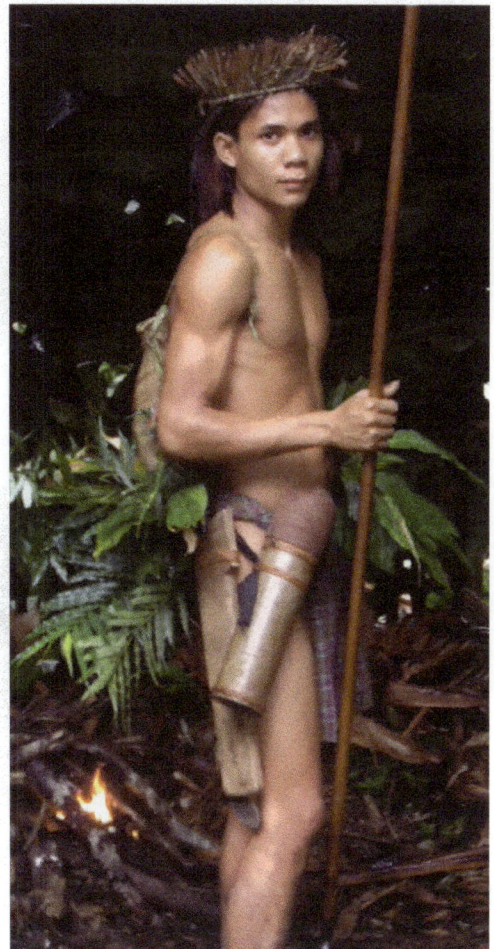

ʔAdiᵏ ʔAbaaŋ of Gawíɨn village models the traditional attire of loin cloth, with the blowdart quiver at the hip. (Credit: Jani ʔAyob)

Batu^k siyab, quartz rocks used for striking iron, were sourced from the mouth of the S'raŋɛ^k River.

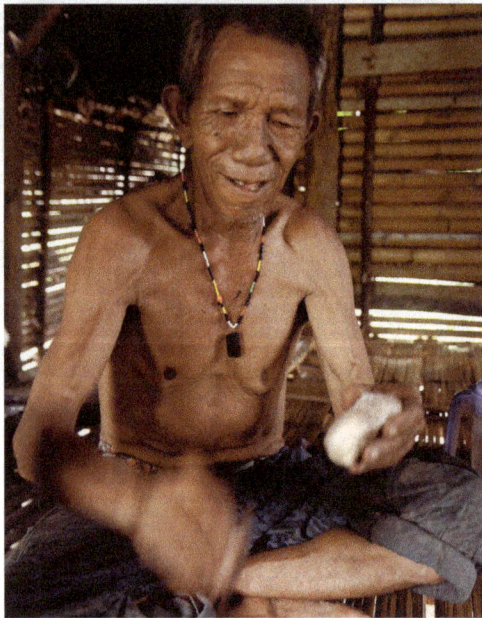

The late Rtd Sgt ʔUda Siyam, here demonstrating how to make sparks with a batu^k siyab, a piece of quartz, and a scrap of metal, in his home at Kacəŋ village.

A stone found at the Pínco'oŋ River, similar to others kept by the Temiars, its use now unknown.

Gasɛᵏ (Credit: ʔAnɛl)

Saməl, a natural cotton once used for lighting fires and for inserting behind blow-darts when shooting, was found either on the towering jííg palm or on the smaller gasɛᵏ palm.

Jííg

(Credit: ʔIdris ʔAsɵd)

The original tools of the Temiars were made of stone and for this reason, their style of horticulture was probably limited by what type of tree they could fell, and how much effort it would take, not to mention if their stones broke now and then. The first iron tools were obtained in the late 1920s by Temiars who found work down on the east-coast railway line, on the Dabong to Kuala Lipis stretch,[1] as payment for their labour. They came back up-river with *jɛx*, adzes, *j'waaj caŋko*ᵏ, spoon-shaped bush knives, and *taro'g*, hunting spears. After the durability of the iron was realised, their stone tools would no doubt have been discarded and no knowledge remains today of how to make them.

Wooden replicas of the first iron tools that the Temiars possessed, and an original spearhead

3.1 According to records found online, the Gua Musang to Kuala Krai stretch of railway was opened in 1931, which means that work on the stretch may have begun in the 1920s.

Great hardwood trees could only be felled with the help of the iron adze.

Stone adzes found in a cave at Gəmbalah that most likely predate the use of iron. Could these tools have been used to fell hardwood trees and bamboo, to enable cultivation of land?

Felling trees at a swidden at Labuᵏ, on the Bərtax River

The *jɛx*, or iron adze, is almost as iconic of the Senoi people as the *b'laaw*, their blowpipe, due to its use by tree fellers throughout their territories. It had a slender blade with a pointed, lance-like tail that was tied to a wooden handle with a tight weaving of rattan skin. The *p'rɛndah*, or handle, was made from a short block of a tree trunk with a protruding branch, of small trees such as *c'yɛd*, *saad* or *caad*. The block was thinned down and the edge away from the branch was flattened to make a mounting. The branch was cut and fitted with a piece of soft *libɔd* wood, to make a grip. When the adze was swung at a tree, the hands felt nothing, because the handle was flexible, taking all the shock, even when swung at solid mahogany. A giant hardwood could be felled in a day's work, often by cutting out wedges from left and right and leaving a centre piece to be cut out last. When cutting a forested plot of land, all the smaller trees below would be cut three-quarters the way through beforehand so that the top tree would knock them all over when it fell. If the adze head turned in its rattan tie, then after a swing at the tree the handle was turned downwards or upwards and the adze was easily straightened.

ʔAŋah Sɛdlíj stands on a scaffold to fell a tree with an iron adze, to clear an area for planting millet.

A platform of poles, called an *ʔulǒw*, would be tied to stand on while cutting at a large tree, in order to reach above the sometimes enormous buttress roots. There are still signs found today of tree cutting made with the *jɛx*, at swiddens perhaps over eighty years old, with great tree stumps still standing there. Iron tools would have been hard to come by in those days (until the British arrived and gave out plenty of them), needing to raft down-river with wares to trade for them or to find work and obtain them as wages. Stories tell of Taaᵏ ʔAmpís and his group cutting a very large swidden at Taməŋ, while they lived at Jaŋrax, on the Upper Puyan. So this must have been no earlier than the year of 1930, unless they had already found them by trading wares. Stones suitable for honing their tools were sourced from the Bayuur River, over the pass at Kasuh, to the east, in today's Pos Pasíg region. A very sharp stone could even be used to shave the beard. It was also discovered that sparks could be made by hitting a certain quartz with the end of the iron adze, and from then on the Temiars would always carry a *batuᵏ siyab*, or fire stone, in their pouch. The S'raŋɛᵏ River was the only source of these stones and they walked there from all over the region, whenever they needed a new one.

3.2 HOME BUILDING

A dwelling place in the time of the early Temiars was typically a single long-house raised above the ground on wooden piles that were set deep in the ground to provide stability. The wood for the piles was chosen from hardwood that would resist rot for ten years or more. There was no specific wood required for any build, but the best available trees would have been sourced, such as *t'ramoᵏ, j'rəg, gaar, k'bəəᵏ pɛrlug, cɛmpɛɛx* or *k'rɛɛw*. They couldn't be over-sized as splitting them would be impossible if too broad, but foot-wide trees could be split. Today the Temiars are aided by chainsaws and can *pag*, or plank, a large *kolím* log. The floor and roof beams, likewise, would have been sourced from nearby forest wood such as young *cah* trees, whereas these days, after so much secondary forest has sprung up, the fast-growing *g'lapoh* tree is chosen for its mixture of strength, light-weight and straightness. The roof was of open gable construction, with the rafters raised to a ridge pole and tied underneath it, making an 'X' in which it sat. The *rabuŋ*, or ridge pole, was first held up by poles stood vertically at the centre (noticeable in the picture on p105), and once it was fixed by the rafters, the poles were removed (a technique still used by Temiars today).

The Temiars had a simple method for enclosing space, used primarily to keep out animals from the swidden and the home. They would cut long bamboo poles and *r'dɛɛd* them, stack them in a vertical wall, tied with rattan to posts set in the ground. On the house, they also added a bamboo slat on the outside of the wall at every post, and rattan was wound around slat and post to clamp the stack of poles tightly. The *dɛix rɛndɛɛd*, or stack-walled house, was preferred over other techniques, such as walls of flattened bamboo, and it still is today. The floor was made of *cɛŋkaar*, or split bamboo slats, tied to underlying skins of *bayas* palm, which made an impenetrable layer. On top of that, *niis*, or flattened bamboo boards, were laid to create a level surface. But often the covering of *niis* was done without, so that they wouldn't sleep too comfortably, and would stay alert at night, to noises in the forest and around the house.

A meeting hall, with half-open walls.

A simple home made of rɛndɛɛd bamboo walls, at Píncoʼoŋ village.

Roofing was made of bɛltoʹp (Malay, bertam), a leafy palm that grew abundantly on some hills. The leaves of one side were folded over the back of the spine and braided with the leaves from the other side, to form sheets. These were tied onto the roof in pairs, each pair overlapping the one underneath, until the top was reached, using up to thirty to forty pairs. The closer the pairs were tied together, the more water-proof the roofing would be and the drier the occupants inside. The roof also needed a fairly steep incline so that rain water shed off. A set of overlapped woven sheets, from top to bottom, was called a *luwaar*, and when a house was built they would count how many *luwaar* were needed to cover one side of the roof, be it six to eight for a small house, or a dozen or more for a long-house. Then they would send off the palm cutters, who would look for the longest and most leafy branches to cut. Ten or so branches would be laid in a pile and the leaves would be gathered, all the way down in a giant braid, to make a long bundle. One man could then carry three or four bundles down to the house.

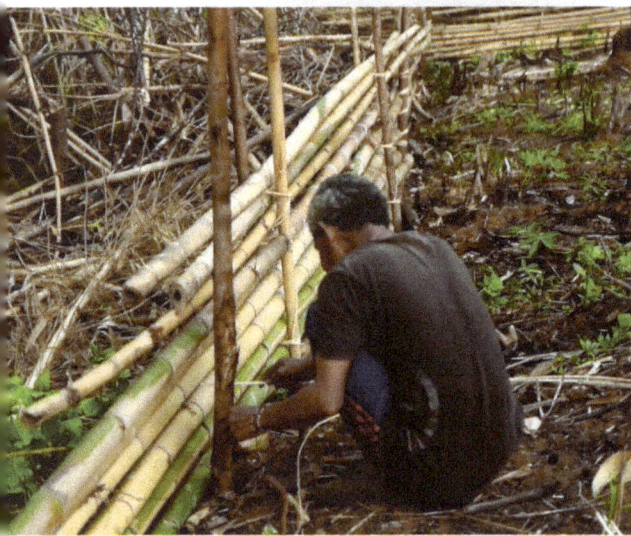

A villager ties a bamboo wall to keep pests out of a new swidden.

A tidy work was made on the wall of this new house.

A house wall is constructed by inserting lengths of bamboo between uprights.

All the village men contribute to the building of their community hall.

A new roof ready for tying on palm sheets.

A man at Tɛmagaaᵏ builds a new house, alone.

The women would then take their turn, braiding the leaves to make sheets and laying them out in the sun to dry. After drying, the leaves would be pulled tight to close the gaps created by shrinking. Once the roof was tied, the fire place would be made at the centre of the house, to dry the palms from the inside. A house with a constant fire going would blacken the roofing with soot and that was desired, so that the roofing would stay firm, without rotting from damp or becoming *j'rɛgliig*, or holed. A new roof might last for up to three years, but repairs could be made if a leak developed, such as by stuffing fan-shaped palms in between the roof sheets.

The complete structure, with the walls and roofing, was held up with lashings of rattan vines, made so tightly that not a single pole could come loose. The vines were sourced from montane forest, where they were pulled down from the trees. To be usable for tying they were carefully split length-wise and thinned down with sharp tools, to remove their pith. This would allow them to flex around any size pole and be pulled tight (rounded vines make too much friction and knots cannott be tied). Varieties such as *s'tɔɔg* and *c'mɛɛs* were standard in building, whereas the finer *riyɛw* or *sɛnsiyɛc* were used in tying fish traps. A typical house could last up to five or six years before the wood was eaten out by weevils, but much longer if good wood was built with.

Often the *k'moòm*, or kin group, would make a move after two years anyway, because the food from the swidden would be used up and a new one would need to be cut elsewhere. If they knew their stay would only be temporary they might not put too much effort into the home to begin with. In ten or twenty years they may come back to the same place and re-use the *l'mog*, the overgrown swidden, especially if the area was suitable for hunting and fishing and had fruit trees that they or their forefathers had planted.

A young Temiar selects palm branches to cut. He then plaits the leaves to make 'bundles' for carrying.

Two women plait the palm leaves to form sheets.

(Credit: ²Anel)

The roofing is tied on with rattan cord to create a perfectly waterproofed interior.

Rattan vines are pulled down from the trees where they hang and wound into coils to be carried home.

The vines are split in two and thinned down on the inside to make flexible cords.

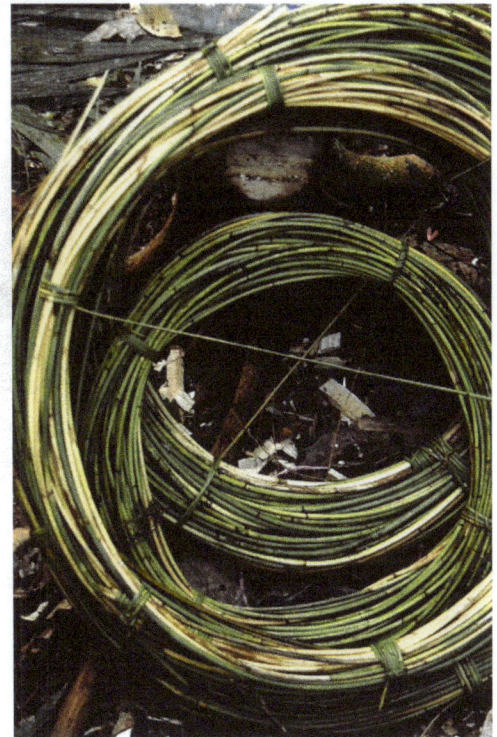

When a new house was ready to live in, they would *juul*, or warm the roof by climbing into the rafters and waving a tray of hot coals, while asking for the *r'waay* of the house to be good to them. Then they could sleep in peace, and always have good health and ample provision of food in the house, with no one getting ill or suffering from hunger.

Tiger-proofing was a vital requirement of home-building, because the big cats prowled the land as if it was all theirs. A menacing tiger wouldn't hesitate to scratch at the walls of a flimsy house, to tear it open and make a meal of those sleeping inside. If one was heard near the house and became a worry, the group could scare it off by shouting and banging on bamboo, or lighting bamboo torches and shining them in its face. But there are stories of people being trapped in their hut all night, huddled together and unable to leave until the morning, for fear of being eaten. In some places, such as Sʼrijooʼh and Paax, on the Bərtax river, they built their homes high up on ten foot stilts, and even up in the trees, needing a ladder to access them.

They also kept strict adherence to the prohibitions, and sought peace with nature through the dances they made, in order to keep safe from the dangers of the wild. For they were constantly aware that their own odour was the cause of danger in regard to *mɛrgɛɛs*, or the beasts of the forest, and they knew they had to be cautious. If they feared there was a *jɛᵏtuux sɛnʔooʼy* about, or a tiger which had been kept by a keeper, but was now roaming free since the death of the keeper, they were extremely wary of it because it could attack anyone.

Bamboo is hacked at the nodes and opened out flat to make niis, or flooring.

Pɛnpəəᵏ, a liana that was used for tying river rafts or fences.

Walls could also be made of palm skins, woven in zig-zag patterns. (Credit: ʔAnɛl)

3.3   FORAGERS OF THE FOREST

As with other indigenous peoples in the tropics, the forest was the great, open pantry of the Temiars, full of nutritious foods they could gather. Wild ferns, such as *bəər sɛndab, bəər sɛnyoˊn* and *bəər sɛjlíj*, would be gathered from all around the dwelling and from along the paths in the forest or along the riverbank. The slender leaves of *bəər camɛɛŋ* that grew on the rocks in the up-stream rivers were picked in arm-fulls, as well as the rough-leafed *bəər k'laab* that grew in places on the forest floor. Wild mushrooms, such as *bəər luux, bəər ˀāntaᵏ* and *bəər poˊoˊg* were picked whenever sighted, as they only lasted a day or two when they sprouted. Oil was extracted from *soˊic* nuts (Malay, perah) by mashing them in a bamboo tube over the fire and this they used to give their ferns a *g'rax* or delicious taste (in the present day they cook with raw peanuts to create a creamy broth).

The Temiars had no manufactured goods in the old days, and the first time they had oil or salt to cook with was in 1957, when the British air-dropped food supplies at the gathering zone at Ranah. All their meat, ferns, and yam roots were boiled or baked inside bamboo tubes and were flavoured with herbs such as the *moˊoŋ* leaf, the *j'maad* root, the *gantən* flower (all three of these are zingiber plants, or wild gingers); *k'bəəᵏ kolím*, a nut from a hardwood tree (*Scorodocarpus borneensis*), the pinkish inside of which has a nutty, garlic taste; *k'bəəᵏ kɛrwoˊoj*, a small berry with a strong citrus smell; and *k'bəəᵏ maŋgoˊoy*, wild aubergine (*Solanum trilobatum*), which has slightly bitter berries that can be baked or boiled, then mashed and mixed with vegetables.

Bəər luux

Bəər poˊoˊg

Bəər ˀapoˊoˊs haaŋ

Bəər k'ˀuux

ʔAŋah Panda^k picks bəər cameeŋ at the Jeŋhuŋ River (left), a plant edible when raw, and cooking the ferns with fish (above), at a campsite.

Bəər panteɣ

Bəər gentox bawaaj

Bəər ʔānta^k

Bəər cameeŋ

Bəər sɛjlíj

Bəər sɛndab

Bəər sɛnyon

Bəər capí[k]

Bəər capaa[k]

Bəər karaax

Bəər kɛnyaar kaaᵏ

Bəər gùx

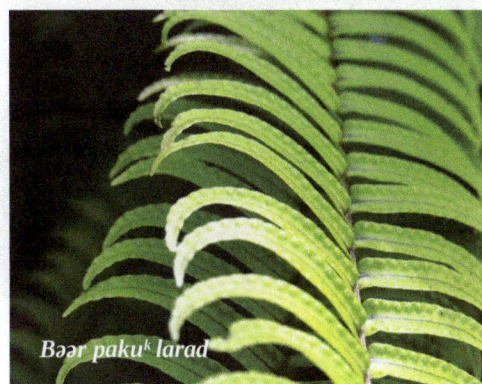

Bəər pakuᵏ larad

In the old days they would cut down the high
bəər sayah fern to pick its leaves.

Bəər sayah

Bəər k'laab

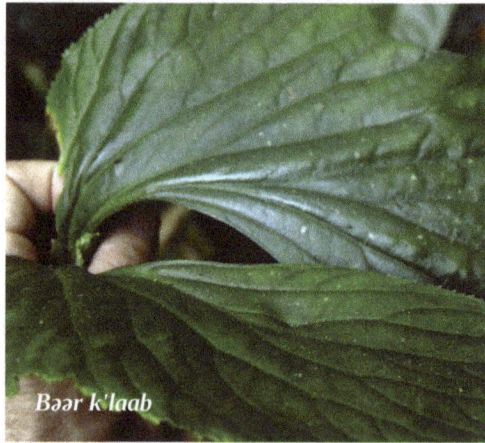

Bəər k'laab

Two kinds of bəər k'laab, that were found abundant on the forest floor.

J'maad

J'maad root

Moʻoŋ

Moʻoŋ and j'maad are two zingiber plants used for flavouring food.

Gantən

Gantən flower   (Credit: ʔAnɛl)

Gantən, a zingiber common with Malay cooking. Its stem and flower were used to flavour food.

K'bəəᵏ kɛrwoʻoj, small berries with a citrus smell, were used to flavour meat and fish.

Kolím

Maŋgoʻoy

Laar

Laar ʔuud

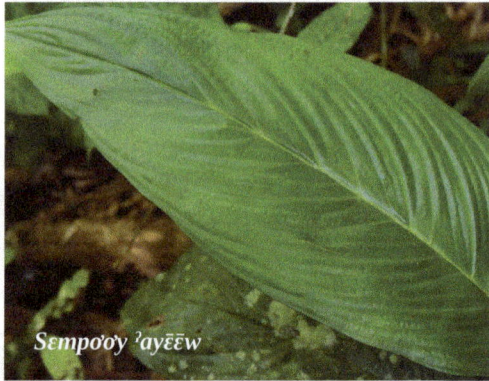
Sɛmpoʼoy ʔayɛ̄ɛ̄w

Smooth, odourless leaves were used for wrapping bats or mushrooms, for making packets for steaming, or to plug the end of a cooking tube.

Pɛnpət ŋoʼor was used for stopping the end of bamboo when carrying fish.

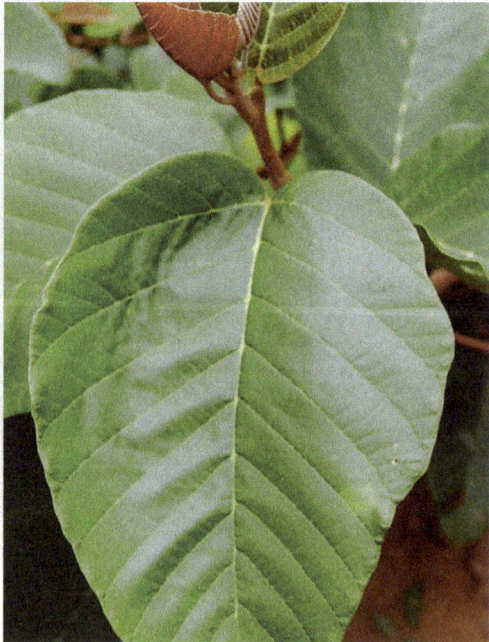
S'laaᵏ baroᵡ, a leaf suitable for wrapping fish.

Fruits played a vital part (and still do) in the Temiars' forest existence and seasonal fruits such as *jiyɛɛs*, *soʿic* and *d'koʿh* were not to be wasted. According to the tradition of their ancestors, the first harvest of the fruit season began with a petition to ʔAlʉj Tampuy, to let the fruit trees know that they were present, and wanted to take of the fruits and so that no harm would come on them (as these fruit trees are believed to have powerful souls). This would be made when the first *jiyɛɛs* tree had ripened, and another petition would be made at the house, with the whole group gathered together, to *kahyax* or celebrate the first fruits. After this, the group was free to gather fruits from the trees, as they pleased. The harvest at the *jiyɛɛs* tree and at other trees like *sɛmpaaᵏ* (varieties of jungle durian, with smaller, more fragrant fruits than durian), *kabaax* (wild rambutan) and *tampuy* (tampoi fruit), were undertaken by the whole kin group.

Several men would climb up with their *ganas*, or hook poles, to twist off the fruits and make them drop below. At a suitable pause in the fruit dropping, while the men shimmied up new boughs in the tree, the group would race in under the tree to *moʿos*, or collect all they could in their baskets, and pile them up outside the slightly dangerous drop-zone. Then the group would sit around the pile and hack open the skins to extract the yellow pips inside. Fully ripened fruits burst open on impact with the ground or could be broken open easily and the juicy, orange flesh was sweet and delicious (the taste is something between orange and mango) but most of the fruits were still half-ripe and hard. The extracted fruit was posted into bamboo tubes and taken back to the long-house to be baked on the fire. The baking softened and sweetened the fruit and also cooked the pips which tasted of nut.

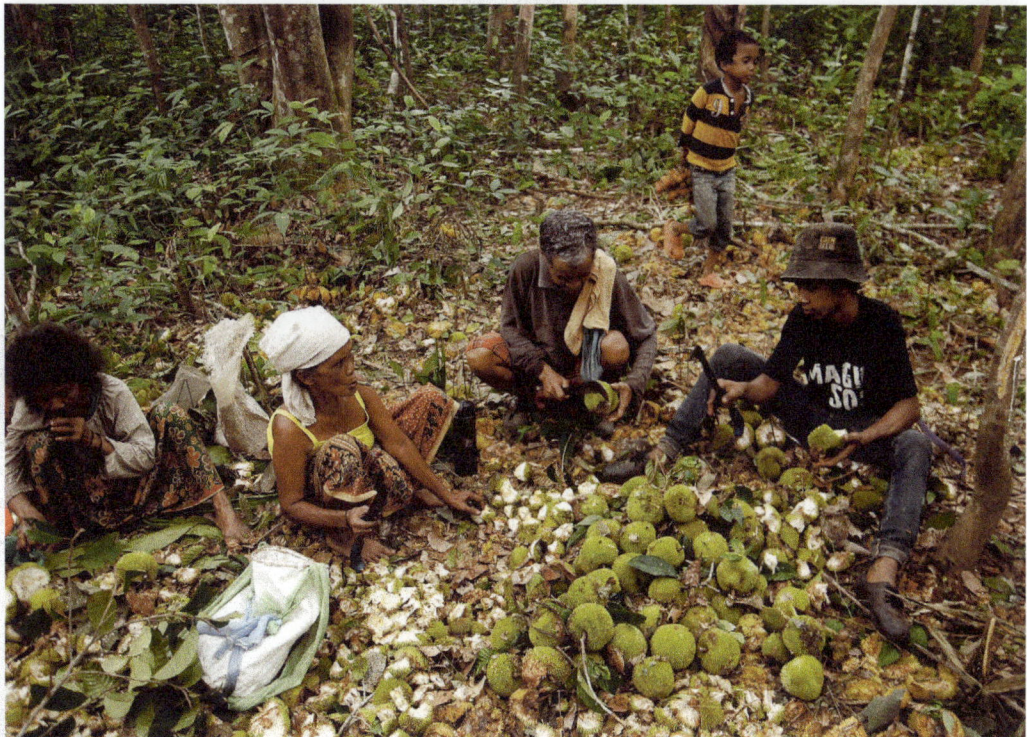

Jiyɛɛs harvest: villagers sit by a pile of fruits to extract the edible parts for cooking.

The fruit pips are taken home in clean bamboo tubes.

Roslan ʔAŋah of Píncoʹoŋ makes petition to ʔAlʉj Tampuy, guardian of the fruit trees, with burning kasay root.

In the fruit season there were so many wild fruits that they called it *tawùn b'rəx*, 'year of fruits'. They lived off their sweetness for three months, feasting each day on *b'rəx nɛgliig*, 'swallowing fruits', and *b'rəx nɛjmuuj*, 'sucking fruits', those sucked off the pip, not swallowed. They would *p'lóg* juicy fruits, or mash them with a stick inside a bamboo tube, to drunk the nectar neat. When the fruit season arrived it was the happiest day of the year for the children, and their mothers painted their faces and gave them little baskets to carry, that they had made specially, so that they could take part in the fruit gathering. It was a celebration of life for the Temiars, and they would wait with eagerness for the first day of the harvest.

Soʹic nuts were also knocked down with hook poles, when the fruits were ripening, because the older folk found them a food well worth savouring. Only the men would go to the soʹic tree, because the fruit was potent and could harm children's or women's souls if they went. They would first make petition to ²Alɨj Lɛn²ɔ͡ʊy, before climbing the tree, to ensure their own safety. The nut shells were cut open at the tree and the white insides were collected, to be grated on sticks and mashed in bamboo on the fire, at home. The hot-tasting cake produced was delicious, but the nut had a strong smell that could make a young person dizzy.

K'bəəᵏ d'koʰ (called maŋkoʻŋ in the old days) was another valuable source of nutrition. It was a wild, autumnal variety of cempedak (*Artocarpus integer* var. *silvestris*), similar to jack but smaller, non-sweet and grew from the tree-trunk. The fruits were cut open and bashed with rods to loosen the stones from the latex-rich husk. These, after boiling, were soft and tasted a little like chestnut. Everyone gladly took their fill of them.

Waiting for the thanksgiving to be made, before indulging in the first fruits of the year.

²Asuh ²Ati packs jiyɛɛs fruits into bamboo tubes for cooking.

Fully ripened jiyɛɛs is soft and sweet when cooked, and very delicious. The less ripened fruits are firmer and less sweet, but are more filling. The cooked pips are peeled and eaten, and taste of nut.

Stones of the d'ko'h fruit, boiled and ready to eat.

Lɛ^k

Rako^k

Pahíd

Raŋsíil

Kɛlwɛɛx

Cɛdro'o'd

P'rago'o^k

Sɛdwɛd

Bɛjsij

Gayax

B'ko'o'd

3.4   SHIFTING CULTIVATION

Swiddening, the cutting and planting of patches of land, became a logical and necessary way of life, combined with age-old skills of hunting and foraging (they were not pure foragers like neighbouring tribes). They learned that dependence on wild roots, fruits and plants for their sustenance could leave them in times of hunger, especially in the seasons of heavy and persistent rainfall that greatly hamper activities in the forest. Several persons in the historical stories are known to have starved to death because they had no means to find food. With the advent of iron tools, either home-made or obtained from trading forest wares downriver, swiddens could be cut each year, according to the seasons, to guarantee a food supply.

Squashes were grown on the swidden and baked inside bamboo.

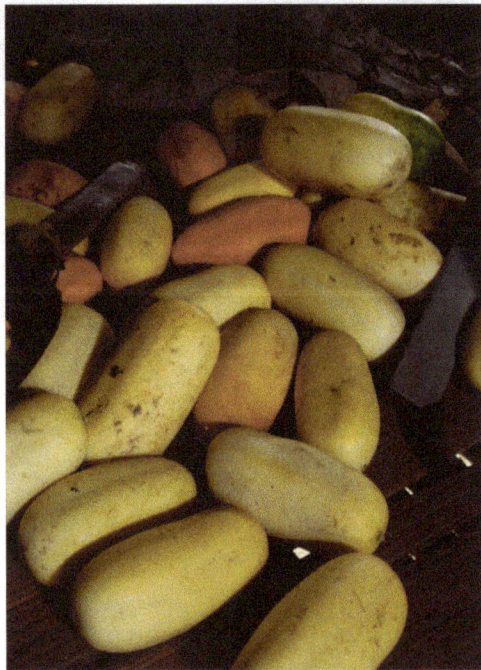

A new swidden is burned, but there are still many cuttings to gather up so that planting can begin.

A giant crop of cucumbers.

(Credit: ʔAnɛl)

A single swidden would make use of two or three acres of forested land, in which all trees and vegetation blocking the sun were felled, left to dry out and burned. The forest grows because of a cycle of humus and dead wood decaying on the ground. So with a swidden, the burn-off adds ash to the ground and the raging fire helps to prepare the topsoil for planting, but in a year the crops deplete the soil's nutrients and the ground also hardens, making it impossible to replant. The thick undergrowth that comes up in the scorching sun is also too energy-consuming to cut down, and so the swiddener must abandon it and move on. He must shift to a new area and cultivate more land, to keep the cycle of food production going.

Previously cultivated land grows over with secondary forest in a few years, and in forty or fifty years with trees seeded from the surrounding unharmed forest, which grow so broad and high that it is hard to tell that the land was once cleared and planted by man. The practice of swiddening has gone on for centuries in the forests of the Peninsula and it keeps in balance with the natural ecosystem, never over-cutting or leaving permanent damage to the environment. The ground itself is left untouched and the rivers continue to flow with clear water—they do not become blocked with tree debris or silted from landslides, which is a standard after-product of mechanised forest harvesting in the modern day.

They planted *k'waay go'oŋ*, a yam with arrow-shaped leaves, and *jawa^k*, or varieties of millet, on the cooler, upriver hillsides. Sweet-corn, rice and peanuts, which today are eagerly planted all across the Temiar region, were not yet acquired in the early days. Planting millet was a simple affair of scattering seed among the logs of a burned swidden and no weeding would be done until the harvest (unlike rice, which needs much more care in order to help the crop produce). Wherever they planted, a long-house would be built for hanging the red-brown bunches of grain heads during the harvest. When the harvest arrived, because of the ample food available each day, with the young people enthusiastically pounding the millet, many visitors would come from the long-houses in the other valleys and they would have merry times in the evenings, decorating themselves and making their *nɛhpɔɔh* dances.

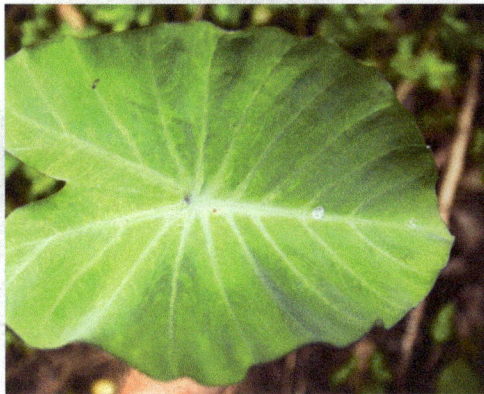

K'waay go'oŋ, a yam that produces large, starchy tubers.

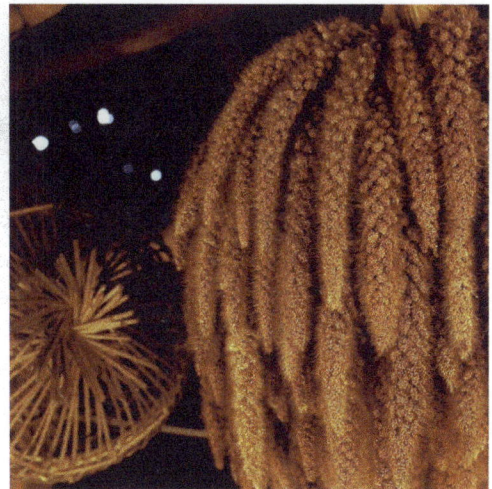

Jawa^k (foxtail millet) hanging at a home at Calɛɛr village, being kept for seed.

The millet was pounded with poles in a *guul*, a mortar carved out of solid wood, to break the husk off the grain. It was an energy-consuming task because of the fine grain, but they would rotate the pounding duty. The women turned the millet in bamboo tubes on the fire to heat it up before the pounding (compared with today's use of a large wok on the fire). Once a mortar-full was all broken and a delicious smell filled the house, it was taken for winnowing on *gadaŋ* trays, to blow away the chaff. Then it was sifted using a *campεj*, a woven tray with a pointed end, to separate the milled grain from the unbroken grain, a skilled job requiring a rhythmic jerking of the hands. The husked grain was sent back to the mortar, to be pounded again until all the pure grain was obtained. Finally, it was baked into a delicious millet cake, inside bamboo.

Jawa^k is pounded in a guul, a mortar carved of wood, and sifted, to make grain for the day's meal.

Jawa^k has been a staple grain crop of the Temiars since time immemorial and they have cultivated over ten varieties. Some of the harvesting and preparation techniques, such as cutting the heads from the top of the stalk, treading the grain in a folded mat, as well as the pounding and baking, have been passed on to the newer cultivation of rice.

Most Temiars say that the first time they obtained rice seed was during the return from their three-year migration downriver, in 1959. But another story is told of rice being found sprouting by itself on a swidden, a long time before then. This would fit into their beliefs that many of the staple foods the Temiars possess were *ʔasal*, or original, given by Nyʉ^k ʔAlʉj, and not imported from outside sources. The first tobacco, for example, was discovered at Batu^k Kamεy, the great limestone stack at B'riix, near Pos Pasíg, probably a few centuries ago, and it has been cultivated everywhere since. Also, if the forefathers had seen the soul of the rice field in dreams long ago (as I mention in Part 1.3, above), they must have known the crop at that time too.

The Temiars know of 22 different rice varieties, all of which they have planted at some time and probably around half of them are still planted today. Most of the names for rice and millet describe the colour and appearance of the variety. For example, there is *cɛᵏcoᵏ*, meaning 'sharp', *j'bad*, 'heavy', *rantɛy*, 'like chains', *ʔuloˀx*, 'yellowish', *ʔamaŋ*, 'black', *cabaax*, 'with branches', *kabaax*, 'red', *sakool*, 'white'.

Tubers and bananas could also be made into a cake which was called *nɛjkiij*, by grating them on rattan sticks, the thorns burned off to leave hard nobbles to grate on. This they scooped into bamboo tubes with a rolled up *laar* leaf inserted beforehand, to keep the pulp from sticking to the tube. Another way was to *sɛrpaad* the pulp, or wrap it in leaf packets, and stuff them into bamboo for steaming. The tube was split open after cooking and the cake was cut and shared out, and was eaten all at once. Packets of food would keep longer, and each person would take as many as they needed. Today they cook home-grown rice in packets to celebrate their festivals.

When manioc was adopted by the Temiars in the mid twentieth century, they learned to grate it and dry it in the sun to make a flour that would keep longer. *Kayuh nɛmkəp* was made by soaking manioc in water for a few days to let it ferment. Once softened it was grated and the pulp squeezed dry, before being baked in bamboo to make a solid cake with a cheesy flavour. This cake could also be kept for a while and added to a meat broth. The easiest method of cooking manioc was to make it *nɛdtoˀd*, or baked, by standing it peeled and scraped in the glowing embers of the fire.

Women grate raw manioc into a pulp on rattan sticks, to be baked in bamboo tubes.

Leaf packets of rice are made. for stuffing inside bamboo and steaming.

Other cooking methods were:

Pɛnʔoˀol   baking without water: tubers, squash and plantains were sliced and stuffed into a tube, and also fruits that were cut open unripe, such as *jiyɛɛs*.

Pɛgtoˀg   boiling with water: ferns were stuffed into the bottom of a tube, with fish or meat added on top, with layers of herbs between; the tube was stood in the fire, resting against a slanting pole, to prevent the water from spilling.

Pɛnʔuux   mixed game and tubers: manioc was boiled with meat to make it soft in a delicious gravy, which was poured out and sipped.

Nɛgroˀg   mashing pulp: grated tubers or perah nuts were mashed and stirred inside the tube, on the fire, using a *ranoˀŋ* stick, the latter taking an hour or two of mashing, to remove the toxicity.

The cooking tube was stoppered with a folded *laar* leaf and turned repeatedly to prevent it burning through to the inside. Foods cooked this way had a caramelised taste from the bamboo, and even today, they are much preferred over foods cooked in aluminium pots.

3.5 HUNTING AND GAME

The Temiars may have had chickens (that looked very similar to jungle fowl) but they never consumed the meat of anything they had reared and fed themselves. Meat was always sourced from the wild and if not monkeys, civets or fish, birds and bats made good meat too. Jungle fowl and pheasants could be caught on the ground with a snare trap, whereas fruit-eating birds could be hunted using *sɛɛp*, sticky gum strands, and a method called *nɛgcoʼog*, 'jabbing'. The gumming strands were made of the outer skin of *bɛltoʼp* palm midrib, and were coated in a gum made from the latex of the *g'tah cɛp* tree, itself a fruit tree where birds were gummed. The white latex was mixed with a vine sap, such as of the *rɛnyoʼl*, *gacɛɛᵏ*, *kɛdrɛd*, or *sɛdɲoʼoʼd* vines, to make it turn sticky and the strands were coated with it by a method called *l'bɛɛᵏ*, dipping them in the gum, inside a bamboo tube, and then dividing and joining them together, over and over. They were then blackened, by holding them over a fire with some burning *gooc*, a tree resin, and this would make them less visible to birds on the tree.

The bird hunter took his sticky strands up a fruiting tree, in the dark of early morning before the birds arrived, and jabbed them along the top of the branches. When the birds flew in to feed, the strands would gum to their feathers and cause them to fall, helplessly, to the ground. The hunters, waiting quietly below, would collect the fallen birds into a pile, until the strands were used up. One may think that catching and eating small birds is rather cruel, especially when one sees the colourful feathers they have (for example, the sapphire blue back of *cɛp pɛjlaaj*, the Asian fairy bluebird), but they turn into a needed meal for all at the long-house, often tasting of the fruits that the birds had been feeding on.

Cuts are made in the tree as far up the trunk as they can reach (Credit: ʔAri Kɛntoʼn)

ʔAri Kɛntoʼn collects latex from a g'tah cɛp tree, for making into bird trapping gum. He makes a cut and waits for the latex to congeal, before wrapping it onto a stick. (Credit: ʔIdris ʔAsoʼd)

A pile of gumming strands are laid in a leaf up the fruit tree, ready for prodded into the tree's branches. (Credit: ʔAnɛl)

Sadəri ʔEmbah prepares gumming strands at a hunters' camp. (Credit: ʔIdris ʔAsŏd)

A hunter spreads gum onto new gumming strands, over a fire with burning resin, to blacken them. (Credit: ʔAnɛl)

Gooc, a brittle tree resin that is burnt to blacken hunting implements.

In the old days they would climb the great *j'lax*, or mahogany trees (Malay, tualang), that towered high and on which the fruiting *k'bəəᵏ luwaaᵏ* creeper grew, to which rhinoceros and pouched hornbills flocked, to feed during the rainy season. These large birds needed thicker gum strands to stick on their feathers, to render them flightless, and much more effort was needed to catch them, but the meat they offered was well worth it. Climbing the large and smooth trunks to reach the canopy of these trees was a task that only the skilled, and brave, could do. They had to *b'lad* the tree trunk, or lash a thick vine to it all the way up, making a climbing pole, and they needed to tie themselves to the tree with cord. In those days, when the fruiting trees and vines were still abundant all over the forest, the sky would be blackened with hornbills, swarming around their feeding places like bats. Today, pouched hornbills arrive each October from their migratory origins, flying up the valley in V-formations made of ten to thirty birds each. In 2017, they flocked to the Puyan, with hundreds of birds arriving each morning, but other years there have been much fewer, perhaps because the fruit trees have gone.

Cɛp guwɔɔᵏ, or bats, were hunted in the caves where they nested and they made good meat and a delicious soup when baked in bamboo. Tiny bats could be extracted from standing bamboo if their nest hole was spotted, and *cɛp lasar*, or giant bats, were to be found high up in great *r'guul* trees. To hunt them in caves they needed plenty of dry bamboo to light as torches, which they carried in their back-baskets. These they first *layuur*, warmed over a fire, to make them super-dry, so as to catch light easily. When one piece was nearly burned down another could be taken and lit quickly. Some of the group would enter the cave and try to hit the hanging bats with their twiggy sticks, or make them fly out to be hit by others waiting at the cave's mouth. Once hit to the ground they would be chased and held by the throat to kill them, and tossed into a pile. To take them home they would sapoʼoˈd them, or wrap them in leaf.

A catch of birds. The bird population has never been affected by the small number of Temiars who hunt. (Credit: ²Anɛl)

Bats from the caves (top) are larger than those found in bamboo cavities (above).

Bat hunting caves. (Credit: Yusman ²Andoᵏ/Rapi)

Squirrels, monkeys and civets were hunted with the *b'laaw* and *s'garr*, the bamboo blowpipe and poison-tipped blow-dart. If the poison was good an animal would fall to the ground in a few minutes, although, a large monkey such as a siamang might fall and get stuck in a tree bough. Their blow-dart poison needed to be fresh to make sure that the darts were effective. Hunters could shoot their darts a hundred feet and hit a bird or tree shrew, having excellent eyesight. It took great stealth to *lɛɛb*, or creep up on langurs because they were always watchful of movement below. They could be found returning to their roost in the bamboo at evening, and a hunter might observe them and wait until morning to shoot them. Small rodents could be caught with snare traps, comprising of a noose of rattan cord and a catapult tree to tug on it (these I describe in greater detail in Chapter 4). Larger tree-dwelling mammals were trapped with a snare trap tied on a branch, high above the ground. Bandicoot rats were water-divers and at night they could be seen jumping about on the rocks in the river, and were easy to whack with a stick.

Rats caught with a kembɔɔd spring and snare trap.
(Credit: ²Anɛl)

Two langurs shot with a blowpipe.

A pot and a bamboo tube of game, cooking at a camp at Gɛjgíjwɛɛd.

Wild boars, serow, muntjac and sambar deer were caught with a snare trap on the ground, or by a spear trap made with a sharpened bamboo blade attached to a horizontal catapulting tree, its presence hardly visible to the eye. Boars were even hunted with iron spear heads tied to poles, with the dogs catching the scent and leading the way. When the rainy season was on they would try their luck at spearing a boar's nest, a big pile of leaves inside which a boar was sleeping. There were other means of catching boars too, such as building a *rɛndɛɛd*, a wall of bamboo poles, to enclose an overgrown swidden where a herd of boars were heard foraging roots. A new manioc patch could be enclosed with walls also, with a trap door that could be sprung shut when a whole herd of boars had gone inside, in order to keep them contained until morning light, when the spearing would commence. But there was always another hunter about, lying in wait for the *taʔoŋ*, the grunting and squealing wild boar, and so the Temiar hunter had to give way when he saw signs of the king of beasts about, and either had to stay up a tree for quite a long while or give up his hunt and slip away silently.

Standing guard at a wall of bamboo, made to trap a herd of wild boars inside.

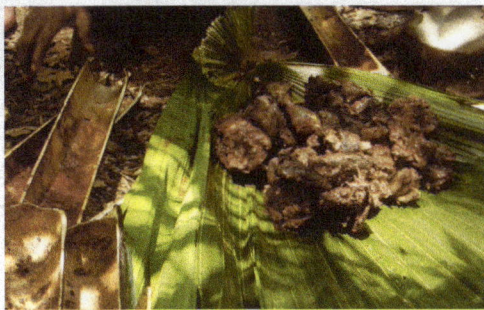

At Ranah, tubes of game are split open and the meat emptied onto a palm leaf, for all the group to eat from together.

The small dogs of the Temiars were vitally important in many ways, from acting as night guards, or for leading hunters to animals such as monitor lizards and even tortoises.

Temiars of B'rog village, lower their fish traps into a pool on the Puyan River.

Fish were abundant in the rivers in the old days and typically they could be caught with a *bubuuᵏ* trap, that was made of split canes, woven together to form a large egg-shape, or a long, bottle-shape. The trap's mouth was fitted with a funnel of sharp strands pointing inwards, to allow fish to enter the trap but to prevent their escape. These were sunk in a river pool with a rock inside to hold it down and usually some fermented manioc as bait. In the early days, fishing hooks were made from the hooked protrusions of the *kadɔɔᵏ-daax* vine (pictured on p197), and fishing line was made by tying many lengths of *bəx* together, that versatile black vine. Later on they used brass wire to make hooks, that had been obtained as wages, again, by the railway workers. The midrib of the *bɛltoˀp* palm made the best fishing rod, and is still chosen today by Temiars old and young. Women preferred this method of fishing, as they could sit and relax while out collecting fern shoots. In modern times, young men are skilled with the harpoon, a sharpened and barbed length of steel with multiple elastic catapult bands tied to the end. They wear a snorkel mask and dive down to look between the rocks where the fish can be found lurking. It is a much more difficult task since the rivers have gone through so much ecological change due to the massive logging operations in recent years.

Methods of catching fish in large quantities, such as for a festival, aimed at scooping up a whole river pool of fish. With the use of certain vine tubers, of the *k'waay nasíᵏ* or *k'waay c'ˀaag*, they would *k'roox* the fish, or stun them, by submersing the beaten tubers and mixing their white sap in the water. This had the effect of de-oxygenating the water, causing all the fish downstream to suffocate. The people then scooped them up in cones made of splayed-out bamboo and tossed them onto the riverbank. But this method was actually seldom used, and if it was, not in a main river, for fear of killing the entire fish stock. Sometimes barriers were built to channel the fish into traps (which I describe in the next chapter). Fish were also speared with the *loˀoj*, a harpoon made from a bamboo pole with a sharpened bone tip, or by submersing a *taŋkuul*, a square-shaped basket, in a deep pool and drawing it out with a catch. If they were camping and fishing away from home and had plenty to take back for the family, they would lay the catch over a fire to smoke it and then wrap it in leaf, semi-dried, in order to preserve it for a few days.

The head-water river fish were only of small varieties and attempts were made to transport fish from the lower valley, but it was found that the fish returned down-river because the water was too cold for them upstream. The large waterfalls on the Puyan and Bərtax Rivers, with their height and powerful plunging of water, are a natural barrier for fish and the rivers upstream used to be without any fish at all. Taaᵏ ʔAmpís transported fish in bamboo tubes from the S'ŋaaᵏ River, just over the boundary, and released them in the Upper Puyan, in order to create a food supply for those living there. And until today, you can still find plenty of small fish in the Puyan, upriver from the waterfalls.

Fish caught with a harpoon gun. (Credit: ʔAnɛl)

Kaaᵏ s'laaᵏ and kaaᵏ t'ŋə̄ə̄s caught in fish traps, in preparation for a feast.

The entire north-west region, up to the mountain peaks of K'jaay, Lírís, Síríŋ, Jɛŋhuŋ, P'gɵy and P'naŋɵ̓w mountains, including Mt Sɵ̓id, was the hunting ground of the Bərtax River Temiars. Likewise, the mountains to the east, including B'dɵx, Hūūlhīl, S'liwaŋ, R'nakɛd, Kəd, and Yaŋʔɵ̓ol were the boundary of the Upper Puyan hunters. A ridge from K'jaay mountain, in the north, all the way down to the Bərtax river-mouth was the interior boundary between these two respective roaming grounds. The hunters would walk in a small group or a pair of men, going bare-foot, with their simple possessions carried in a small ʔalɛɛg, or back-basket, and would camp several nights away from the swidden to hunt wild animals with traps and blowpipe, or birds with their sticky gum strands.

A nɛysɵ̓ɵ̓y, or temporary shelter with a lean-to roof would be quickly assembled on arrival, at their favorite camping spot in the forest, sometimes on a mountain ridge where it was dry and the forest sounds could be heard, or near to a river where there was access to water, frogs and fish. To make this they would use the branches of the *kamaa*r palm (a similar but smaller variety to *bɛltɵ̓p*), stacked together leaning against a beam, held up between trees. Other types of palm branch could also be used in the same way, such as *cacuh*, *cɛmcɵ̓ɵ̓p*, *bayíᵏ* or *balɵ̓ŋ*. Or they could overlap the broad, fan-like leaves of *hariyuw* (a *julux* species but safe for men to cut its branches), or paddle-like leaves of *koor* palms to create a dry shelter, if they were found in the forest nearby. The floor inside was spread with more *kamaar* branches, or *ŋɵ̓ɵ̓r* leaves, or even with wild banana leaves. If the ground was particularly uncomfortable, wet or crawling with ants, they would lay poles together, making a hard bed to lie on, slanting up from the fire-place. Then they could warm themselves and chant their slow recitals during the cold of night. Hunters would climb up on a boulder, if there was one in the area, such as Batuᵏ Saɲɛ̄ɛ̄n at a swidden on Soʾid mountain and Batuᵏ Bʾtaar at Labuᵏ, on the Bərtax, to sleep the night in more safety. They drank water from the streams, scooping it up with a 'hat' made of a folded leaf. If they were on a ridge with no river-source nearby, they could cut open the nodes of standing bamboo to seek a cool drink of the pure water inside, or cut lengths of *kadɔɔᵏ-daax* or *c'moʾg* vine and hold them upright to drain clean water from them straight into the mouth.

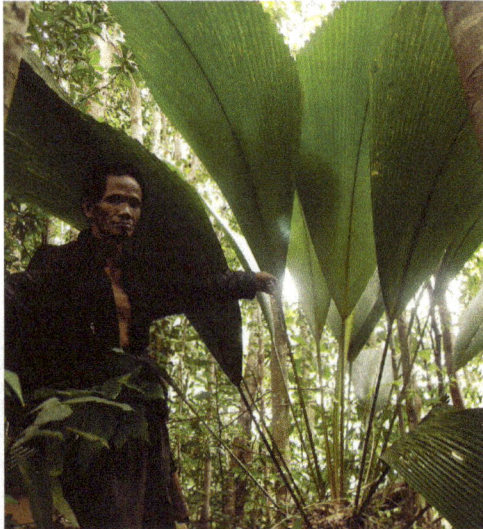

There are many types of palm leaf that can be utilised for building shelters, if they are found nearby a campsite, such as this paddle-shaped *s'laaᵏ koor*.

A *nɛysoʾoy*, a shelter made of leaning branches, cut from *kamaar* palms, where hunters might stay for a few days.

The *cacuh* palm, found at higher elevations than *bɛltoʾp*.

Pɛnpət, a palm used for laying to make bedding.

A shelter built to live in while cutting a swidden.

A young Temiar ties a roofing of bɛltʊp palms, for a more permanent shelter.

Tiʔux, fresh water contained inside live bamboo, was a life-saver when thirsty. It could also be drunk to remedy a fever.

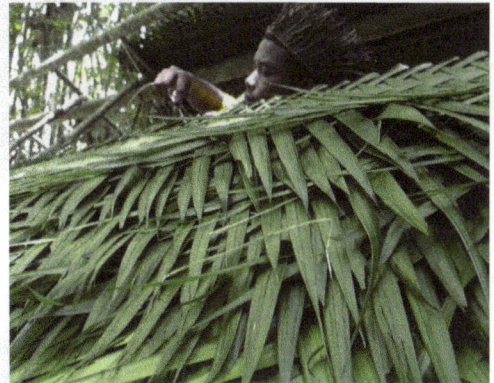
The kadɔɔ^k-daax vine holds drinkable water.

3.6   A THOUSAND UTILISATIONS OF BAMBOO

ʔAwɛn, bamboo, was (and still is) the most versatile resource available to the Temiars and it had dozens of practical uses, other than its importance in house-building. It has strength, but at the same time it is easy to cut and split, and depending on the variety, it is also completely clean inside. For one, they carried their water from the river in *gɛnhuŋ*, newly cut bamboo of three or four nodes in length, knocked through on the inside with a closed bottom node to make a single, long tube. It was so called because the water inside made 'hun-huŋ' sound as it sloshed about, that often amused. If there was a nearby stream then water could be transported via a *tɛnlo'or*, an aqueduct made of bamboo poles raised above the ground, with the nodes knocked out, each length dropping water into the next until it reached the house. Many foraged foods were carried home inside bamboo, such as fruits like *sɛmpaaᵏ*, jungle durian, which they extracted from the fruit skins near the tree to save carrying the prickly things home, or wet foods such as fish and frogs. Dry foods however, such as bats or mushrooms, they would *sapɔɔd*, or wrap in a parcel, using a suitable broad leaf and tying it with a vine, or fastening it with its own stem.

Fresh tubes were cut from standing, live bamboo each time they needed to cook food. The bamboo wouldn't burn before the food inside was cooked, although it would become charred black from the fire. When the tube steamed it was the sign that the food was cooking and soon they could *huuc*, or sip, the hot soup from *ʔabaag*, bowls made of segments of bamboo split in half. The fire was fueled with *karuᵏ*, dead bamboo. The fire-place was made with a *k'rɛnwaaᵏ*, a square frame of four interlocking bamboo bars that was filled with earth to make a mound, called the *waal*, that insulated the floor from the fire's heat. Fire logs were laid on the mound, their ends pointing towards the middle from all sides. The *waal* was the gathering place, where elders discussed what work they should do, or where they should hunt, and where people sat to talk after dark. The *ranoŋ* stirring stick was made from *ʔawɛn p'laᵏ*, a variety of montane bamboo without a cavity.

Clean water could be transported to the house via a bamboo aqueduct.

A *takoᵏ* was a short tube of green bamboo, that was used for a drinking cup. A *símiluᵏ* was a knife made from the sharp edge of split bamboo and it was used to cut up meat or green tobacco leaves, which were rolled up and sliced on a bamboo pole. A smaller knife called a *sɛnyaag* was used to cut a baby's

Nasiᵏ s'rɛmpaad, rice in packets, steaming in bamboo tubes, the everyday cooking pot of the Temiars.

umbilical cord after birth. The *b'laaw*, or hunter's blowpipe, was made of thin, straight bamboo, sourced from montane forest.

Certain traps utilised bamboo as well, such as the *raaj*, the spear trap, *c'rox*, the trap made with lethal stakes in the ground, and the *p'raŋ-lʉh*, a warning signal made of a split bamboo pole that whacked shut when set off. A fish scoop was made by splitting the end of a bamboo length and splaying out the splits with vine to make a funnel. The river raft was made almost entirely of bamboo poles, with rattan cord to lash them together. Even the *sikad*, a hair comb, was made of a short piece of bamboo with teeth carved out along the grain. The Temiars sourced at least fourteen varieties of bamboo from the forest to meet all their needs, the most durable of which being *k'yool*, *liyaax*, *poᵏwaᵏ*, *b'sííᵏ* and *banun*. Another variety, *s'mɛɛy*, was used for weaving trays, and another, *pōōg*, for making the blow-dart quiver, due to its large size.

K'yool

Liyaax

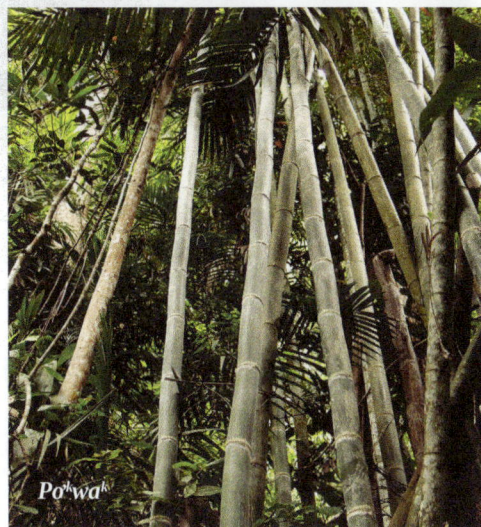

Poᵏwaᵏ

B'sii^k

Balaar

Banun

Pɔ̄ɔ̄g

S'mɛɛy

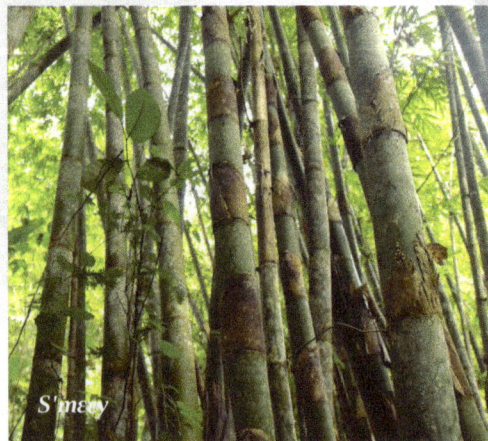

Varieties of bamboo used by the Temiars.

Hair combs made of bamboo. The fruit of s'kɛᵏ haar, a pandanus, which had hard hairs inside it, was also used as a comb.

Dry gourds such as these were used to carry water.

S'laaᵏ cɛŋloʼox

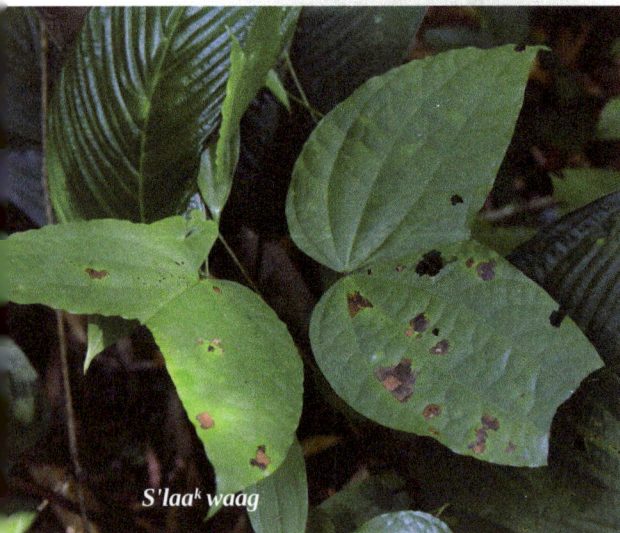

S'laaᵏ waag

Certain leaves were ideal for tobacco-rolling.

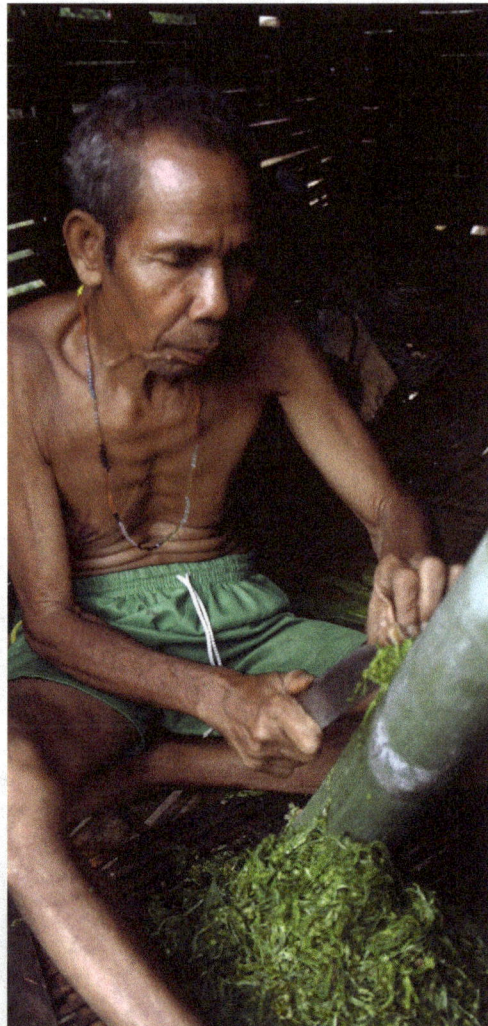

²Aluj Soʼid cuts tobacco leaves on a bamboo pole.

Even with its great strength and abundant availability, bamboo did have a major shortcoming as a material, in that it was susceptible to weevils. With temporary items such as a cooking tube, or cup, dish, knife and so forth, the item could be discarded after use. But certain items needed keeping for months and even years and couldn't afford to be degraded so quickly, eaten into powder by the burrowing beetles. House-building components such as floor slats were laid in the sun before fastening, and they were also made from the longer-lasting varieties, but cutting them at the wrong time of their growth could cause them to deteriorate quickly as well. The blowpipe and dart quiver were hung above the fire place, in order for the smoke to preserve them. Likewise, fish traps made of bamboo or palm skins were hung up in the smokey roof-space to ensure they lasted long enough for many fishing trips, as they were time-consuming to make new.

3.7 NATURAL RESOURCES

The bamboo of the *b'laaw*, the Temiar blowpipe, was of a special thin and straight variety, such as *b'laaw s'woʻor*, and was sourced from high altitude forests on mountains such as Paw and Kasay in the Bərtax region, B'ras, Hüülhil and R'nakɛd in the Upper Puyan region, and Bərlɛɛy and Pɛnrɛɛw in the Píɲcoʻoŋ region. The ancestors also planted it in lowland areas around the swiddens, to create a nearby source, and there are still clumps of *p'lakuj, t'hɛl, t'mííŋ* and *hatar* varieties growing in those places today. These varieties were used to make the inner barrel of the blowpipe, whereas the montane bamboo was used for the outer barrels. Each bamboo length would need heating over a fire and *nɛndoʻt*, bending and twisting, to correct its flaws.

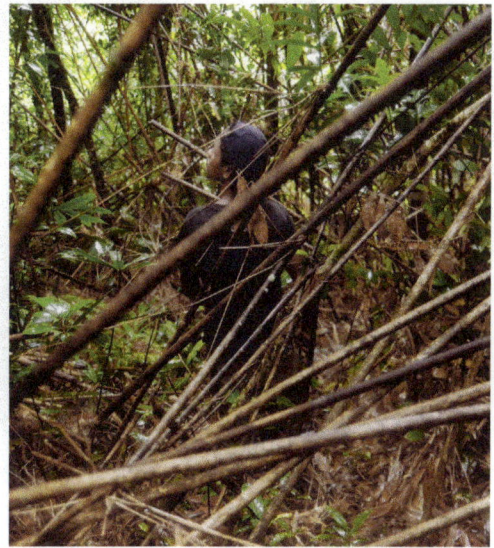

b'laaw s'woʻor, or blowpipe bamboo, grows densely on some mountains over 1600m, and suitable lengths are cut by Temiars to be crafted into the barrels of new blowguns.

The outer barrel of the blowpipe would take all the knocks and was suitably large to carry in the hand or rest on the shoulder. The inner barrel was made of two parts, joined at the centre, and was rubbed with a rattan brush on the inside to make it smooth, for the blow-darts to shoot with speed. At the end of the *b'laaw* they made slits and tightened them inward with *bəx* vine, so that the *b'laaw* would make a 'swish' sound with the blow of a dart. The *t'boʻox*, or mouthpiece, was made of a piece of carved *dayix* wood, shaped like an inverted bowl, about as large as an 'O' made with thumb and forefinger. Its upper part was inserted into the mouth when shooting.

The Temiar b'laaw is decorated with hand-carvings.

A blowpipe tip is tightened with a winding of bəx vine.

A Temiar looks for a suitable length of blowpipe bamboo to cut.

A fully loaded blow-dart quiver, with saməl cotton in the lid..

Tali^k talùd, the soft pith of which is used to make blowdart flights.

A dɔʾg tree, at the Kʾlɛɛr River, showing scars from years and years of tapping by the Temiars of Gɔɔb, for making blowdart poison.

The latex from kɛdrɛd vine was used as a gum, to stick the cones of blow-darts on and to stick the barrels of the blowpipe together.

The blow-darts were made from thinned down sticks of *bɛltoʹp* palm midrib, sharpened at the point, with little cones called *basùx*, of the soft inside of the *talùd* vine, stuck onto the end, and smoothed toward the front, to aid propulsion. The darts were kept in the *ləg*, a large bamboo tube that was carried at the waist, whenever they walked in the forest, and which was covered by the *c'rɛŋkəb*, a lid made of woven vine. The lid contained a wad of *saməl* cotton, used for loading behind the dart in the blowpipe to enable the air to push it. The blow-dart poison was tapped from the *doʹog* (Malay, ipoh) tree. The brown latex was first collected in a *takoʹk*, or short bamboo tube, and was then boiled in a large bamboo *abaag* over a fire, reducing the fluid and turning it clear and black. A scum remained on the surface, and to obtain the pure poison, the bamboo container (today, a cooking wok would be used) was tilted until about to spill and a filter of bamboo shavings would be dipped into the liquid, causing it to seep through and drip into another tube, leaving only solid residues behind. The hunter would also be careful not to come in contact with the lethal substance himself. With a tube of poison prepared the hunter would make his new darts, and once he had enough to fill the quiver (because there was no where else to store darts with poison on), then he would *laas*, or paint their tips with the *doʹog*, and set them to dry by the fire. After that they would

Doʹog, or ipoh poison, just tapped from the tree.
(Credit: Rapi)

Cooked poison is filtered off through a sponge of bamboo shavings.

Blow-darts, with poison-coated tips, drying by the fire.

Dried palm skins are split into new blow-darts.

be inserted into the quiver, which had a ball of *bɔx* vine stuffed inside it that would hold them securely, and hung up over the fire, ready to fasten on the waist when needed.

The *bɛriyɛl* vine could also be tapped to obtain blow-dart poison, but it was not as strong as *doʹog*, and would only be used to hunt squirrels, as with larger animals it would have little effect. *Doʹog* was needed for hunting primates and civets, to make sure they fell from the trees. There were two varieties of the vine, one being *cɛrgoʹr*, which was found in the lowland, and another, *poʹkwaᵏ*, which was found in the mountains and was the more potent of the two.

Kajaɖᵏ (Credit: Rapi)

S'kɛᵏ baluᵏ

S'kɛᵏ jaroʹw

S'kɛᵇ tanɪən

The pandanus palms were vital resources used for weaving many everyday items of the Temiars.

The long, thorny leaves of *s'kɛ^k*, the pandanus palm, were braided into useful items, such as baskets for carrying manioc, pouches for tobacco or betel nut, sleeping mats to lay out in the evenings, and even women's wrap-around skirts. They had at least seven varieties of *s'kɛ^k* that could be woven, including *jaro̊w* and *taməŋ*, montane varieties, which made fine strands and were made into intricate pouches and soft back-baskets. Others such as *kajaax* and *k'lí^k* made coarse strands and were ideal for weaving mats, which needed more thickness. *S'kɛ^k balu^k* was not preferred because it made the fingertips sore. To prepare for weaving, the leaves were first stripped of their thorns running along the edges and slit into strips, which were then softened by stroking with a blade or some split bamboo. To create their coloured designs they first boiled some of the strands in dyes made from *sumbaah* flower pods. They also painted their pouches and baskets yellow with *r'mɛɛd*, or turmeric root.

Another craft that was loved by Temiars was the *c'no̊o̊s*, a bracelet made by braiding a single length of rattan skin into itself, to create a circular band. A zig-zag pattern was made all the way round by interweaving a darker coloured rattan skin. They made small *c'no̊o̊s* to fit the *b'laaw*, for a holding grip, and also for the handle of the adze, to prevent the soft wood of the grip from splitting. They were even made to hold the wooden fore-piece on the shotguns given by the British. A special one was the *c'no̊o̊s hukom*, a woven band that turned in and out of itself like a figure of eight. A *tataa^k* would bring this along to help settle a dispute, telling the displeased persons to take time and try to find the end of his *c'no̊o̊s* first, before they continued to vent their anger!

ʔAlɛɛg, the Temiar back-basket, was soft but durable, and was carried everywhere.

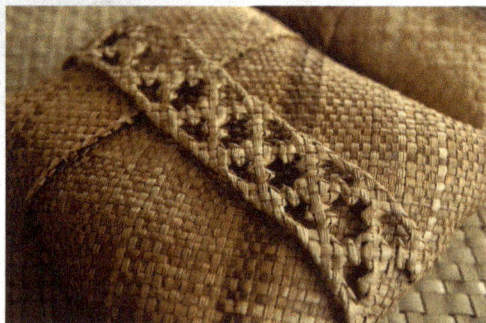

The late ʔAbo̊o̊ŋ ʔAbus of Jadɛɛr village, works on a basket of pandanus.

Every handiwork fits a specific purpose, such as the ²apoᵏ, the betel nut pouch (previous page). ²Apííl floor mats (left) were used for sleeping on and treading grain.

The bark of the cɔɔx tree was stripped off and tied to baskets for straps.

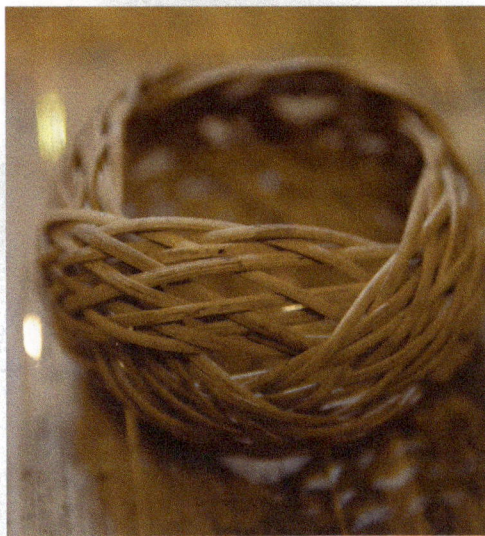

The c'noʹós hukom, or judgment bracelet, was used by an elder to settle quarrels.

The Temiar c'noʹós, a bracelet braided from a single length of rattan skin.

3.8   DANCE AND FESTIVALS

On the day of a *nɛhpɔɔh* dance, the group would start early making preparations, dispersing into the forest with large *ʔambooŋ* baskets strapped on backs to gather fragrant leaves of zingiber plants, needed for arrangement of the dance hall. Returning with their baskets overflowing they would tip them on the floor and prune off the dead leaves. They cut them with their stems so that they could be hung dangling, just above head-height. Citrus-smelling plants, called *boʼod*, were collected for tying in bunches, or for the hair decoration of women. Flowers were picked from around the house, such as red and yellow *carax* (*Celosia plumosa*). purple *tahoʼn* (*Gomphrena globosa*) and the fragrant, green *k'ralad* (all pictured on p47), which were used to weave into *tɛmpɔɔᵏ* headbands for the men, and to tie with the *boʼod* leaves into *caloon* bunches, for waving about during the dance.

The women would *coʼod*, or dab patterns on each other's faces with sticks dipped in different plant saps—from the *ʔɛsʔoʼo*'s vine, which made an orange-brown colour, and the *d'rəəp* tree, which made yellow. Yellow was also made with the juice of the *ʔuloʼx* root and red was made from the seeds of the *sumbaah* flower pod. They adorned their hair with beautiful flowers, such as the red-orange *buŋaaᵏ rajōᵏ*, a ginger flower (similar to *Zingiber officinale*) or the yellow *buŋaaᵏ c'naap*, or ginger-lily (*Hedychium flavescens*), together with red of *carax*, and green of *boʼod*, so that their heads resembled the plants of the forest at each dance.

caŋwo'oj

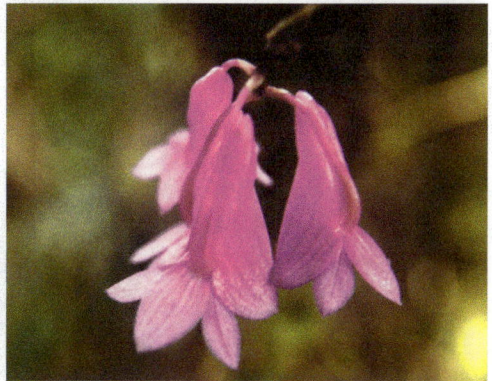

Orchids are a favourite flower for hair adornment, though many are only found in the cool montane forest, a long walk from home.

(Credit: ʔAri Kɛnton)

l'mo'oŋ

Loŋɛɛw

Hɛrkoy

T'lɛy

Suŋkut

Suliy

Tanjɔɔx jərnɛy

Bal

(Credit: ʼAnɛl)

Maŋlɛᵏ

Rajo

Tanjɔɔx

Jɛnjix

Gapɛh

Gɛlpap

Miloʔr

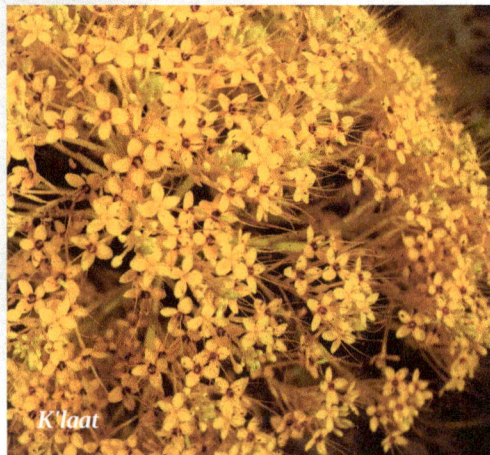
K'laat

Pine fronds and flowers from the mountains are much favoured for decoration of headbands and hair. Traditionally, Temiar girls are named after forest flowers such as these, including luhɛɛw, luŋɛɛw, hɛrkoʸy, miloʔr, rajōᵏ, suliy. (Credit, miloʔr: Rapi)

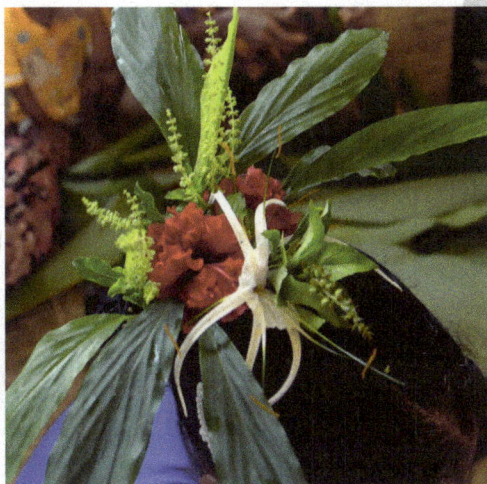

An elaborate hair decoration made with leaves and flowers.

ʔUloʾx

Dˈrəəp

ʔAŋah and ʔArif Pandaᵏ wear their fragrant headbands, before ascending to the mountain peak.

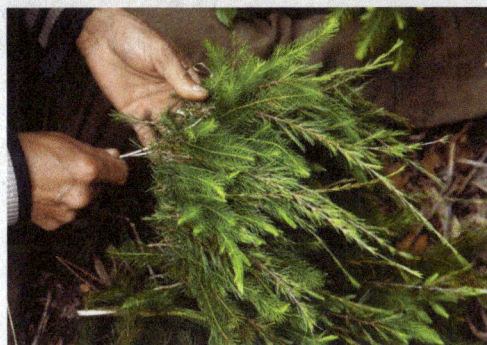

A new headband is made with pine tree fronds, by a Temiar on Soʾid mountain.

Sumbah

Face paints were made from natural sources such as roots and tree sap (top) and flower pods (above).

A bunch of picked fragrant plants: kayaaᵏ, hɛntəl, barʔoʼb.

Boʼod luwaɡ

Boʼod cʼmərdam

Boʼod kɛriyoʼl

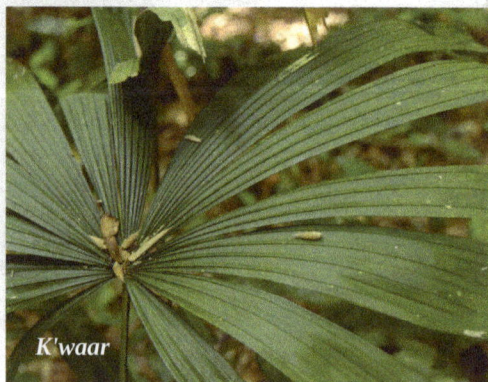

Kʼwaar

Fragrant leaves were located and collected to wear at the waist or to tie in bunches, to bring their fragrance into the dance hall. in the dances.

The kʼwaar leaf was used by great mediums to make elaborate headbands.

A bunch made of fragrant leaves and k'ralad flowers.

Hanging the cɛnlaay leaves in the dance hall.

Necklaces and bands of threaded *kariyɛl*, or 'Job's tears', the shiny grey seeds of a river-side grass, had been made beforehand and were worn on the dance day *tɛgwaag*, or hung over each shoulder and across the chest. The men wore their best headbands, either made with threading flowers and leaves along a single cord, or with strips of dark green and brown *sataax* leaf, woven in and out of five or six strands of rattan with the ends neatly cut off at the top. They all looked exquisite in their decorations, ready for their evening dance, and an air of excitement hung over them as they looked at one another, joking and laughing.

The late ˀAtíh ˀAloŋ, of Tanjuŋ village, sorts kariyɛl seeds, for threading on strings.

A tɛnwaag, or chest band, made of kariyɛl.

Tɛmpɔɔᵏ headbands made of sataax grass.

The dance was held after dark, and was opened with a *pɛntaaᵏ* petition of an elder or a soul-medium, while holding incense in a split bamboo half, burning on a few hot embers. It continued with many elaborate songs from dreams until the medium had sometimes entered a trance, or they had felt the ritual had reached a good place of harmony. Songs were appreciated at other times as well, for example while walking far, up a mountain, or while rafting down a calm, peaceful river, or during the still of night. They had several home-made musical instruments with which to carry on the sounds of their *g'nabag* songs, such as the *joríg*, a mouth-harp carved out of *bɛltoˀp* palm, that was held between the lips and tugged on by a cord to make its needle vibrate, resonating a twang sound in the mouth. Another was the *k'rəp*, a bamboo guitar having two rattan strings, that was strummed while holding its end on the belly, and lifting it off in a rythm, making a high and low note, similar to the bamboo percussion of the dance. The *siyoˀy* nose flute was made of thin *k'yool* or *b'sííᵏ* bamboo, and was played with tremendous musical talent, mimicking the calls of the wild.

Latíf ²Abaaŋ twangs a joríg mouth harp.

Layíís ²Ayob plays a bamboo flute.

A joríg, the Temiar mouth harp, complete with a porcupine quill tug.

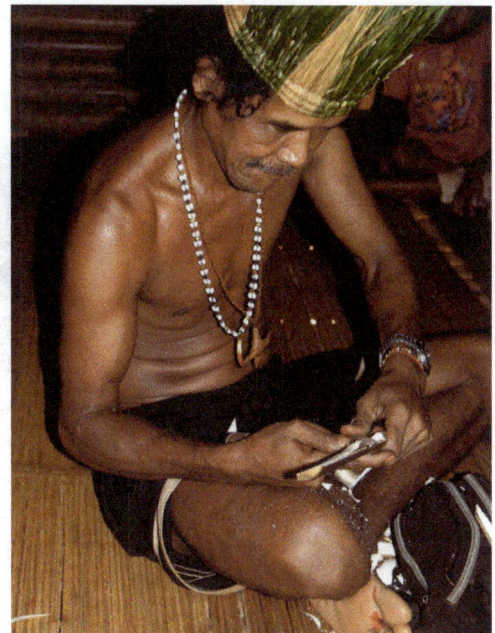

The late ²Amɛᵏ ²Abɛy, of Gawíín, strums a bamboo harp.

²Ayoᵇ Bərlɛɛy carefully crafts a joríg from palm skin.

The Temiars had three notable *ʔanʔiwoʔh*, or festivals, that they celebrated annually, by preparing a mass of food for a large crowd. The first was held to mark the New Year, which fell on the first day of the millet or rice harvest. The swidden owner would cut only a symbolic amount, like a sack-full, or enough for everyone to eat that day, with the real harvest beginning the day after. The second was held at the end of the harvest, to mark its *k'rɛnma*s or completion, and to celebrate the *s'maŋat canaaᵏ*, the life of the crops. The third was held on the day the planting begun, in September for rice, or later in the year for millet. A *k'rɛnmas* party would also be held when receiving someone home who had been away for a long while. Preparations for a feast began a few days early with the men going out to *t'goʔs*, or gather in game, either from setting fish traps in the river, shining frogs at night with fire torches, or hunting game in the forest, such as langurs and civets. In the old days the feasts could cater for hundreds of people because there was such an ample supply of game, especially fish. Following the feast, they danced in the evening to enjoy themselves and to petition Nyʉᵏ ʔAlʉj for protection and a good harvest or a good crop. At the new year, the rains gave way to the dry season and with the emergence of cicadas, chirping noisily in the heat, the fruit trees would begin flowering, signaling that the seasons had been set in motion again.

Preparations are made on a festival day, on which the first ripened rice will be eaten with plenty of meat and fish.

3.9 GENDER ROLES

While certain tasks would be undertaken by the menfolk of the group, such as hunting with the blowpipe, tree felling and swidden cutting, or shouldering heavy wood for house piles and firewood, the womenfolk took care of some very physical tasks as well, and they would even shoulder a log if they needed to. All planting would be under their supervision, when they didn't need to abstain due to taboos, and sometimes they would be left entirely to themselves, for example, with planting manioc stems in a new swidden. Even the other crops might have been planted by the women alone, but if the field was large or the women were too few then the work would involve everyone. Women would take charge of the swidden in many other ways and especially in the duty of harvesting. The men would only harvest crops if they were on a camping trip and had a remote yam or manioc patch they had planted, or if the women were not able and food was needed immediately. The harvest of millet and rice was undertaken by all who had the skills to cut the heads of the grain with the *taman*, a little hand-blade. The men would tread the heads to collect the grain and the women would heat the first grain over a fire to prepare it for pounding. The pounding of grain was always a joint effort, the more hands the better, but the men might not be available to help if they were out hunting. Likewise, the women would often take care of winnowing the chaff, as well as the highly skilled work of sifting the grain.

Women were never involved in hunting of large animals or trapping of tree-dwelling animals such as langurs, but they could set traps for rodents, sink fish traps in the river, dangle a hook on a line, or go sifting for shrimps in the streams. At night they would hunt frogs with a burning bamboo torch, unafraid of meeting large snakes in the water or tiger eyes on the bank. They excelled at foraging for foods in the forest, such as wild mushrooms and fern shoots, and they would gather fruits that were cut or knocked down by their menfolk up the trees. Some women were good tree-climbers too but they would have to be extremely brave to shinny up a betel palm or a high *jiyɛɛs* tree.[2]

3.2 Due to the general segregation of males and females in Temiar society, that began as soon as persons reach adolescence, the women often carried out activities on their own, such as foraging fruits, while the men took on the task of hunting game further afield (see also, Footnote 1.4).

Two women catch newts on the river rocks.

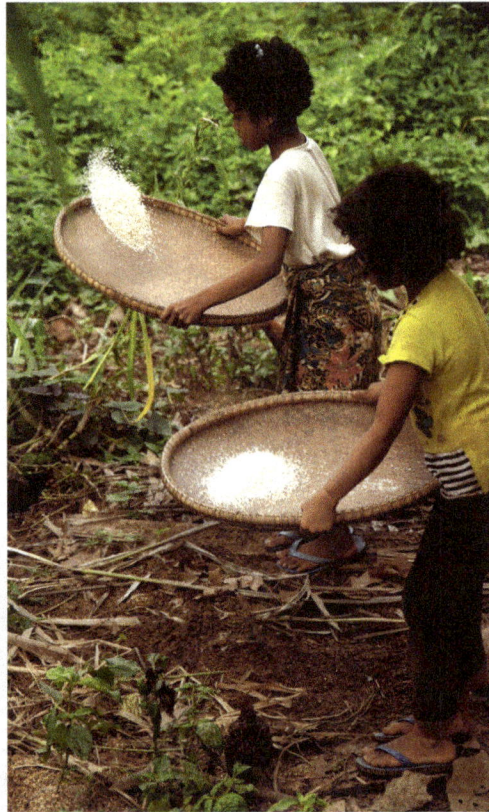

Women pound rice grain in a wooden mortar, while two girls winnow the grain to separate the chaff. Another woman sifts the pounded grain on a tray. Rice is a new staple, however, as in the old days they only had millet.

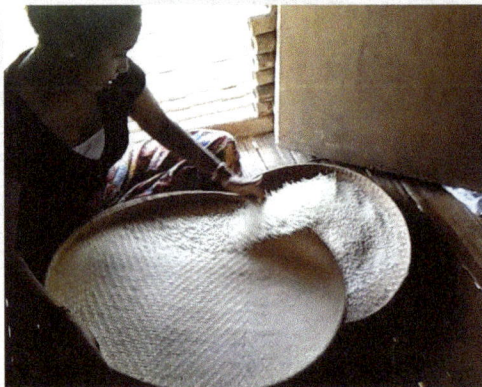

Pεngooh, or cooking of food in bamboo, was normally the task of the women, and they would sit by the fire, turning the tubes of steaming meat, fish, frogs, manioc or yams, while the men who brought the catch home would be chatting about the day's walk and which paths they had followed. The cooking for a feast would be shared out, with the women washing meat or fish and filling the bamboo tubes for cooking and stuffing others with split manioc or yams, or grated tubers in leaf packets. The men would line up the tubes against a large fire, twenty at a time, turning them to prevent burning while trying not to scald themselves with hot water. *Sabat* meat and other taboo foods would be prepared only by the men and away from the home. Fetching of water was the task of the women, and they would also cut the long bamboo tubes for this purpose, as well as tubes for collecting fruits in and for cooking.

Midwifery was a skill held by some of the older women, by those who were brave enough and had the experience. They knew how to feel the child in the womb, by pressing with the fingers, and by doing so they would know if it was in the correct position for birth. If it wasn't, they would help position it head-down. Their assistance was greatly valued and a mother would always pay them for their service, after the child was safely born. At birth, the *tulag*, or midwife, would normally only massage the womb, pulsating it, to help the mother give birth. But in case she did intervene and deliver the child, getting her hands covered with the afterbirth, she would then have to observe the same taboo period as the mother, in which they would abstain from certain foods (as described in part 2.3). I have heard of occasions when an expectant mother had no time to call for help, but gave birth at the swidden, or on the path coming over the mountain. Some women preferred their privacy and would go off into the bushes, to give birth alone.

Both genders were skilled at craft-making, with the men using palm skins to weave into *gadaŋ*, or the *bubuu*[k] fish trap, and also the *c'noʔ's* bracelet of rattan. The women were at home with the pandanus palm leaf, which they wove into mats, baskets and pouches. They were also tasked with threading grass beads to adorn both men and women at dances. Only men made the blowpipe with its poison-tipped darts, and it was their task to collect the bamboo from mountain-tops and then work the lengths over a fire to correct flaws. Men would also collect the blow-dart poison and the latex for making bird gum. Both men and women would collect, prepare and apply medicinal herbs for those in need, especially their own children. Collection of fragrant plants and flowers was another task for all, and tying of the men's headbands could be done by either gender. Temiar men were not fierce or warrior-like, but they were gentle and caring and never dominated over their womenfolk. They saw the provision for and safety of their children, their brother's children and all the grandchildren as paramount in their forest existence. A father was always on hand if a child was sick and he would not go out anywhere until the child recovered, or he would cancel a camping trip and come home if news reached him of his child's illness. He would carry a child in a sling on the back just as a mother would.

Children were included into the chores of the home and swidden at early ages and were given tasks to help with, such as the picking of ferns and harvesting manioc, but the real skills, such as weaving or hunting, would take years to acquire. Boys would know how to shoot the blowpipe by the age of seventeen, perhaps, but to attempt making their own they would need to observe

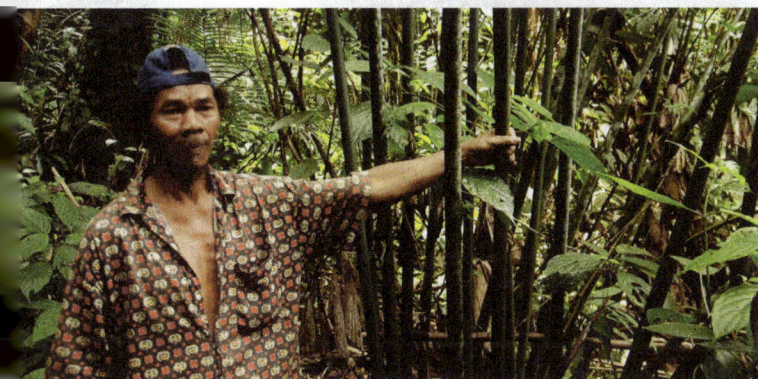

ʔAnyɛh P'di[k], *the new penghulu of Tɛmagaa*[k], *shows the stems of the r'tam plant, the skins of which are good for making fish traps, rice trays and other crafts.*

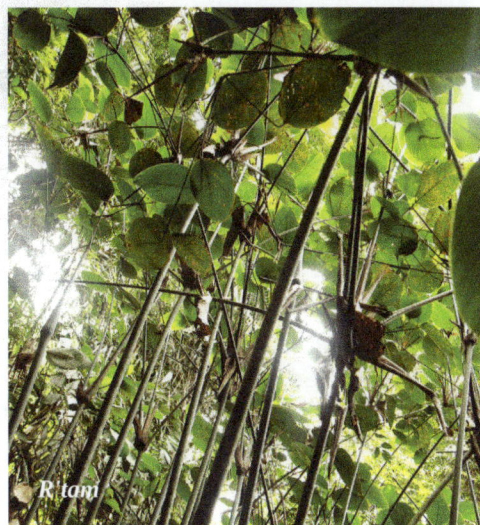

the handiwork of their elders until they understood the techniques involved and were willing to source their own bamboo from the mountain. Girls also, would not learn how to weave a basket until they were old enough to be married and to manage their own swidden, as otherwise they would leave this task to their grandmothers! I have seen girls of eight years of age helping with the weaving of roofing palms, and boys of fourteen able to tie roofing onto a house with rattan cord. In today's villages, I often observe a group of teenage boys building their own small hut to sleep in, which would be the first test of their construction skills.

In all, Temiar society in a river valley kin group was close-knit, and most roles, if not too dangerous, could be shared out between men and women if necessary. In ritual practices, such as invocation of the souls of the fruit trees and mountains, it was often the men who took a leading role—and especially so with great mediumship, involving the taming and placating of a dangerous tiger soul. But there were always some women who arose as more vocal, who would be called ²abaaŋ, or jolly-spirited, always talking and laughing, and they would contribute greatly to the community. They could lead the *gabag* or song at the dances, and were always ready to make their opinions heard at discussions. A *towaaᵏ's* or chief's, wife would also be a leader among the womenfolk, if she accepted her responsibility, and together they would demonstrate good *hukom*, teaching others respect and generosity. In today's changing Temiar world, gender roles are largely unchanged from what they have always been. But the adoption of mobile phones and movie-watching and music-playing has done much to negate and replace the traditional ways by which the Temiars would find expression of the soul life, and perhaps even to undermine values of Temiar *hukom*, and the importance of everyone contributing equally to the effort of survival.

²Alʉj Sisam shows his gadaŋ work, using a clamp to hold the ring to the strands, until it is tied on and the strand ends cut.

A Temiar of B'rᴏ́g village weaves the board of a new rice tray.

One weaving pattern used for a rice tray.

3.10 THE FIRST TEMIARS OF THE PUYAN

The earliest known Temiar settler of the Puyan River was one Taaᵏ Galoŋ, son of Taaᵏ Batɛl, with his son, Taaᵏ ˀAmpís. He arrived possibly in the late 19th Century, and found the land inhabited by Jehais (from the north), with migrant Menriqs (from downriver at the B'rơơx). He and his son understood the importance of connecting with the spirituality of the land and through their dreams they were able to live in harmony with the souls in the mountains and rivers, without infringing on their boundaries. It is said that the former Jehai inhabitants often succumbed to natural catastrophes, such as the earth turning over on them, according to the stories, because they didn't know how to avoid conflict with or how to placate the spirits in the land. Apparently, they had no soul-guides to teach them.

Taaᵏ Galoŋ likely came from the Bəər River (the region called, ˀAsal Gɛrlơơx, where the Temiar people are said to originate from). He came to the Halaaᵏ River, in the Pɛriyas valley, and from there he ventured up the Puyan until he came to the Bərtax (so named because its water has a reddish or earthy colour; *bar-tɛx* in Temiar means 'earthy'). He followed this river further up and saw that the land was ideal for a hunter to inhabit, with Bərlɛɛy and Sơïd mountains on either side of it, and its source curving round toward a ring of great mountains, including P'naŋơw (2180m), P'gơy (2108m), Pagar (1734m) and Síríŋ (1866m). The climate was cool with plenty of rain, perfect for growing millet. He had easy access into Perak via the mountain passes and over to the neighbouring R'kơơb River. He could walk over Ndaŋkaaᵏ ridge to the tributaries of the the Upper Puyan, just three or four hours away, where there were good hunting grounds, teeming with wild animals, or he could come down the Bərtax to its mouth (at today's Pos Gɔɔb area) where the fish were abundant. Other Temiars joined Taaᵏ Galoŋ's family, such as Taaᵏ Kíndan, and they lived together and roamed with freedom, walking, hunting, cutting and planting wherever they deemed suitable, and visiting each other's long-houses to hear news or discuss a fishing trip, to share fruits and to tell their dreams. It was Taaᵏ ˀAmpís who cut the first swiddens with the iron adze, over at the Tampaal River, and he would have planted yams, manioc and millet, as well as tobacco.

A crossing point on the Bərtax River, near to the old village of Sapɛd, which led to a route along the ridge line and another along the Puyan, that both reached the Perak border.

The reddish water of the Bərtax River, which gives the river its name, meaning 'earthy'.

Looking up the boulder-strewn Bərtax from a hunters' camp at Layaŋ island.

The crystal clear water of the Upper Puyan River, near Ranah.

Puran waterfall, on the Upper Bərtax.

The clear, cool water of the Palɛɛs River.

Taaᵏ P'naŋoʼw, son of Taaᵏ ʔAmpís, lived and died during the years of peace, when life followed the seasons, blissfully unaware of the world outside. He never saw the turmoil caused by the Communists pressing on the Temiars and the British arriving to chase them about all over the jungle. His son, Taaᵏ K'lusar, was the leader of the Bərtax clan, with Taaᵏ Pandaᵏ the leader of the Puyan clan, when the Temiars were gathered and relocated by the British Army in 1957. These two were the first to be made *pəŋhuluᵏ*, or headmen, in the Puyan valley, being appointed by an officer of the British administration, whom they named, 'Taaᵏ S'nop'. But before there was ever such an institution, each *k'moʼom* or kin group lived together often in a single long-house, holding their important discussions around the communal fire mound. The appointing of headmen was a new order imposed on the Temiars and, being alien to their own custom of sharing opinions and deciding on matters together, it didn't significantly change the way things were done from generations before. The most it did was put a name to the different groups from the different ancestral river valleys, to which the authorities could call when they had directions to give.

There were never any fights between the Temiars, as the elders said that fighting was fruitless and if they squabbled and acted selfishly they would not survive long. Jealousies still arose between people and sometimes these became so severe that they used *pɛnsuuᵏ* sorcery against those they feared were doing better or were more vocal. But even so, the Temiars have really never known violence and they have never fought with other peoples (that is, until the British thought it good to enroll them into the Senoi Praaq commando unit[3]).

They had no need of government, or ministers, or police, or jail, or deeds to the land where they roamed and planted. They lived with freedom and each respected the other's area of hunting and gathering. But there was ample game to hunt and fruiting trees to gather from in the old days. They moved about wherever they could to find food and to stay alive, because they knew well that there would be times of hunger too. There were no markets or shops from which to buy food, they went out and gathered everything they needed from the forest around. They had to hunt monkeys or dig yam roots each day or else they would starve and become too weak to forage. Even when it was raining they would need to dig yams or hack open jack fruits to find food for the stomach. So they were never idle. They used their skills in trapping birds with gum, or monkeys with a twisted rattan trap that was tied to the branches of high trees. The forest was virgin and untouched by human intervention, except for small patches where the natives had cut down trees to plant crops. The rivers flowed with crystal-clear water, teeming with large mahseer carps that could be harpooned, taken with a hook, or even tickled out of the water.

To communicate, people walked over the mountains to visit their relatives' long-houses in the other valleys, always returning to their home valley after a few days. The path from the Puyan valley tht reached the R'koʼob River, a main tributary of the Pɛriyas, passed near Mount P'goʼy, and was followed all the way into Perak, to reach Kimaar. The northward path that followed the K'jaay River, a tributary of the Jɛŋhuŋ, or the parallel path going up Ndaŋkaaᵏ Ridge, and over the Mount K'jaay pass, were used to reach Ciyuŋ, in Perak. The path that followed the Puyan reached the Taloʼŋ and S'ŋaaᵏ Rivers in Perak, via the mud bog of L'baax Sɛnduŋ, and it was the preferred route as it was practically level all its way.

Other paths branched off the Puyan path, going up mountain ridges to B'doʼx and Hūūlhīl, and there were also paths heading eastward from the Puyan, reaching the Bayuur River via Bawoʼl, Kasuh and Tanaaŋ. Likewise to the west, the path that climbed Mount Bərlɛɛy followed the ridge-

3.3 This commando unit comprising of Orang Asli soldiers was originally proposed and organised by Richard Noone, and was used to seek out the Communist insurgents in the 1960s.

line up to P'naŋoʹw, the highest mountain of the region, and descended via P'goʹy or S'pɯɯh to the R'koʹoʹb River. They roamed the whole river region, wherever there were plenty of fish, birds or monkeys that they could shoot or trap. They might walk over to Perak for five days of fishing, just so that they could stay alive.

A Temiar points to the path that leads down from the boundary, towards the Ciyuŋ River, in Perak.

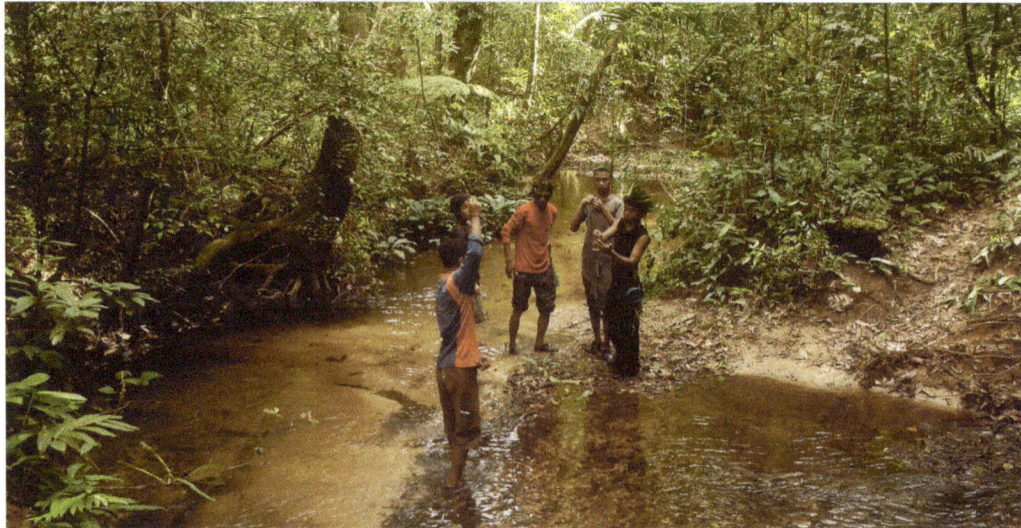

Temiars from Gɔɔb stand in the Taloʹŋ River, at its source.

3.11   TAAᵏ Gᴇɴᴅᴏᴡ AND THE TIGER ATTACK

Taaᵏ Gᴇɴᴅᴏᴡ, son of Taaᵏ Tukaŋ, caught a monkey in the Upper Puyan area, using a *bako'oᵏ* trap up a tree. When he had cooked the meat he poured the soup into new bamboo tubes to take home, thinking it was too delicious to waste by pouring it out. He carried the bamboo tubes on his back and when he came to a tree leaning across the path, he bent down to go under it and the hot soup spilled on his neck, scalding him. And in Temiar custom this is a taboo (called *pɛl'ax*), which causes a smell of offense that attracts the tiger. A person who has broken it carries a smell on them for a number of days, and even if they were to walk with a group of people the tiger would single out the person having the smell on them. Sure enough, when Taaᵏ Gᴇɴᴅᴏᴡ went out again, before the smell had worn off, the tiger found him and ate him, there at 'Amparr 'Ɛij, a sloping rock on the river.

When he did not return that night and the tiger was seen prowling about under the house, his children understood what had probably become of him. At so, at dawn, Pandoᵏ fled with his two sisters down the river-side path, to find safety. Desperate to save themselves and hearing noises of the tiger taunting them on the path behind, 'Abo'oŋ put down her younger sister, 'Asuh, by a jungle durian tree, as she could no longer carry her. The tiger found the child, and after eating her it bellowed, which sounded like a yawn—and thus the place where 'Asuh was eaten was called Kɛyho'y, 'yawning'. The two survivors reached the Kɛnsɛy River, where they crawled into the mud bog and slept. Pandoᵏ was still a child, perhaps just ten years of age. The next day they made it to the house at S'po'oy, where many people were dwelling, and they were safe.

'Ampar 'Ɛij, the rock slope where Taaᵏ Gᴇɴᴅᴏᴡ was killed by a tiger.

The badoʻox tree at the J'ríx River, where the evil tiger soul was imprisoned by Taaᵏ ˀAmpís.

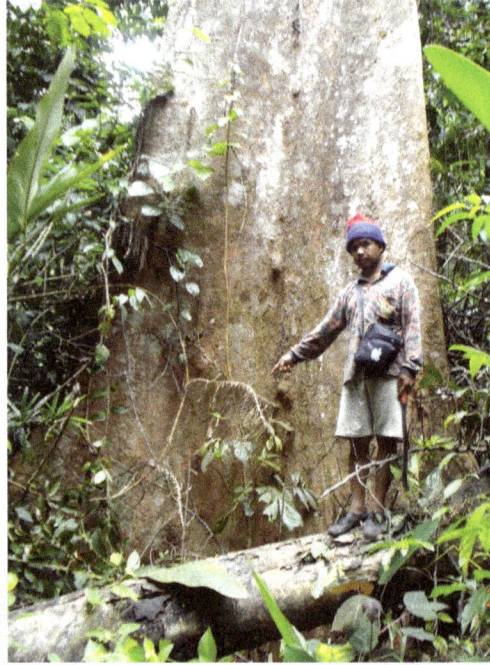

The jungle durian tree at Kɛyhoʻy, where the tiger ate Asuh's baby sister.

Later on, Taaᵏ ˀAmpís performed a ritual dance and he saw the soul of the tiger that had attacked Taaᵏ Gɛndow. He then banished it to the *badoʻox* tree at the J'ríx River, near the place of the attack, and until today, the tree has a great scar down its trunk where it closed up on the tiger soul. After a week they heard that a tiger had been caught in a spear trap over in Perak, which was believed to be the same one that attacked their fellow Temiar, because it was ill fated after Taaᵏ ˀAmpís had performed his dance.

After that, Pandoᵏ lived with Taaᵏ K'lusar at Labuᵏ, on the Bərtax River, and was gathered with his clan to Ranah, by the British Army, and was relocated with them down-river. His son ˀAŋah was born, in 1952, at the encampment of Jɛnɛɛs, during the return to their original homeland. In the following years, he lived with Pəŋhuluᵏ P'diᵏ at Lɛŋraaŋ, and used G'ləəŋ for hunting camps, all the way up to Capɛɛr, where he also cut jelutong rubber to float down-river to trade. He made a swidden at J'waaŋ, near G'ləəŋ, where he planted hill rice.

(Told by ˀAŋah Pandoᵏ)

3.12   JAAᵏ SƐNAYIH

Years before the Emergency of the 1950s, there were Chinese bandits roaming the forest and the Temiars viewed them as dangerous. A tragedy occurred at the Upper Puyan when a group of Temiars were living at Jaŋrax, with a large swidden at Taməŋ. Bandits approached the home with guns and the Temiars fled for their lives. Jaaᵏ Sɛnayih, daughter of Taaᵏ ʔAmpís, and mother of Pəŋhuluᵏ Boŋsu, was left behind as she was too weak to run and the bandits abducted her. Boŋsu hid in the forest and watched where they took his mother, and then he ran to call for help. The bandits had taken her and tied her to a pole where they tortured her, and possibly they also ate her flesh, because they were ruthless. Only her skull and bones were found when the group returned to find her. When it was quiet they collected her remains and buried them at Taməŋ hill. The tree that they tied Jaaᵏ Sɛnayih to was a *tampaal* tree, and thus the river there was also named the Tampaal.

(Told by Jambu ʔAlaŋ)

The late ʔUda Siyam stands at the Tampaal River, near where Pəŋhuluᵏ Boŋsu's mother was butchered by bandits.

4 | TEMIAR ANIMAL TRAPPING

The Temiars' trapping skills were both technical and effective, allowing them to catch birds, reptiles, fish and mammals from the wild, to provide meat for their families. The hand-crafting of traps for different purposes was taught by the elders to each new generation, thus preserving a hereditary knowledge that would be impossible to obtain by any individual alone. Other hunting techniques, such as shooting with the blowpipe, are also evidence of the intricate knowledge that the Temiars have held for thousands of years. Many of the techniques they employ bare close resemblance with, or are identical to, those of the Semais, including blowpipe construction, the tying of snare traps, the spear trap and all types of fish trap, indicating that these age-old traditions have perhaps stemmed from the same ancient ancestors. I once met a Bateq man, from a tribe that neighbours the Senoic peoples (Temiar and Semai in particular) but whose traditions vary somewhat, who had never tied a trap for rodents before. When I asked a Semai in the village to demonstrate the tying of a *kɛm* trap, he was baffled by it. Which goes to show that, if a person does not grow up seeing and learning such skills, it would be difficult to make them second nature, or add them to their head band, so to speak.

Common to nearly every trapping technique, excluding those for fish and birds, was the catapulting tree system. The catapult was made from a young, flexible tree that was either tied to a branch or jabbed into the ground, and was bent over toward the trap like a bow. A cord tied to its end held it down to the trap and the cord's end was secured to the trap by winding it round part of it and catching its tip by a stick laid across the trap. The trigger mechanism for most traps was made using a strand of a fine, black vine, called *bɔx*, obtained from under the drooping arms of the *jííg* palm (*Arenga pinnata*), that was tied to the base of the trap and to the stick catching the tension cord. Because this vine was practically invisible to animals, the wandering rodent, civet or primate would walk straight into it, pulling down the stick tied to its end. With skill, a trapper would set the trap so that the vine would only need to be touched and the trap would spring, catching the animal by its neck or foot.

A kɛm trap, set on a leaning bamboo pole.

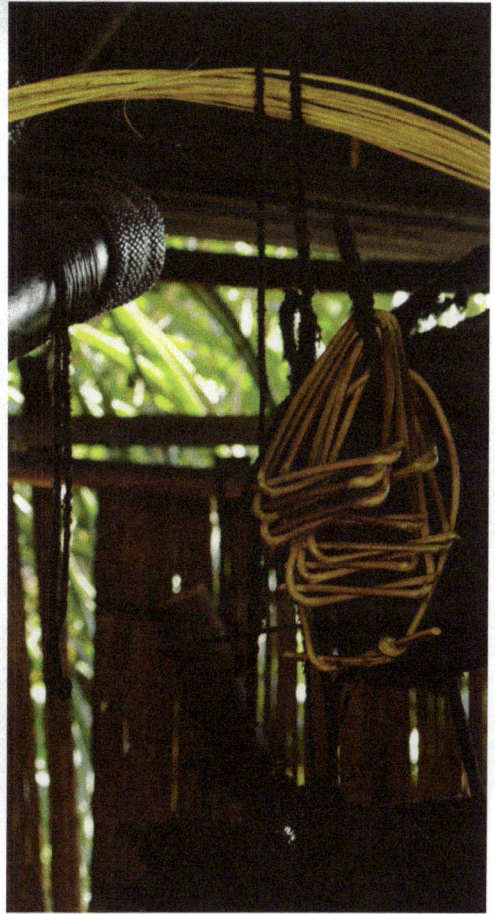

Rattan triangles hang over a fire place, with a bundle of tug cords, in preparation for tying traps.

The kɛm utilised a catapulting tree to pull a cord that slid up the trap and constricted the rodent in its top.

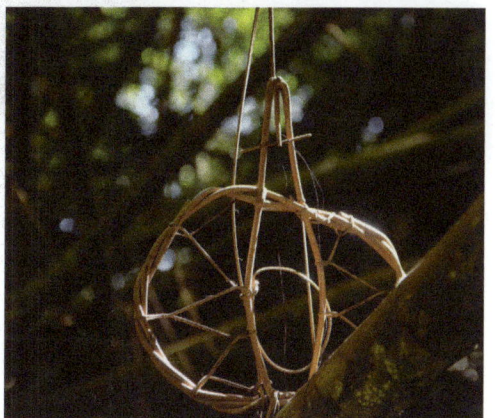

A kɛm trap with 'ears', that prevent the rodent running around the side.

Nine of the twelve mammal traps (refer to Table 4, p189) used a catapult and noose technique, with the *kɛm balɛh* (sometimes just called *kɛm* or *kap*) being slightly different in that it utilised a cord that slid up the sides of the trap and caught the rodent in the apex of its triangle shape. The *kɛm* was also the simplest of these traps and it was tied wherever rodents were seen using a pathway, usually along a slanting bamboo pole or tree leaning over a waterway, called a *píŋgoʼw*. The trap could be used at any time of year, or when the trapper thought that rodents were active, such as in the fruit season.

A variation of the *kɛm* trap was the *kɛm gɛntoʼx* (*kɛm* with ears), which had wings on its sides to prevent rodents from running around them. It was tied on top of branches in the fruit trees where squirrels were seen feeding, or on branches leading to those trees. It also used a snare inside the trap instead of the *kɛm's* sliding cord. The larger version of this trap was the *bakoʼoᵏ*, which was made of thicker rattan wound around a larger centre piece, that had wings up to 60cm across. Of the *bakoʼoᵏ* there were smaller ones for catching civets and broader, heavier ones for catching primates and bear cats. These were tied onto branches at high level where these tree-dwelling animals would be moving or in areas where primates such as langurs were heard chattering, which was often a longer way from the home. The trapper had to be aware of the signs, such as dropped fruit peels and urine on the ground, that would tell him where these animals might be roaming.

Other traps were set at ground-level, for catching animals such as porcupines, or jungle fowl. The sab *k'lɛg*, the porcupine snare, was made with a noose tied inside an inverted 'V' of bent liana, that was stuck in the ground, with a wall of sticks and foliage on its sides. A length of *bəx* vine ran up through its centre that would be pushed by an animal, in the same way as the aforementioned three traps.

The porcupine trap, hidden between walls of foliage.

Certain traps were made without a trip-wire but their release mechanism was made in similar fashion, with a stick holding the end of the tension cord, that would be dislodged by an animal's intrusion. One of these was the *kɛmbɔɔd* trap, which utilised bait on a stick, or put behind the stick, poked into a hole in the ground, that once tugged and moved would slip off a cross-wise stick and set off the bent tree that yanked on a noose. The *t'lóg* trap was a bamboo tube with some manioc tied inside, that when eaten through would release the tension cord. It was set beside waterways, where water rats would be caught. Another trap, the *sab k'woʊ̓ᵏ*, was set on the ground for catching jungle fowl and it was constructed with a pressure pad, that a bird would stand on, with a noose overlaid on it, hidden by leaves. Large ground-dwelling mammals would be caught with the *sidiŋ*, a variant of the jungle fowl trap, but more robust, which would be set along animal paths or around the swidden, to catch wild boar as they came to dig up the manioc.

The kɛmbɔɔd, or bait-in-a-hole trap, caught rats when they wobbled the bait stick.

Sóic nuts were collected by trappers and stored up for later in the year.

The sóic nuts left at a baiting place on a trapping line.

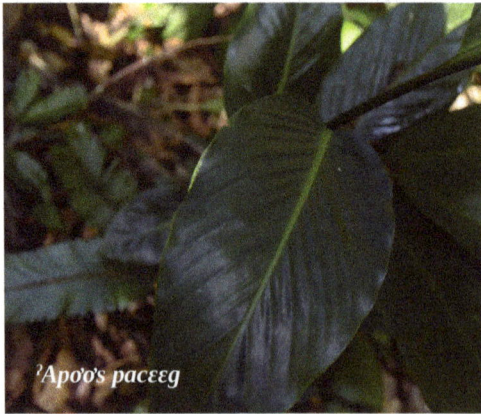
ʔApoʼoʼs pacɛɛg

Apart from dedicating much time to setting traps, the Temiars walked the forest looking for signs of animal activity, with blowpipe at hand, and they could mimic the calls of monkeys, squirrels and birds, in order to attract them or make them show themselves in the trees. The leaf of the *ʔApoʼoʼs pacɛɛg* was held in the mouth to *sɛgpiyɛg*, or make squirrel noises.

In each trap, the tension cord, called the *línís*, which held down the bent tree, the *lamuŋ*, was wound around the trap's apex and was caught by a stick placed cross-wise. The stick was tied to a fine black vine called *bəx*, which itself was the secret of the trap's success. As an animal stepped through the trap, it pushed into the vine and pulled down the stick, thus setting off the trap. The *bakoʼoʼᵏ* trap would be up to four times the size of the *kɛm gɛntoʼx*.

The kɛm trap

línís

s'nəg

bəx

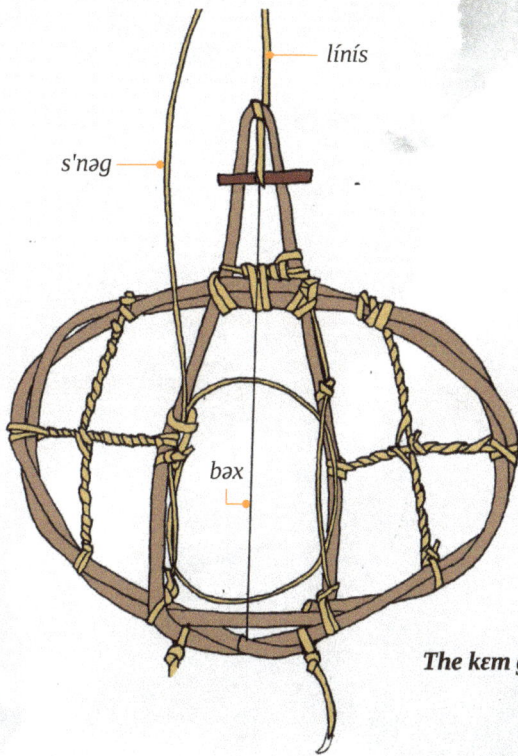

The kᴇm gᴇntoˀx trap

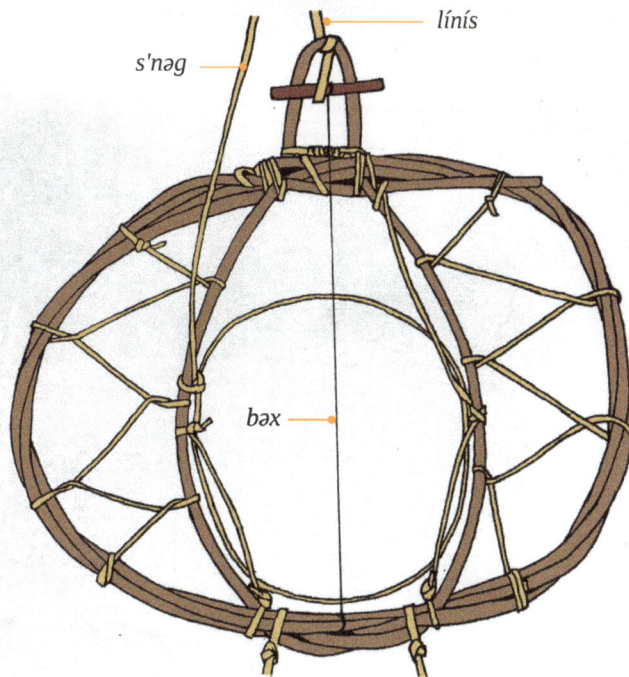

línís

s'nəg

bəx

The bakoˀoᵏ trap

The *kɛmbɔɔd* made use of a hole in the ground with a noose laid around it and some *p'rat*, or bait (of fermented manioc or *soˈic* nut), on a stick, the *canɔɔg*, poked inside. The cord holding the catapult tree down was wound around a pole, the *s'landow*, inserted across the trap, and its tip was caught against the stick with the bait. When a rat, or sometimes a civet if the trap was larger, entered to nibble at the bait, it pulled the stick like a lever (it being pinched by a third stick, the *kɛnalɛix*) and the *línís* cord was released, causing the bent tree to yank on the noose.

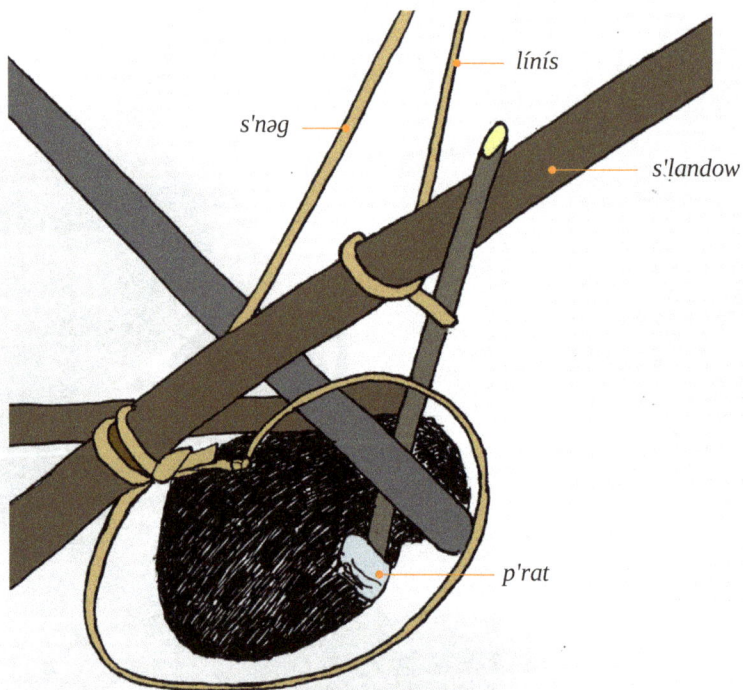

The kɛmbɔɔd trap

The *t'loɡ* trap made use of a bamboo tube, open at one end. The *línís* cord extended from the bent tree into a hole in the top, and was held down by some bait tied at the end inside the tube. Another cord, the *s'nəg*, extended from the bent tree to a hole at the front and had a noose at its end, opened out inside the tube. The rat would enter the tube and chew through the bait, releasing the cord from the trap and setting off the bent tree, thus yanking the noose and catching the rat.

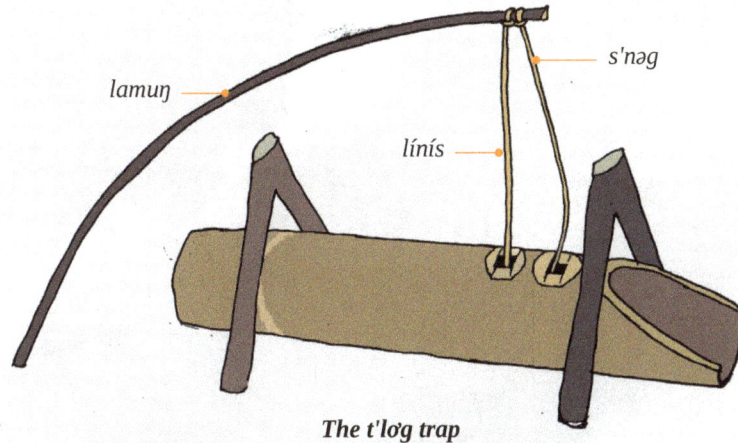

The t'loɡ trap

The *sab k'lɛg* was made with an opening, the *lanaŋ*, through a wall of obstacles called *pɛncɛɛr*, set along the track of small animals such as porcupines. The animal walked through it and pushed the *bəx* vine, tied to a stick sunk in the ground, that pulled on the stick catching the tip of the *línís* cord, releasing the catapult in a similar way to the *kɛm* and *bakoʼoᵏ* traps.

The sab k'lɛg trap

The *sab k'woʼoᵏ* made use of a pressure pad, with a row of sticks laid against a stick set across a forked branch that was stuck in the ground. The catapult tree was held down by a tension cord, which had a short stick at its end that hooked under the fork. When an animal trod on the trap the stick across the fork was pushed down and the *línís* whipped free, causing the bent tree to yank on the noose, laid out on the sticks. Everything was carefully hidden under leaves and the end of the *lamuŋ* with a bamboo cuff. This trap was laid for pheasants, whereas the similar *sidíŋ* trap was for catching wild boars (it was exactly the same in design, except that a stronger noose cord and larger bent tree were used). They both had *sakarr*, or walls made of sticks and branches to create a pathway, the *cɛnrux*, for an animal to walk through, into the trap.

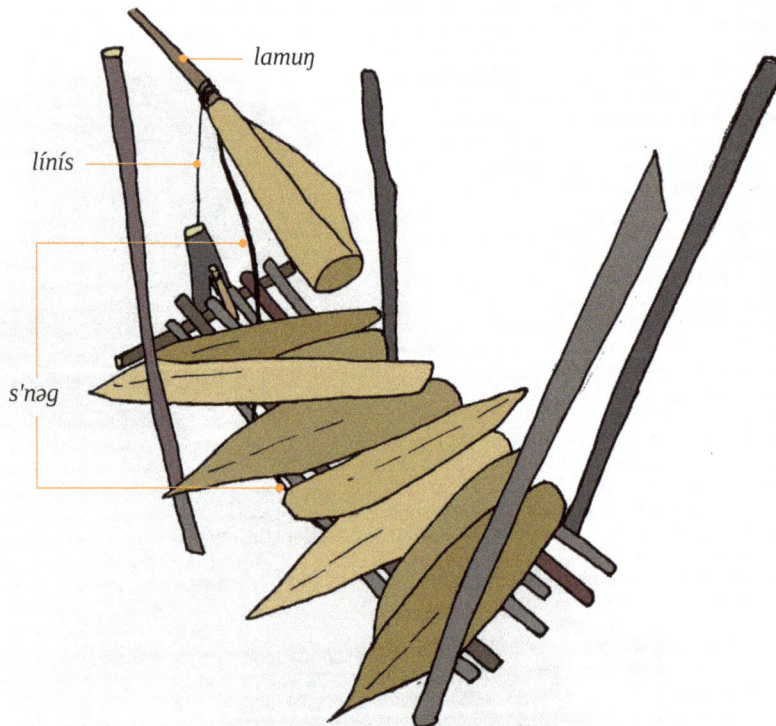

The sab k'woʼoᵏ or sidíŋ trap

Trapping, as well as hunting with blowpipe or spear, often depended on the right season to be successful. Birds flock to the trees that are fruiting and so the trapper would walk the forest looking for signs that different kinds of fruits would be ripening. When a particularly advantageous tree was found, attracting birds, he would then plan a bird-gumming day. Firstly, he would collect the *c'borr*, or new latex from the gum tree, as well as the sticking agent to mix with it, and then he would make his gumming strands from *r'tam* palm, for the prodding. When langurs were observed feeding, then he could wait below with the blowpipe. The ability to identify wild fruit trees was vital to their success at hunting, and without it they wouldn't be able to catch anything with their traps.

The luwaa^k is a creeper that grows up hanging from a giant j'lax (mahogany) and spreads out all over its canopy, where its fruits attract hornbills and primates.

Tajaar

Tajaar

Tɛlbal

Gɛrhaar

Baaɣ

Mɛmhiim

ʔIpəəs

Kʔuux

G'tah cɛp

J'rix

Guwaaŋ (Credit: B'roɡ)

J'raŋkoŋ

Wɛj

S'lɛjmɛj

K'roʿx

Sɛg

Saweh

Jaŋrax (Credit: B'roɡ)

Lumag (Credit: B'roɡ)

Some of the species of wild fruit trees that are known to the Temiars.

Luwaaʰ

T'lambax

Baay

Gɛrhaar

J'rix

Kɛnwəəl

Tɛlbalwe

Lɛrwɛɛr

The trees are easily identified by their fruits.

Ground-dwelling rodents were easier to trap when the fruit season was over and food was more scarce. Around August, a trapper would collect a sack or two of *sŏic* nuts, which all kinds of wild animals feed on when they scattered from the abundant *sŏic* trees. Come the wet season, he would leave these nuts at set places along a trapping line, to lure brown rats. And after a week of laying the bait, he would then set kɛmbɔɔd traps for a couple of nights at all the baiting places, returning in the morning to collect the catch. With this method he, together with the other trappers, could take home baskets full of rats to share out.

The rodents would be fur-singed in the house, gutted, and roasted or cooked in bamboo with tubers or *d'kŏh* pips. The trapping could only be carried out in the black of a moonless night, as if the moonlight shone on any of the trap cords and sticks the rats would not dare scavenge for the bait. Another technique was to build a *bajaa*x, a little hut in the forest, in which the bait was left each day for a week. Once rats were familiar with the food source, the trappers would hide themselves at night under a special floor and tug on rattan cords to catch rats as they nibbled on the nuts.

At other seasons, when baiting wouldn't work so well, rodents would be caught on their paths across small water courses, or up in trees. The trapper had to have good eyes and senses to know where the animal tracks were and where the animals were scavenging. With fish, the trapper would observe which pools the fish were lurking in and, in the case of sinking the *bubuu*ᵏ trap, it was also advantageous when certain trees were fruiting, such as *jadaar*, which fish feed on. Its branches would be used to cover the trap, that was sunk in the water with a rock inside, and lure all the fish toward it.

Setting the traps needed special care and much skill, to make sure an animal could be caught and that they wouldn't find an empty trap. Any cut ends of wood, that the animal could see, had to be covered with a leaf. The tip of a spear had to be hidden too and anything that a clever wild boar could see, as being fixed by human hands, they had to properly *gᵾh*, or cover over with bamboo and leaves. A rat wouldn't notice a trap on its path and would bumble straight into it, and hence the kɛm and kɛmbɔɔd make no use of covering anything up. But squirrels, civets and langurs were all much more cautious, and thus the traps used for them (small and large *bakŏo*ᵏ traps and the kɛm gɛntŏx, practically a miniature *bakŏo*ᵏ) were crafted with wings made of interwoven rattan cane around the sides, to block the sides and to force an animal to go through the opening at the centre. The traps for pheasants and wild boars (*sab k'wŏo*ᵏ and *sidíŋ*, also known as *j'rad*) both utilised the same method, whereby they were set off by an animal's foot treading on a platform of sticks, with a noose laid on top of them, and these needed hiding carefully.

To call someone to join the trapping they would say, "*Jo*ᵏ, *ʔam-juwah*," let's go and play, for to mention the name of the trap, or that they were going to trap animals, would cause them bad luck. A trapper might also say, "*Yím-bəx tali*ᵏ", I'm going out to tie cords. After setting traps, the trappers had to *t'laa*ᵏ, or forego food until dark, because if they went home and had a meal they would be sure to catch nothing. A *bakŏo*ᵏ trap could sit ineffective on its tree branch for two weeks, until it dried out and the catapult lost its spring, if they had broken any rules required by the trap. In the home of a trapper, dozens of rattan triangles were hung up near the fireplace, to keep them stiff and ready for use on a trapping day. There would also be no lack of caught rodents hanging above the fire and each morning meat would be chewed with manioc before attending any chores.

Trap	Quarry	Location	Technique	Strategy
Sɛɛp	*cɛp* – birds	branches of a fruit tree	gum strands	landing area
Bubuuᵏ	*kaaᵏ, sɛgnug* – fish, turtles	sunk in a river pool	containing	baiting
Kilooŋ	*kaaᵏ* – fish	across a river	containing	chased
Marɛɛx	*kaaᵏ* – fish	across a river	containing	chased
Kɛm balɛh	*k'dííg man* – brown rats	bamboo pole across stream	catapult sliding knot	pathway
Kɛm gɛntóx	*k'dííg s'koˊoˊr etc* – squirrels	branch of a tree	catapult noose	pathway
Kɛmbɔɔd	*k'dííg man* – brown rats	hole in ground	catapult noose	baiting
T'loˊg	*k'dííg ˀen-ˀoˊoˊx* – water rat	river-side	catapult noose	baiting
Bakoˊoᵏ loox	*k'dííg ˀɛn-balíx* – small tree-mammals (giant squirrel, linsang)	branch of a tree	catapult noose	pathway
Bakoˊoᵏ ˀaay	*ˀaay ˀɛn-balíx* – large tree-mammals (langurs, civets, bearcat)	branch of a high tree	catapult noose	pathway
Sab k'lɛg	*j'kəəs, tood* – porcupines	on ground in forest	catapult noose·	pathway
Sab k'woˊoᵏ	*k'woˊoᵏ, pugaaᵏ, d'naᵏ* – great argus, pheasant, jungle fowl	on ground in forest	catapult noose	pathway
Sidíŋ (j'rad)	*taˀoˊŋ* – wild boar	animal track in undergrowth	catapult noose (using wire)	pathway
Raaj	*lawuᵏ* – large mammals (wild boar, muntjac, deer, serow)	animal track in forest	catapult spear	pathway
C'roˊx	*taˀoˊŋ* – wild boar	animal track behind log	sharp stakes	descent

Rɛndɛɛd	ta²oŋ – wild boar	around manioc swidden	containing	baiting
Pad	sɛn²o'oy – humans	by side of a track	catapult bar	pathway
P'raŋ lʉʉh	sɛn²o'oy – humans	by side of a track	clapping shut	pathway

Table 5. Eighteen types of trap that the Temiars set for different quarry.

Traps set for humans were made for prevention of intruders, not for catching people! The *pad* trap could effectively maim a person by hitting their legs with a powerful blow, and the *p'raŋ-lʉʉh* trap, made of a split bamboo pole, held open by a stick, would whack shut when an intruder walked into a tripwire, alerting people at the house. The *pad* trap is still used today by villagers when they feel fearful that strangers could be lurking around at night. The rule is, if you have to approach a village after dark, then you don't sneak up quietly, you give a loud call to let people know you are coming. That way could save you being hit by a trap or bitten by dogs, or worse yet, shot with a blow-dart!

An example of the P'raŋ lʉʉh trap, that gave early warning of intruders.

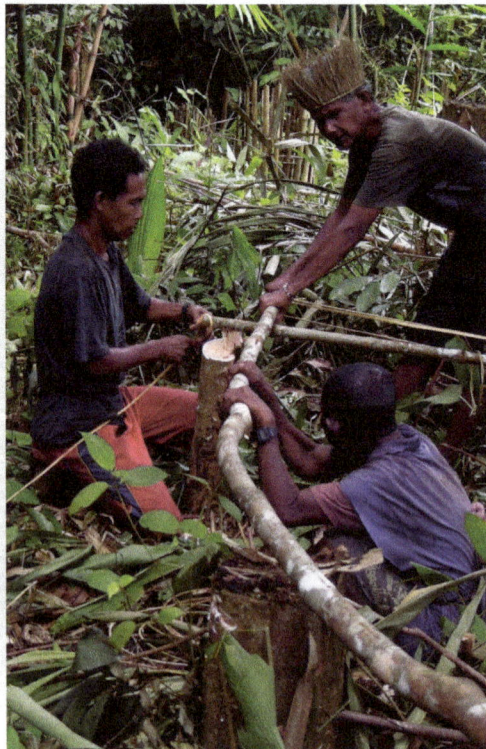

Temiars construct a pad trap, which is similar in design to the raaj trap, but without the spearhead, only a pole.

The línís stick is inserted into a cord and bent down, to hold the catapult in place.

The raaj spear trap, with the komax ring holding down the release stick clearly seen.

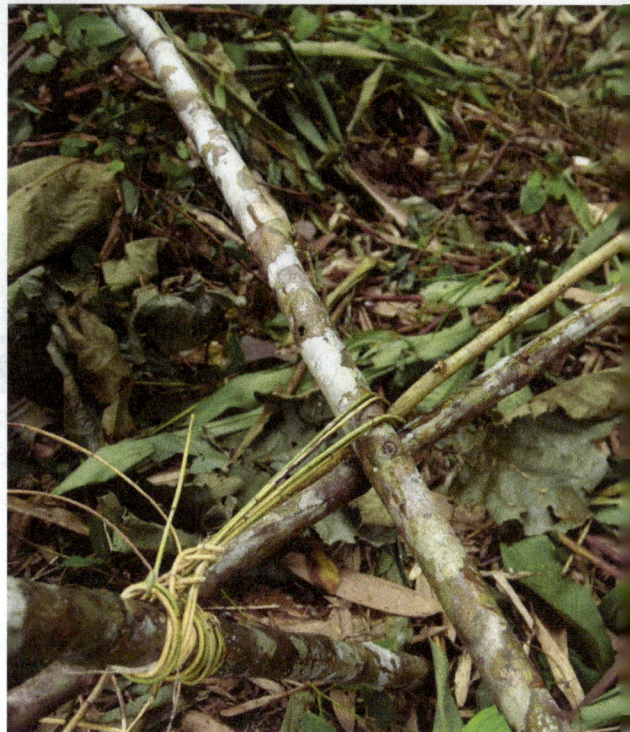

The trap is set, ready to strike at an intruder.

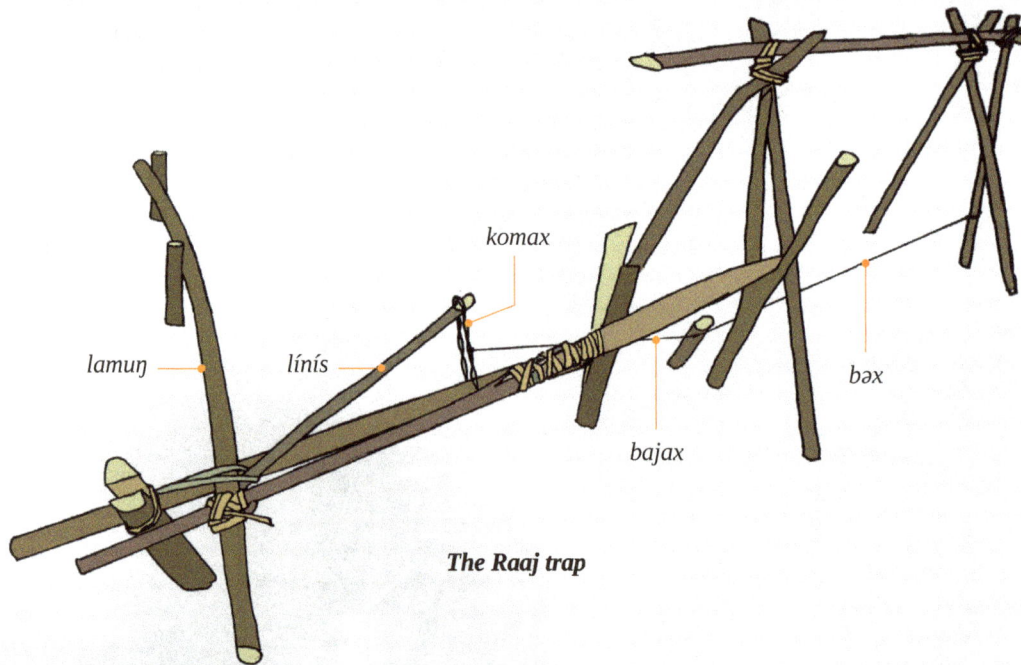

The Raaj trap

The *Raaj* trap was different to the other traps in that the *lamuŋ* or bent tree traveled horizontally above the ground and thrusted rather that pulled on the trap. Instead of a noose there was a sharpened spearhead, the *bajax*, made of *ʔawɛn t'mííŋ*, a variety of fine blowpipe bamboo, which was tied to a shaft, the *coʼow*, that was in turn tied to the *lamuŋ*. To hold the *lamuŋ* back in its bent position, to set the trap, a strong cord, the *taliᵏ boʼox*, folded over it and a stick, the *línís*, went through its loop and under the *lamuŋ*, to hold it down. The *línís* stick was prevented from flying off by a ring of rattan, the *komax*, catching its tip. The *bəx* vine was attached to the *komax*, and it ran right through the trap to the other side. When an animal walked through and pushed the vine with its foot, the *komax* would be tugged and it would slip off the tip of the *línís*, which would fly off, causing the spear to thrust instantly into the torso of the animal. The whole apparatus would be carefully concealed with bamboo branches laid over it so that nothing was visible to animals. Even the tip of the spear would be covered with a bamboo cuff. Because of its lethality, it would be dangerous for humans (though the spear would likely tear into a person's calf or thigh) and would never be set anywhere near the village. The Semai also use this trap, which they call the *dax*, and they always make a cross sign on the path if there is trap further up. The Temiars also refer to this trap as the *ʔoʼmooh*, which refers to both the path through its centre and the hole it makes in the side of a pig, and thus they avoid calling its real name so that the trap will be successful.

The *bubuu^k*, or fish trap, was essentially a bottle-shaped trap made of *bɛltoʹp* or *cɛmcoʹoʹp* strands woven together with cord, with a *cɛmpoʹg*, or funnel, made of sharpened strands tied into conical shape and fastened inside an opening at the end or in the side. Fish entered through the funnel, attracted by bait, and would be trapped inside.

Two traps, the *bubuu^k loox* and *bubuu^k gəət*, were long, cylindrical traps that were sunk in the river with the mouth end facing downstream, for fish swimming upstream to find their way into them. The first had only one *cɛmpoʹoʹg*, while the latter had two, with one at its opening and another one tied inside at its head. Fish would be extracted from these two traps by untying the *katɛ̄ɛ̄ɲ*, a woven cap at the base of the trap (the pointed end).

Two other traps, *bubuu^k pacō̄ō̄^k* and *bubuu^k gəəl*, were more egg-shaped and had a *cɛmpoʹoʹg* tied inside a hole at the side. The latter differed to the *pacō̄ō̄^k*, in that the strands of one end were drawn out in a long tail and the strands at the other end were tucked inside the trap, so that the trap could be stood upright in the water with the tail tied to tree roots above it. With these two traps, the fish were extracted by removing the *cɛmpoʹoʹg*.

Bubuu^k loox

Bubuu^k gəət

Bubuu^k pacō̄ō̄^k

Bubuu^k gəəl

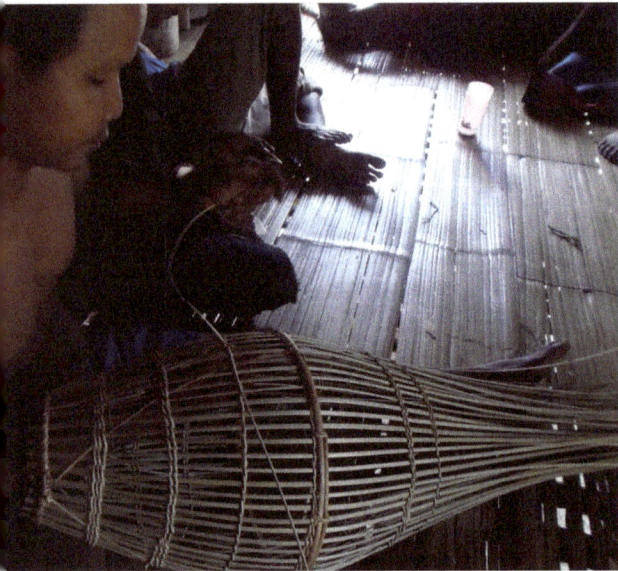

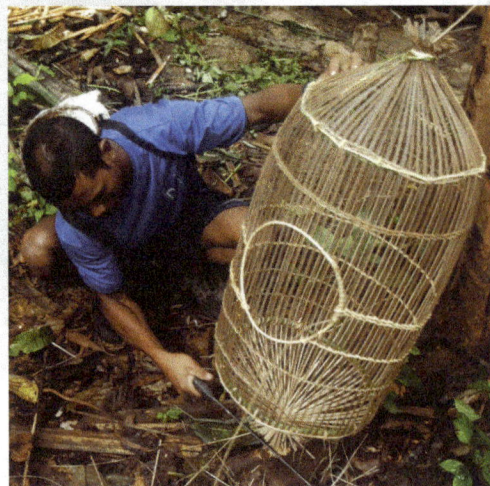

Egg-shaped fish traps were preferred for sinking in river pools.

Before going to *goʔp*, or sink, a fish trap, the trapper would ask someone to soak the manioc for him to use as bait, as by doing it himself he would not keep his luck intact. The *bubuuᵏ loox* was difficult to make a catch with anyway, and if the trapper was not *t'nɔɔᵏ*, or apt enough, he would catch nothing with it and return *siyal*, or empty. The other traps would make a catch much more easily.

A marɛɛx, an ingenious method for stranding fish. (Credit: Jadɛɛr)

K'waay cʔʔaag.

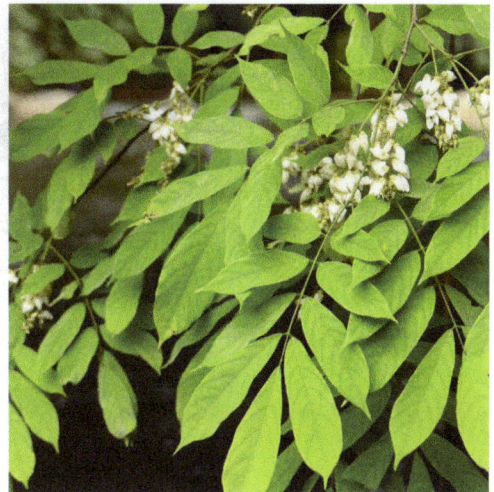

The jadaar tree; its leaves were used for covering a sunken fish trap and its berries attracted fish.

When fish were abundant, the river could be cleverly channeled with barriers so that fish would be forced into a trap. One method was the *kilooŋ*, which could be constructed by just two men. It employed a barrier of bamboo slats made at each end of a river pool, with the up-river barrier having a gap in it, with a trap door, that the fish entered by, and the lower one an opening into a channel, running into a large *bubuuᵏ* trap. The trappers would feed the fish with manioc for some time, while being careful to stay out of sight, until the fish learned to enter the enclosure and large fish could be seen swimming inside. Then, at the right time, they pulled on a long rope to drop the trap door, causing all the fish to flee for fright, down into the *bubuuᵏ*.

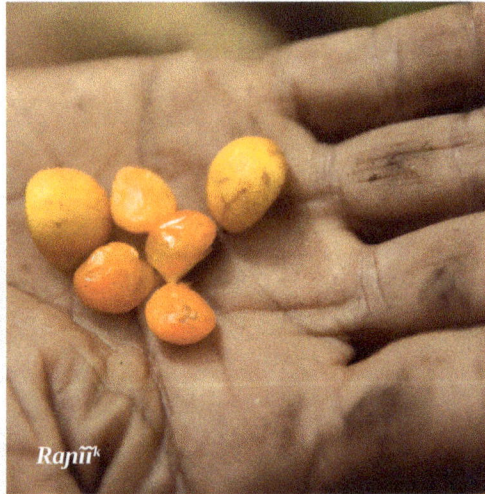

Wild berries were used to bait fish in small rivers.

Another method, the *marɛɛx*, involved constructing a bamboo dam with a weir, and needed a group of men to build it, as so much bamboo had to be cut and tied. It would also only be worthwhile if the river was teeming with fish (hence it has not been used in the last thirty years). Boards of flattened bamboo were fixed along the riverbank and drawn in toward the barrier, where an opening allowed water to drop down a level, into an enclosed platform of bamboo poles, similar in appearance to a river raft. To make the catch, the trappers split lengths of green bamboo in quarters and threw them into the water. On seeing the white of the bamboo, the startled fish would flee down to the weir, a fake waterfall, where they dropped down into the enclosure and were trapped.

A method for catching the fish in small rivers was to *k'roox*, or suffocate, them by mixing the sap of certain vines into the water, which deoxygenated it. This activity, not carried out very often, needed plenty of hands to help scoop out all the fish that would float dead. The tubers of the *k'waay cˀʔaag* or *k'waay nasiᵏ* vines, the former also being edible but bitter, were sources of fish 'poison'. Fishing with hook and line was carried out whenever out walking on a path that followed a river. They would *p'gəp*, or sink a line in a deep river, using mud worms or flying insects as bait, or *kupas*, tug a line in the water, at smaller rivers, using wild berries as bait. Fruits that were eaten by fish included *boʼox, gɛncɛɛy, gɛnraac, kanyu, padax, raɲĩᵏ, rɛɛd* and *tɛŋbiyɛx*.

Above: two Temiars catch fish by tugging a line in the water, while walking toward the river source. Below: the barbs of the kadɔɔᵏ-daax vine were used in the old days for fishing hooks.

Padax

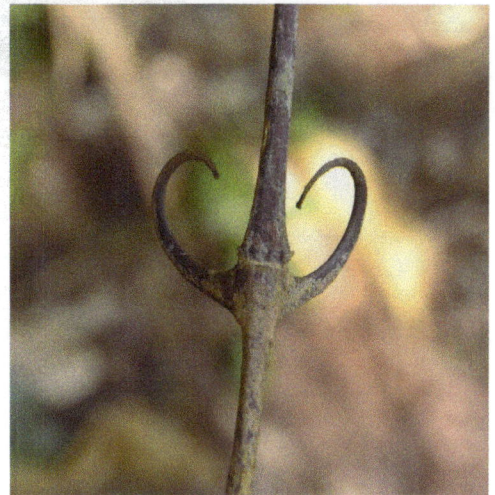

Species of the forest known to the Temiars

The lists of species in the table below, containing over a thousand names, were compiled over the last ten years through interviews with Temiars of Pos Gɔɔb and Pos Símpor, and the names have been checked over many times for their accuracy. There still remains much work to be done in identifying the trees and plants with scientific names and many known plant names are yet to be discovered. Identification of birds and animals was made showing picture books to the Temiars. Alternative names, avoidance terms or nicknames are given in parentheses.

Category	Names of Species
J'huuᵏ j'rəs – Forest trees	badoͦx (jelutong), bakoͦw, barway, balon, bayur, bɛrboͦw (Moluccan ironwood), biceh (canol), bilih, b'luŋɛy, b'runih, b'sar, cabol, cah (meranti), cah k'pùx, cah kalaŋ, cah kucíŋ, cah sagùb, caŋel, calyɛx, cɛmpɛɛx, cɛŋkər, cɛrmɛr, ciyɛx, coͦx, c'rɛŋloͦx, doͦog (ipoh), gāŋyah, g'lapoh, g'rōᵏ, guul, haraaŋ (gempas), hɛmrɛp, jɛx, j'lax (mahogany), j'rəg, j'waŋ, kabuᵏ, kasaw, katuᵏ, katuŋ, kijax, k'miŋam, kolím tɛmagaaᵏ, k'rɛɛw, kulíd, laŋgoͦᵏ, lɛᵏ, lɛrwɛɛr, lir, liyoͦy, l'noͦsdoᵏ, mɛnkoͦod, nɛgsag, pɛlkoͦp, pulɛy, ralɛh, r'guul (tualang), r'lap, rumpay, rusow, sakoͦb, sanoͦl, sanyoͦg, s'daal, sɛŋsiŋ, sɛrwəər (mengas), s'waŋ, s'pʉʉh, sugiᵏ, tampaal, tanaaŋ, taŋlùn, taŋlɛy, taraᵏ, tɛrmín, tɛrsaaŋ, tɛrsíŋ, t'lor, t'límboᵏ, t'ramoᵏ, wɛj, yuyor.
K'bəəᵏ nyam/ K'bəəᵏ cɛp – Wild fruit trees (fruits eaten by animals and birds)	²ajɛɛl, basux, batus, baay, b'dax, bɛnhíc, b'loͦij, boͦt, boͦox, b'raŋsax, canuul, catoͦod, cɛrmɛɛr, cɛx, c'goh, cíntoͦl, c'makah, c'tax, dulaŋ, gariyɛd, gaax, gərcaᵏ, gɛncɛɛy, gɛnraac, gɛntoͦx, gɛrhaar, g'míír, g'raaw, g'rutɛx, g'sax, g'tah cɛp, guwaaŋ, hooŋ, ²iŋcag, ²ipəəs, jadaar, jaŋrax, jɛrnaŋ, joŋ, joͦt, j'raŋkoŋ, j'rɛnluc, j'rɛɛw, j'ríx, jul, jurɛy, jutat, juy, kanyuh, katoͦoᵏ, kɛgwɛg, kɛlbaax, kɛlpuŋ, kɛlwoͦoy, kɛnalax, kɛnɛgwɛg, kɛnwəəl,kɛriyɛɛh, kɛruwoͦc, kijɛl, k'joͦx pacoͦr, k'lɛntoͦg, k'mirɛy, kopɛc, k'rɛmnum, k'rɛmnum bajax, k'rɛᵏbuᵏ, k'rɛᵏmad, k'roͦox bɛrcēh, k'roͦox ²ɛ-coͦog, k'roͦox gɛrbɔɔᵏ, k'roͦox sɛrluur, k'rudoᵏ, kusap, kumhaŋ, k²uux, ladaᵏ, lɛrwɛɛr, loͦon, lumag, luhɛɛw, luwaaᵏ, mataᵏ, maŋsul, mɛmhim b'siiᵏ, mɛmhim poᵏwah, mɛmhim sawyɛh, mɛmhim tabar, mɛŋsoͦl, moͦoŋ, nyɛs, padoͦx, pahux, pahoͦg, pamhuŋ, pɛncɛd, pɛnpoŋ, pɛrlùg, p'lacɛᵏ, p'ragoͦᵏ, p'raŋkup, p'rəəᵏ, p'rɛslɛs, p'rigoͦy, rabuᵏ, raŋsííl, rɛjnaaj, rɛnwal, rɛɛd, rood, rusʉw, sagam, sagəər, salɛɛg, saloͦg, samoͦg, santəəj, sator, sawɛh, saŋyal, saal, sɛdwɛd, sɛg, sɛgsɛg, sɛntɛb, sɛhpuwah, sɛŋluwac, sɛŋrɛx, sɛnsat, sɛntɛb, sɛrlor, siruy, siiw, s'lɛjmɛj, s'lɛmnam, s'luwaŋ, s'maliyɛx, s'mɛh, s'mɛrluŋ, s'paad, s'ríj, tab tajuuᵏ, tagɛɛs, tajaar, tampax, tampuuᵏ, tanbay, tapɛy, tapoŋ, tawuᵏ, tɛlbaal, tɛljɔɔp, tɛŋbiyɛx, tɛŋwɛx, tihɔɔᵏ, t'layax, toͦt, t'rih, yahpih, yahyɛh.
K'bəəᵏ nɛdpoͦod – Large fruit trees (edible)	²aŋrəəy (niring), bagan, biraax, b'taar (petai), cəl²el, c'mp'daᵏ, dɛriyan, gaar, ha²oog, jiyɛɛs, kolím, k'laat, k'lɛidaŋ, k'nalag, lɛᵏ, l²ɛɛg (sapuŋ), maŋkuŋ (d'koͦh), maŋkuŋ tād, ndaŋkaaᵏ (jack), pɛnpuŋ, pɛrgəəs, soͦic (perah), s'poͦoy, t'koͦy, tɛnjug.
B'rəx – Small fruit trees (edible)	²ataag, bajaw, bɛjsíj, b'koͦod (salak), b'rɛgnoͦog, calaag, caŋoͦod, cɛlpɛl, cɛŋcoͦox, cɛrmɛɛr, c'riykay, cumpuh, gayax, gɛsəər, gíncɛy, g'ldɛɛs, g'ruh, g'woͦom, hakoͦor, jantaal, kabaax, kɛrmal, kɛlwɛɛx, k'maluŋ, kubax, kuriiᵏ, l'cax, lɛɛg, limoͦw, maloŋ, pacɛɛy, pahíd (caŋeh), píŋgoͦw, p'latow, p'ragoᵏ, p'ragun, p'rɛgnaag, rakoͦᵏ, rambɛy,

B'rəx – continued	*raŋkíh, raŋsííl, raŋīī^k, raroʰh, rɛmmaŋ, r'loʲj, r'yɛl, sɛdwɛɛd, s'taar, s'tool, tabu^k, tampuy, tanbay, tapɛl, tərlɛŋ, tɛrhii^k, t'ŋo^k, wʉʉd.*
Tɛŋtɛɛx – Rattan	*cɛrwíís, c'mɛɛs, c'moʲg, cuwaag, gahtííd, gərtas, g'rah, haag, jɛrnaŋ, k'law cowa^k, l'but, lɛ^k, manjɛɛr, manoʲw, mɛntɛ, māāh ²alaaj, pantɛy, papan, pɛŋpəəx, p'nɛhsɛh, p'níntɛs, riyɛw, sakuul, sɛnsiyɛc, s'garr, s'tɛg, s'toʲog, suŋkal paya^k, talùd.*
Tali^k – Vines	*baro^k, bawə^k, biyaax, galər, g'rɛmtoʲp, kacíp, kadɔɔ^k-daax, kalox, kason, kɛdrɛd, kɛldoŋ, manaar, papan, píŋgoʲw, p'níntɛs, p'rago^k, rɛnyoʲl, r'naloʲj, t'now, tayug, ²urad.*
²Awɛn – Bamboo	*balaar, banun, b'síí^k, b'toŋ, gantaaŋ, hawurr, jɛr'wad, k'dɛx (no cavity, montane), k'yool, liyaax, p'lax, pōʲ^kwa^k, pōōg, sah, sɛndəx, s'mɛɛy.*
B'laaw – Blowpipe	*hataar, pɛnrɛɛw, p'lakuj, s'woʲor, t'hɛl, t'mííŋ.*
S'kɛ^k – Pandanus	*balu^k, g'racɛŋ, haar, jarow (montane), kajaax, k'li^k, p'rah, tamuŋ.*
Kɛnroʲob – Roofing palms	*bayí^k, bɛltoʲp, cacuh, cɛmcoʲop, kamaar, k'labɔɔb, manta^k, pacɛh, salah.*
C'kəər – Palms (*edible pith)	*baloŋ*, bayas*, bayí^k, gasɛ^k, hariyuw, j'rox, koor, kuwuy, k'waar, l'goʲog*, pacɛɛy*, tadùg, ta²oʲo^k.*
Buus – Canes	*²abow, b'tí^k, c'lakah, ciyuh, gantaŋ, hadow, k'moŋ, k'tam, pɛnyaaw (laŋɛɛd), po^k, tabaar, tɛŋtɛɛx.*
²Apoʲos – Zingibers	*boʲt, cadag, gancɛɛr, gapəd, haaŋ, kapoʲo^k hayom (torch ginger), kāyōōd, kɛnwoʲox, k'rag, ləwɛɛy, pus, rajōō^k, tahoʲr, tapix, ²uup.*
Cɛnlaay – Fragrant leaves	*bar²oʲob, cɛlcool, c'mərdam, jalar, kamaar, k'waay, kayaa^k, liyoʲy, pɛnhɛg, pɛnpɛt. rəŋow, rəx.*
Boʲod – Decorative flowers	*bɛrɲɛŋ, carax (celosia), c'naap (ginger lily), d'rəp, gapɛh, gɛlpap, gɛlpəd, hɛntəl, hɛrkoʲy, hubɛɛw, jampox, j'rɛmsɛɛm, k'laat, k'mujoʲo^k, k'ralad, locɛɛw, luŋɛɛw, maluu^k, maŋlɛ^k, milor, mɛ^k cɛŋkɛy, ²okɛt (orchids), pɛriyo^k (jùx ²ití^k), p'rawas, pʉʉt, rajōō^k (officionale), rayə (hibiscus), saguu^k (canna), s'dùx, síríŋ, s'lɛmdam, s'rudɛb, suliy, suŋkut, tahoʲn (globosa), tambus (marigold), tanjɔɔx, tapix, t'lɛɛy.*
S'laa^k – Plants	*bal, bar²oʲob, bayas, barox, b'lɛŋgaŋ, b'rawɛɛŋ, catax, cihoŋ, dudug, galox, g'rah, jarííj, karaax, kasay, k'rudu^k, lagoh, lambu^k, laar, laar ²uud, l'bag, lɛmpux, mɛnsat, moʲoŋ, pahu^k, pɛnlaay taŋən, pɛnlu^k goʲb, pɛnpət, r'pɛy, r'tam, saɲēēn.*
Bɛjsíj – Irritable plants and creatures	Plants: *bəər gù^k, bəər kɛh, bəər rayax, bɛjsíj ²awɛn (bamboo hairs), bɛjsíj padi (rice leaves and husk), hēēd, k'waay goŋ, lalaŋ (elephant grass), rambaŋ (grass), s'laa^k rumpɛy, s'laa^k koŋha^k, s'laa^k lambo^k, s'laa^k pɛnpət, s'laa^k rumpay, s'laa^k s'lɛntí^k.* Trees: *j'huu^k cɛrwɛɛs, j'huu^k patah, j'huu^k sɛrwəər.* Caterpillars: *k'maay gííp, k'maay k'laad, mamə^k.*

Bǝǝr bɛɛx – Edible plants	*bǝǝr ʔampùg, bǝǝr camɛɛŋ, bǝǝr capíᵏ, bǝǝr cɛŋkɛh kaaᵏ, bǝǝr gùx, bǝǝr gɛᵏ, bǝǝr karaax, bǝǝr kɛh, bǝǝr kʼlaab, bǝǝr latax, bǝǝr lawaar, bǝǝr lɛntaag sɛgnug, bǝǝr pacɛh, bǝǝr pakuᵏ, bǝǝr patooŋ, bǝǝr sayah, bǝǝr sɛjlíj, bǝǝr sɛndab, bǝǝr sɛntɛᵏ taroʼox, bǝǝr sɛnyoʼn, bǝǝr sup, bǝǝr taʔoʼoᵏ, bǝǝr tawarr.*
Bǝǝr nɛnlut – Edible mushrooms	*bǝǝr ʔamís (bǝǝr lɛglug), bǝǝr ʔāntaᵏ, bǝǝr ʔapus, bǝǝr ʔarap, bǝǝr bɛgyug, bǝǝr boʼt, bǝǝr bʼrɛŋbux, bǝǝr cʼrikay, bǝǝr gasɛᵏ, bǝǝr luux, bǝǝr pasih, bǝǝr poʼg, bǝǝr saboʼh, bǝǝr salud, bǝǝr sʼbùn, bǝǝr sǝǝt, bǝǝr sʼgarr.*
Kʼwaay – Yams	*ʔakɛɛs, ʔantoʼh, bʼrɛɛw, cʼʔaag, cʼŋǝǝl, dagax, daran, gɛnsuul, kʼdííg, kɛnsiŋ, mantoʼh, maŋkɛl, nasiᵏ, takob, toroᵏ, woh.*
Jaay – Banana (*inedible)	*ʔabuh, ʔamboʼn, balaŋ, balít, balít nor, bʼraŋan, buŋaaᵏ, gadiᵏ, hudĩĩl, jʼlíy, kamow, kapal, kʼlaat, kwaay*, mambiŋ*, mamoᵏ*, mas, ndaŋkaaᵏ, puntoᵏ, ragaᵏ, ranjɛs*, rʼlog, santíír, sʼmatuh, tanlon.*
Kayuh – Manioc plants	*ʔadɨᵏ, ʔanit, ʔasal, bɛhkooh, bʼlaŋūūd, cɛrmɛɛr, hɛrwɛɛᵏ, katɔɔᵏ, kʼlah, kunyíd, luhɛɛw, pulud, sakaaᵏ, sujɛw, tampaal.*
Sǝǝh – S. potatoes	*ʔagaay* (white), *ʔayoʼoʼd* (orange), *cʼmaroᵏ* (yellow or red), *loʼoʼj, pʼriih* (white).
Jawaᵏ - Millet	*ʔamaŋ, ʔasíh, bɛlʔíc, cabaax, cɛŋcoʼox, gɛrlɛn, kabaax, sakool, sitǝr, sɛyjoʼy, ʔuloʼx.*
Padi – Rice	*badaᵏ, bidor, bɛrjɛɛr, bɛrtih, capǝr, cɛᵏcoʼᵏ, coríŋ, gajoh, hɛryas, jʼbad, kawín, kɛnlas, kɛnrǝŋ, kʼlah, kuroᵏ, lɛmbùᵏ, pulud ʔaraŋ, pulud manís, pulud papan, rantɛy, ʔuloʼx, waŋiᵏ.*
Cɛp – Birds	BIRDS OF PREY: *kʼlaax bajaw* blyth's hawk-eagle; *kʼlaax cɛpiyɛw* wallace's hawk eagle; *kʼlaax kʼrʼhuy* changeable hawk-eagle; *kʼlaax sɛmpǝl* grey-faced buzzard. HORNBILLS: *balyɛx* bushy-crested hornbill; *dʼku*g (burung lilin); *kahkuuh, kahkōōh* white-crowned hornbills; *kʼhāār* black hornbill; *hʼnwaaŋ* great hornbill; *hʼlaŋ* (*ragaŋ*) rhinoceros hornbill; *taʔǝ̄ǝj* wreathed (pouched) hornbill; NIGHT BIRDS: *caŋwoʼoʼj* brown wood-owl; *jʼkoŋ* brown boobook; *togtɛbaw* nightjar; JUNGLE FOWL: *cʼkum* crested fireback pheasant; *dʼnaᵏ* red junglefowl; *dɛddud* (*kaduud*) greater coucal; *dɛŋdoʼoŋ* a partridge; *puyuh* barred button-quail; *kʼwɔɔx* great argus; *pugaaᵏ* a pheasant; DOVES: *bɛrkooh (bɛrkoʼg)* mountain imperial-pigeon; *bʼrawɛl, bʼrawoʼl* green-pigeons; *jʼrɛgpaag* a dove; *mɛnyut* emerald dove; *rɛgwoog* little cuckoo-dove; *tǝkukur* spotted dove; PARROTS: *bɛrlɛɛŋ* blue-crowned hanging-parrot; MALKOHAS: *cʼmoʼg* green-billed, red-billed malkoha; *sɛgduwa*g chestnut-bellied/breasted malkoha; TROGONS: *ʔakul* scarlet-rumped trogon; *bʼrɛlkuul* red-naped trogon; KINGFISHERS: *caguᵏ* blue-eared kingfisher; *coʼrís (poʼx bʼlaaw)* rufous-backed kingfisher; *pʼragaaᵏ* stork-billed kingfisher; *woʼoʼy* black-capped kingfisher; BEE-EATERS: *bíríg* blue-tailed bee-eater; *kɛkoʼg* red-bearded bee-eater; BARBETS: *tagùt* yellow-crowned barbet; *togroʼh* golden-naped barbet; *tʼraad* fire-tufted barbet; *tʼwaal* golden-throated barbet; WOODPECKERS: *tahwah rahrɛh* rufous woodpecker; *tahwah tahtoh* banded woodpecker; *taŋ ʔalaaᵏ* common flameback; *tʼranɛᵏ* chequer-throated woodpecker;

Cɛp – Birds	BROADBILLS: *biyoʻy* black-and-yellow broadbill; *gagoob* silver-breasted broadbill; *tamboʻoj* (*ʔamboʻoj*) whitehead's broadbill; *tɛŋtaŋ* black-and-red broadbill; *t'raad* long-tailed broadbill; SHRIKE-BABBLERS: *cɛw* white-browed s.-babbler; *cicarr* black-eared s.-babbler; *poʔajɛɛl* javan cuckooshrike; *jɛŋwɛɛr* white-bellied empornis; *tabaar* tiger shrike; *hɛhoʻoh* short-tailed green magpie; MAGPIES: *biraay* oriental magpie-robin; THRUSHES: *g'rɛɛs pəŋkul* (*b'laŋaaᵏ*) blue whistling-thrush; *p'rokow* black laughing-thrush; *rukow* spectacled laughing-thrush; ORIOLES: *hoʻldoʻx* black-naped oriole; *sakooh* black-hooded oriole; *tantas* black-and-crimson oriole; DRONGOS: *tɛŋtoʻox* ashy racket-tailed drongo; *wɛdwāād* white-throated fantail; SPIDER-HUNTERS: *cɛdcad* little s.hunter; *cɛragah* streaked s.hunter; *k'licah* yellow-eared s.hunter; *sɛŋuwɛɛŋ* var. sunbirds; *tɛgtɛg* yellow-breasted flowerpecker. NUTHATCHES: *yaaᵏ ʔɛŋkuuᵏ* blue/velvet-fronted nuthatch; FLYCATCHERS: *laŋkɛj* little pied flycatcher; *sɛŋluwaj* asian paradise-flycatcher; BULBULS: *barow* n. straw-headed bulbul; *ʔɛsʔēēs* ocraceous bulbul; *g'raloʻg* stripe-throated bulbul; *g'royoʻj* black-crested bulbul; *hēēr* scaly-breasted bulbul; *kərkoʻr* olive-winged bulbul; *pohwɛh* hairy-backed bulbul; *tajaar* black-headed bulbul; WARBLERS: *rɛɛs* yellow-breasted warbler; BABBLERS: *hooŋ* rail babbler; *k'ruduᵏ* chestnut-backed scimitar-babbler; *p'lɛɛw* blue-winged siva; *siyɛɛy* everett's white-eye; *yaaᵏ-t'bax* short-tailed babbler; TAILOR BIRDS: *cəriyɛj* dark-necked tailorbird; *j'raglag* yellow-bellied prinia; LEAFBIRDS: *p'jlaaj* asian fairy-bluebird; *sɛŋloʻx* leafbirds; OTHER BIRDS: *cintaap* white-rumped shama; *ciyoŋ* common hill-myna; *ʔɛgʔaag* crow; *jawiyɛɛr* swiftlet; *kukor* bornean whistler; *layaŋ* barn swallow; *lɛmsap* a black bird; *sɛgsɛg* scarlet minivet; *sɛlsɛɛl* chestnut-naped forktail; *s'merloŋ* white-winged black jay; *tabaar* tiger shrike; *tɛrhɛr* scaly-breasted munia; LOWLAND BIRDS: *baŋow* heron; *k'dɛy* tree sparrow; *kubah* common myna; *tayɛt* eastern yellow wagtail.
Kaaᵏ – Fish	*ʔabus*, *ʔayoʻm* (*ʔahɛɛx*, *pərgeŋ*, *sabat*, *cɛŋləx*) mahseer, *b'lɛmbad*, *bawol* (*cɛᵏcoʻᵏ*, *sumnag*) a fish with no scales, *bawol k'lulaŋ*, *bawuᵏ*, *bɛgbag*, *bɛl*, *bujuᵏ*, *c'mp'raas*, *cicōʻit*, *daroʻᵏ*, *gahoʻᵏ*, *jadaar*, *jɛnraᵏ jawaᵏ*, *j'lawaŋ*, *juroh*, *kaluuy*, *kərju*, *kɛnrab* (*s'dɛl*, *ʔagas*) sandy catfish, *k'lisoʻh*, *k'nɛŋroʻŋ*, *k'ranaᵏ*, *k'rɛh*, *k'ricit*, *lampəəᵏ*, *lɛᵏ*, *línjuwar*, *nip-t'luuy*, *p'rɛd*, *p'ridoŋ*, *pulín*, *ranyoŋ*, *s'baraw*, *s'bran*, *s'laaᵏ* (*daun*), *sayir*, *səᵏbatan*, *sɛdŋoʻd*, *sɛlawaŋ*, *sɛlwooj*, *sikaŋ*, *siyɔɔᵏ*, *tapah*, *t'ŋɔ̄ɔ̄s* a large silvery fish, *tiŋalan*, *tuman*, *ʔulubatuᵏ*.
Sɛgnug – Lizards	*bagɛɛt gɛgrag* (*kabùg*, *pɛhroh*, *p'rɛŋ*) rough-necked monitor, *buhyaaᵏ* crocodile, *cicaᵏ* gecko, *c'ʔug* giant gecko, *daloʻox* crested green lizard, *gɛriyɛx* (*p'daŋ*) water monitor, *haloʻox* flying lizards, *takoʻoy* angle-headed lizard, *taroʻox* skink.
Sɛgnug – Turtles	*ʔawaaᵏ*, *koʻoh* spiny turtles, *kajēēᵏ* a mud-dwelling turtle, *karaac* Malayan box turtle, *k'noʻg* (*batuᵏ*, *p'risay*) Asian giant turtle, *labiiᵏ* river turtle, *manɛg* terrapin, *pɛlɛd* (*limíír*, *sɛdyɛg*) soft-shelled turtle, *səəl* large land tortoise.
Sɛgnug – Frogs	*ʔaŋkuuy* (*ʔaŋkoŋ*, *bəsɛŋkoʻoᵏ*, *b'həᵏ*, *poh palɛy*) an edible river frog that has poisonous skin, *barhíj* a yellow frog, *barj'roᵏ* an edible green frog, *bɛŋboŋ*, *bɛrtoŋ* found in mud, *dɛmdup* river newts, *karsoʻit* has a call like a phone ringing, *kɛŋkax* has pointed eyebrows, *pɛŋpāc* a small frog that climbs up the wall, *pɛnpoʻn* a mountain frog, *s'maag* pond frogs, *sɛɛŋ* (*j'rusiᵏ*) has dappled skin, *tabɛɛg* (*caŋkay*) bull frog.

ʔɛn-ʔɔ́ɔ̀x – River creatures	*gantaam* crabs, *kaaᵏ k'nɛŋrɔŋ* bull fish, *k'maay wad* water grub, *sùmboŋ* river shrimp, *waap* cockle.
Tajuuᵏ – Snakes (*venomous)	*b'ʔoh* brown-tailed racer, *b'rəᵏ* a flying snake, *b'rɛŋcɔ́ɔ̀x* ribbon snake, *ʔɛmpid** spitting cobra, *kabooᵏ** pit vipers, *kabooᵏ hɛ̄ɛ̄d* whip snake, *kariyɛl* banded krait, *k'buux* short python, *padax* dog-toothed cat snake, *rɛgsɔg, r'laay* reticulated python, *sayib** (*kadɔd lus*) king cobra, *sɛnlor mad-ʔis** malayan striped coral snake, *t'duuᵏ** sumatran cobra, *təŋwaax** red-headed krait.
K'dííg – Rodents	*k. ʔabíír (ʔaraaj), ʔajóɔ̀r, b'rawaaŋ* tree shrews, *ʔacaam, ʔadɛɛŋ, ʔajɛɛl* squirrels, *ʔakəəm, ʔaŋaaŋ (sabat), k. bapaax (cəŋc'raan, t'rawəg)* prevost's squirrel (*prevostii*), *cadɛᵏ* red-cheeked squirrel, *caᵏlɛᵏ* giant squirrel, *c'dcɛɛd* white-toothed shrews, *cɛŋkɔb d'kóh* a yellow rat, *k. ʔɛn²ɔ́ɔ̀x (bɛybay)* bandicoot rat, *j'nalɛᵏ* brown rat, *k. kariᵏ jagox* lesser treeshrew, *k. kasar j'laaᵏ* rats, *k. k'lubɔŋ* a small mouse, *k'rɛdlaad (na-s'laaᵏ)* giant squirrel, striped, *k. kuwɛh (b'jalíᵏ, ca²ɛ̄ɛ̄ᵏ)* bamboo mouse, *k. man-rayaaᵏ* white-bellied rats, *k. səlaiman* moonrat, *k. sirɔŋ* himalayan striped squirrel, *s'kóɔ̀l* variable squirrel (*finlaysoni*), *s'kóɔ̀r* plantain squirrel (*notatus*), *k. s'laaᵏ liyaax* red spiny rat, *k. talaad (ʔapóx)* mountain treeshrew, *k. tukaŋ* a giant squirrel.
K'dííg hɛŋhɛɛx – Flying mammals	*ʔancɔ̄h* flying lemur, *cɛp lasaar* giant bat, *cɛp rəx* flying fox, *cɛp tapəər* bats, *pupów* arrow-tailed flying squirrel, *kayiix* flying fox, *l'jəx (ʔāmpax, gɛnhooŋ)* flying squirrels.
ʔAab – Jungle cats	*ʔaab ʔamparr (ʔaab parr)* leopard, *ʔaab bɛɛy* leopard cat, *ʔaab kɛŋwóɔ̀x (ʔataaŋ, balíŋ, jɛᵏtuux, mamùg, sadaam, s'líj rɛŋbóɔ̀x, tataaᵏ b'rɛncaaŋ)* tiger.
Cɛgcóg – Civets	*cɛgcóg lalaŋ* little civet, *cɛgcóg səəh (s'magar, jaraw batuᵏ)* large Indian civet, *ʔɛs²ɔ́ɔ̀s (jajoᵏ, lɛdlɛɛd, lɛnlut)* masked palm civet, *ʔiloŋ* common palm civet, *kɛnsɛᵏ (na-dɛswas)* small-toothed palm civet, *rɛgrɔɔg* yellow-throated marten, *taŋlín* banded linsang.
ʔAay – Primates	*ʔamaŋ (ʔanyɛᵏ, jɛljóɔ̀l)* siamang, *bawaaj (ʔapoŋ, ʔapóɔ̀s, sɛntɛᵏ b'kawɛ̄ɛ̄ŋ)* pig-tailed macaque, *j'lɛɛw (k'raah, tííl-batuᵏ)* long-tailed macaque, *raŋkuuᵏ (rampoh)* banded langur, *tabəəx (b'sííᵏ)* dusky langur, *tawɔɔh (ʔaŋwóɔ̀d)* gibbon.
Nyam – Mammals	*ʔamɔɔᵏ* serow', *b'coᵏ (cɛᵏcoᵏ bal)* mouse deer, *coŋ hadaaᵏ* crab-eating mongoose, *cowəʔ c'lóɔ̀x* dhole, *j'kəəs (k'lɛg, lantɔ̄h, lanag)* East Asian porcupine, *kasíŋ* sambar deer, *kawííb (cɛg ʔapóɔ̀s, kawóɔ̀l)* sun bear, *kùnjoh (ʔajoh, ʔanjɛŋ, jɛɛd)* muntjac, *tampɛl (pɛrpəər)* slow loris, *ta²oŋ (ʔahaab, ʔambóɔ̀j, gaw, kaləh, sab, sidíŋ)* wild boar, *ta²oŋ badóɔ̀t* bearded pig, *tɛnyùx* bear cat, *tood (pacóɔ̀r)* brush-tailed porcupine, *wɛjwooj* pangolin.
Sɛn²óɔ̀y rayaaᵏ – 'Big people' animals	*ʔalul (ʔalaaj)* 'has arrived', *ʔatííŋ* 'large-sized', *g'dɛl* 'tusks', *rayaaᵏ kɛɛd* 'big ass', *rɛᵏyaaᵏ yəᵏ* 'big footprints', *yəᵏ gadaŋ* 'footprints as rice trays', *tataaᵏ rayaaᵏ* 'big old man', *gajah)* elephant, *barɛɛw (baroŋ)* tapir, *hagaab (karaas)* rhinoceros, *s'ladaᵏ* gaur.
Cɔ̄ɔ̄ᵏ – Pets	*ʔamɛ̄ɛ̄w (kucix)* cats, *ʔayam (cɔ̄ɔ̄s)* chickens, *cowaᵏ (ʔacɛ̄ɛ̄ᵏ)* dogs.

Tabəl – Black bee	*bus, kɛnsɛ^k* smallest variety, *jaŋwaar* the largest.
S'muj – Wasps and bees	*b'la^k* nest looks like bread, *b'raŋsax* nests in the wall, *gaŋroʻom* tiny black bee, *hɛŋwaŋ* black hornet with orange stripe, *hoom* night wasp, *hug* a 'flying ant' wasp, *jɛŋjax* stinging wasps, *k'poog* nests under the house, *laŋiir, lɛŋyɛɛr, r'jaw, sala^k* small wasps, *lɛntag gajah, luwɛɛy (padaw)* honey bee, *mɛniyɛɛr* small bee.
Cɛp tawùn – cicada	*ʔɛndral, hornyɛŋ, jawíís, k'waray, lɛɛ^k.*
K'maay – Grubs	*k'maay bahul* found in earth, *k'maay g'por* a long, white, hairy caterpillar, *k'maay gəp* a caterpillar, *k'maay gííb* a large, brown caterpillar, *k'maay jalaa^k* a black caterpillar; *k'maay k'laad* grubs found inside giant bamboo, *k'maay mamə^k* hairy caterpillar, *k'maay t'rulu^k* a large, green/white caterpillar, *k'moʻrr* a small spiny caterpillar.
Talaay – Millipedes	*talaay* a red millipede, *talaay mərtar* a black millipede, *k'lɛdbad* swarming millipedes, *k'rɛlbool* pill millipede, rolls up into a hard ball.
K'ʔɛɛb – Centipedes	*g'mayaa^k* tiny with luminous excretion, *k'ʔɛɛb babow* a short, blueish centipede that runs like a spider, *k'ʔɛɛb k'lah* a red centipede, grows up to 20cm, *k'ʔɛɛb sɛlor* a white-legged centipede.
P'lɒp – Leeches	*babuh, cɛɛr, lintah, sɛnlɛyɛg.*
Caciŋ – Worms	*baad* black gut worm, *g'lɛɛŋ* black earthworm, *taci^k* earthworm.
Kapurr – Snails	*katū^k* land snails, *katoŋ* water snail.
Kabɛd – Ants	*garuuj* termites, *kadu^kdaax, kajɛx* fire ants, *katɛd, kayʔoʻox* red/black ants, *kasoʻod* red ants which climb fruit trees, *ko^k cuwa^k, s'moʻor* swarming black ants, *tagoŋ* big black ants, *takur, tampəəl.*
K'bù^k – Mosquitoes	*capɔɔd biting* fly, *galul* river mosquito, *k'bù^k* mosquito, *k'bù^k jaag* giant jungle mosquito, *r'way* fly, *s'bíc* sand flies.
Insects etc.	*b'ralaŋ* grasshoppers, *bubùg* weevil, *cawāās* stag beetle, *cɛ^k* lice, *gantūūs* dung beetle, *garɛɛd* cricket, *garoop* burrowing cricket, *gasoʻr* jungle cockroach, *g'lumíír* fruit flies, *jalííd* firefly, *kancoʻoŋ* preyinng mantis, *k'səg* stink bug, *maŋaay* scorpion, *maaj* fleas, *saŋɛy* chicken mites, *sɛŋwaar* tree creeper, *sɛɛd* biting cricket, *s'kuwoʻoy* moths, *soʻr* small cockroach, *taləx* carpenter bee, *tanoŋ* dragon flies, *tawāāg* butterflies, *tawiix* spiders, *tawiix ʔamaŋ* tarantulas, *ya^k ganas* stick insect.

Table 6. Names of species from the plant and animal kingdoms that are known to the Temiars.

BIBLIOGRAPHY

———

Adi Haji Taha. 1983. Recent Archaeological Discoveries 1976-82. *Journal of the Malaysian Branch, Royal Asiatic Society (JMBRAS)* 56(1): 47-63.

_____. 1985. The Re-excav*ation of the Rockshelter of Gua Cha, Ulu Kelantan, West Malaysia.* Federation Museums Journal 30.

Bellwood, Peter. 1993. Cultural and Biological Differentiation in Peninsula Malaysia: The last 10,000 Years. In *Asian Perspectives* 32: 37-60.

_____. 1997. Prehistory of the Indo-Malaysian Archipelago. 2nd ed. *Honolulu: University of Hawaii Press.*

Benjamin, Geoffrey. 1966. Temiar social groupings. *Federation Museums Journal* 11: 1-25.

_____. 1967. Temiar Kinship. *Federation Museums Journal (new series)* 12: 1-25.

_____. 1968. Headmanship and Leadership in Temiar Society. *Federation Museums Journal (new series)* 13: 1-43.

_____. 1974. Prehistory and Ethnology in Southeast Asia: some new ideas. Working Paper No. 25, Sociology Department, University of Singapore.

_____. 1976. Austroasiatic subgroupings and prehistory in the Malay Peninsula. In Philip N. Jenner, Laurence C. Thompson & Stanley Starosta (eds), *Austroasiatic Studies, Part I,* Honolulu: University Press of Hawaii, pp. 37–128.

_____. 1979. Indigenous religious systems of the Malay Peninsula. In *The Imagination of Reality: Essays in Southeast Asian Coherence Systems,* edited by A. Becker and A. Yengoyan. Norwood, NJ: Ablex. Pp. 9-27.

_____. 1985. In the long term: three themes in Malayan cultural ecology. In K.L. Hutterer, A.T. Rambo and G. Lovelace (eds), *Cultural values and human ecology in Southeast Asia,* pp. 219-278. Ann Arbor MI: University of Michigan Center for South and Southeast Asian Studies.

_____. 1987. Ethnohistorical Perspectives on Kelantan's Prehistory. In *Kelantan Zaman Awal: Kajian Arkeologi dan Sejarah di Malaysia,* ed. Nik Hassan Shuhaimi bin Nik Abdul Rahman. Kota Bharu:Perbadanan Muzium Negeri Kelahtan, pr.pl. 108-153.

_____. 2001. Process and structure in Temiar social organisation. In Razha Rashid & Wazir Jahan Karim (eds), *Minority Cultures of Peninsular Malaysia: Survivals of Indigenous Heritage.* Penang: Malaysian Academy of Social Sciences (AKASS), pp 125–149.

_____. 2014. Temiar Religion, 1964–2012: Enchantment, Disenchantment and Re-enchantment in Malaysia's Uplands. Singapore: NUS Press.

_____. 2015. Who gets to be called 'indigenous', and why? Text of keynote address at *International Conference on Access to Justice for Indigenous Peoples,* Centre for Malaysian Indigenous Studies (CMIS).

_____. 2016a. Indigeny–Exogeny: The Fundamental Social Dimension? *Anthropos: International Review of Anthropology and Linguistics,* 111: 513–531.

_____. 2016b. Indigenous peoples: indigeneity, indigeny or indigenism? In Christoph Antons (ed.), *Routledge Handbook of Asian Law,* pp. 362–377.

Bowen, J. 2000. Should We Have a Universal Concept of "Indigenous Peoples' Rights"? Ethnicity and Essentialism in the Twenty-first Century. *Anthropology Today,* 16(4): 12–16.

Bulbeck, David. 2004. Indigenous traditions and exogenous influences in the early history of Peninsular Malaysia. In *Southeast Asia: From Prehistory to History*, ed. Ian Glover & Peter Bellwood. London: RoutledgeCurzon, pp 314-336.

Carey, Iskandar. 1976. Orang Asli: the Aboriginal Tribes of Peninsular Malaysia. Kuala Lumpur: Oxford University Press.

Cole, R. 1959. Temiar Senoi agriculture: a note on Aboriginal shifting cultivation in Ulu Kelantan, Malaya. *Malay Forester* 22: 191-207; 22: 260-71.

Dentan, Robert K. 1965. Some Senoi Semai dietary restrictions: A study of food behavior in a Malayan hill tribe. PhD diss., Yale University.

———. 1978. Notes on childhood in a nonviolent context. In *Learning non-aggression*, ed. A. Montagu, 94–143. London: Oxford University Press.

———. 1979. The Semai: A Nonviolent People of Malaya. Fieldwork edition. New York: Holt, Rinehart, Winston.

———. 1983. A dream of Senoi, special study no. 150. New York: Council on International Studies, State University of New York.

Dentan, Robert K., Kirk Endicott. Alberto G. Gomes & M. B. Hooker. 1996. Malaysia and the 'Original People': A Case Study of the Impact of Development on Indigenous Peoples. Boston: Allyn & Bacon.

Domhoff, G. William. 2003, Senoi Dream Theory: Myth, Scientific Method, and the Dreamwork Movement. Revised Domhoff 1985, http://dreamresearch.net/Library/domhoff_2000e.html

Endicott, Kirk. 1979. Batek Negrito Religion. The World-view and Rituals of a Hunting and Gathering People of Peninsular Malaysia. Oxford: Clarendon Press.

Endicott, Kirk, and Peter Bellwood. 1991. The possibility of Independent Foraging in the Rain Forest of Peninsula Malaysia. In *Human Ecology* 19: 151-185.

Fortier, J. 2014. Regional Hunter-gatherer Traditions in Southeast Asia, in V. Cummings, P. Jordan and M. Zvelebil (eds) *The Oxford Handbook of the Archaeology and Anthropology of Hunter-gatherers*, Oxford: Oxford University Press, 1010–1030.

Jennings, Sue. 1985. Temiar dance and the maintenance of order. In *Society and the Dance*, ed. Paul Spencer. Cambridge: Cambridge University Press, pp 47-63.

———. 1995. Theatre, ritual and transformation: The Senoi Temiars. *London: Routledge*.

Leach, Edmund. 1989. Tribal ethnography: past, present, future. In Elizabeth Tonkin, Maryon McDonald & Malcolm Chapman (eds), *History and Ethnicity*, London: Routledge, pp. 34–47.

Leary, John. 1995. Violence and the Dream people: The Orang Asli in the Malayan Emergency, 1948-1960. Athens OH: Ohio University Center for International Studies.

Lim, Teckwyn, David P. Quinton, Alicia Solana-Mena, Yen Yi Loo, Vivienne P. W. Loke, Rizuan Angah, Husin Sudin, Muhd Tauhid, Param Pura. 2017. Short Notes – Temiar Bird Names. In *Malayan Nature Journal, Special Ed*, 2017:21-24.

Lye, Tuck-Po. 1994. Batek hep: Culture, nature, and the folklore of a Malaysian forest people. MA diss., University of Hawaií at Manoa.

———. 1997. Knowledge, forest, and hunter-gatherer movement: The Batek of Pahang, Malaysia. PhD diss., University of Hawaií at Manoa.

———. ed. 2001. Orang Asli of Peninsular Malaysia: A comprehensive and annotated bibliography. CSEAS research report series no. 88. Kyoto: Center for Southeast Asian Studies, Kyoto University.

———. 2011. A history of Orang Asli studies: landmarks and generations, In *Kajian Malaysia*, Vol. 29, Supp. 1, 2011, pp 23–52.

Noone, H. D. 1936. Report on The Settlements and Welfare of the Ple-Temiar Senoi of the Perak-Kelantan Watershed. *Journal of the Federated Malay States Museums* 19: 1-85.

Noone, R. O. D. 1954-5. Notes on the trade in blowpipes and blowpipe bamboo in north Malaya. *Federation Museums Journal* 1 & 2: 1-18.

Quinton, David P. 2022. Comments on Temiar Religion, 1964-2012 (Geoffrey Benjamin, 2014). Figshare, https://doi.org/10.6084/m9.figshare.20166767

————. 2022. The Temiar Ritual Belief System (from chapters 1 & 2 of this book). Figshare, https://doi.org/10.6084/m9.figshare.20383668

Rambo, A.T. 1980. Of stones and stars: Malaysian Orang Asli environmental knowledge in relation to their adaptation to the tropical rain forest. *Federation Museums Journal* 25: 77-78.

Schebesta, Paul. 1926. The Jungle Tribes of the Malay Peninsula. Translated by C. O, Blagden. *Bulletin of the School of Oriental Studies.* University of London 4: 269-278.

Sieveking, G. de G. 1954-5. Excavations at Gua Cha, Kelantan, 1954. Part I. *Federation Museums Journal* 1 & 2: 75-143.

Skeat, W. W., 1953. Reminiscences of the [Cambridge University] expedition [to tile North-eastern Malay States and to Upper Perak. 1899-1900]. *Journal Malay Branch Royal Asiatic Society* 26.9-148.

Skeat, W. W., and Blagden, C. O. 1906. Pagan races of the Malay Peninsula. 2 vols. London: MacMlllan and Co. (Reprinted 1966, London: Frank Cass and Co.)

Slimming, John, 1958. Temiar jungle: a Malayan journey. London: John Murray.

Solheim, W. G. 1980. Searching for the origins of the Orang Asli. *Federation Museums Journal* 25: 61-75.

Stewart, Kilton. 1947. Magico-religious beliefs and practices in primitive society: A sociological interpretation of their therapeutic aspects. PhD diss., University of London.

————. 1951. Dream theory in Malaya. *Complex* 6: 23-24 (Reprinted 1972 in *Psychological Perspectives. A Quarterly Journal of Jungian Tnought* 3: 112-121.)

————. 1954. Mental hygiene and world peace. *Mental Hygiene* 38: 387-403.

Trevor, J. C., and Brothwell D. R. 1968. The human remains of Mesolithic and Neolithic date from Gua Cha. *Federation Museums Journal* 7: 6-22.

Trigger, D. S., and Dalley, C. 2010. Negotiating Indigeneity: Culture, Identity, and Politics, *Reviews in Anthropology*, 39(1): 46–65.

Tweedie, M. W. F. 1957. Prehistoric Malaya. Revised ed. Singapore: Donald Moore.

Wawrinec, C. 2010. Tribality and Indigeneity in Malaysia and Indonesia, *Stanford Journal of East Asian Affairs*, 10(1): 96–107.

Wells, C. 1925. Six years in the Malayan jungle. Singapore: Oxford University Press.

Wilkinson, R. J. 1926 The Aboriginal Tribes. *Papers on Malay Subjects, Supplement*. Kuala Lumpur: Federated Malay States Government Press.

Williams-Hunt, P. R. 1952. An introduction to the Malayan Aborigines. Kuala Lumpur: FMS Government.

Winstedt, Richard O. 1927. The great flood, 1926. *Journal Malay Branch of the Royal Asiatic Society* 5: 295-309.

ABOUT THE AUTHOR

David P. Quinton, born in England, in 1977, was introduced to the Malay communities of Kelantan in Malaysia when he was only 19 years old. Ten years later, he made his first acquaintance with the Temiar people, at Kuala Betis, on the Nenggiri River. Later, in 2010, he reached the hinterland Temiars of Pos Simpor and Pos Gob. His fascination with their way of life and the knowledge of the environment they held, being so isolated from the outside world, not to mention their gentleness and deep beliefs, led David to begin a journey of investigation into their origins. This is described in the Preface of Vol.1, about his trekking in the forest, and interviewing the old folks among them. In 2016, David married a Temiar and settled down at the Pinchong River, near Pos Gob. They now have two young children, who are growing up in the Temiar way, surrounded by forest and waterfalls.

David's wife, Ella, has been an invaluable source of information regarding Temiar culture, and her guidance has helped to steer the book writing on many occasions. Her father, Samsudin B'ked, and her grandparents, ˀAbus Sisam and ˀAsuh ˀAti, and great uncle, ˀAlʉj Sisam, who are all pictured or mentioned in the book, have provided not only a wealth of knowledge that would have been impossible to discover otherwise, but they have also offered unceasing support to David while he has been living among them. David has planted over 50 fruit trees, from durians to coconuts, and each year he also plants manioc and peanuts. But with elephants on the rampage at night pulling up the manioc and pushing over banana trees, David has experienced first hand the difficulties that now face the Temiars in their endeavor to find food for their families.

The author welcomes feedback on his work and can be contacted by the email address in the front of the book. He is currently working on a grammar of Temiar and a dictionary with some 4000 entries and hopes to publish these in the near future. He also posts some of his latest work on Figshare, including videos of the Temiars and audio recordings of traditional dance music and folktale telling.

Link to his Figshare profile: https://figshare.com/authors/David_P_Quinton/12966872

Above: The author holds an interview with the elders of Píncoʾoŋ village. From left to right: the late ʔAhíŋ Bərlɛɛy, ʔAlʉj Sisam, Samsudin Bʼkəd and ʔAbus Sisam.
Below: ʔElla Samsudin sits with her mother ʔAndaᵏ ʔAbus, and her grandmother, ʔAsuh ʔAti.

9 781739 134433